Parking Cars in America, 1910–1945

TWENTY-FIRST CENTURY WORKS
BY KERRY SEGRAVE AND FROM MCFARLAND

Begging in America, 1850–1940: The Needy, the Frauds, the Charities and the Law (2011)

Vision Aids in America: A Social History of Eyewear and Sight Correction Since 1900 (2011)

Lynchings of Women in the United States: The Recorded Cases, 1851–1946 (2010)

America Brushes Up: The Use and Marketing of Toothpaste and Toothbrushes in the Twentieth Century (2010)

Film Actors Organize: Union Formation Efforts in America, 1912–1937 (2009)

Parricide in the United States, 1840–1899 (2009)

Actors Organize: A History of Union Formation Efforts in America, 1880–1919 (2008)

Obesity in America, 1850–1939: A History of Social Attitudes and Treatment (2008)

Women and Capital Punishment in America, 1840–1899: Death Sentences and Executions in the United States and Canada (2008)

Women Swindlers in America, 1860–1920 (2007)

Ticket Scalping: An American History, 1850–2005 (2007)

America on Foot: Walking and Pedestrianism in the 20th Century (2006)

Suntanning in 20th Century America (2005)

Endorsements in Advertising: A Social History (2005)

Women and Smoking in America, 1880 to 1950 (2005)

Foreign Films in America: A History (2004)

Lie Detectors: A Social History (2004)

Product Placement in Hollywood Films: A History (2004)

Piracy in the Motion Picture Industry (2003)

Jukeboxes: An American Social History (2002)

Vending Machines: An American Social History (2002)

Age Discrimination by Employers (2001)

Shoplifting: A Social History (2001)

Movies at Home: How Hollywood Came to Television (1999; paperback 2009)

Tipping: An American Social History of Gratuities (1998; paperback 2009)

Baldness: A Social History (1996; paperback 2009)

Drive-in Theaters: A History from Their Inception in 1933 (1992; paperback 2006)

Parking Cars in America, 1910–1945

A History

Kerry Segrave

McFarland & Company, Inc., Publishers
Jefferson, North Carolina, and London

LIBRARY OF CONGRESS CATALOGUING-IN-PUBLICATION DATA

Kerry Segrave, 1944–
　　Parking cars in America, 1910–1945 : a history / Kerry Seagrave.
　　　　p.　　cm.
　　Includes bibliographical references and index.

　　ISBN 978-0-7864-7007-5
　　softcover : acid free paper ∞

　　1. Parking facilities — United States — History.　2. Automobile parking — United States — History.　I. Title.
TL175.S44　2012
388.4′74097309041— dc23
　　　　　　　　　　　　　　　　　　　　　　　　　2012020792

BRITISH LIBRARY CATALOGUING DATA ARE AVAILABLE

© 2012 Kerry Segrave. All rights reserved

No part of this book may be reproduced or transmitted in any form or by any means, electronic or mechanical, including photocopying or recording, or by any information storage and retrieval system, without permission in writing from the publisher.

Front cover design by David K. Landis (Shake It Loose Graphics)

Manufactured in the United States of America

McFarland & Company, Inc., Publishers
　Box 611, Jefferson, North Carolina 28640
　　www.mcfarlandpub.com

Table of Contents

Preface 1

Introduction 2

1. Banning Begins 5
2. Other Measures 33
3. The General Problem and Solutions 45
4. Garages 85
5. Parking Lots 99
6. Other Facilities 108
7. Parking Meters, the First Two Years 117
8. Parking Meters, Part 2 134
9. The General Problem and Solutions, 1945–1950 156
10. Conclusion 165

Notes 173
Bibliography 182
Index 190

Preface

This book deals with the subject of the parking of automobiles in America from 1900 to 1945. With America's car culture generating more and more problems, I wanted to look at one of the problems created by the automobile — the issue of where and how to store it — in an earlier time period. How the question of automobile storage was dealt with in those first few decades of the car's existence laid the groundwork for what followed in America after World War II when the car culture really took hold. Car parking is covered from the first time it was discussed in the media — around 1910 — until the end of the Second World War.

This book is concerned with the reality and perception of automobile parking as found in the pages of the popular newspapers and magazines of that time period.

Research was conducted in Vancouver, British Columbia, at the University of British Columbia, Simon Fraser University, and the Vancouver Public Library. Sources used were hard copy indexes such as the Readers' Guide to Periodical Literature and online databases such as the Proquest historical newspaper databases, and other newspapers from that period.

Introduction

This book examines how America dealt with what was generally viewed as the most pressing part of the automobile problem — their storage or parking — in the period of 1900 to 1945. How America dealt with the parking of cars laid the groundwork for a decentralized and sprawling society that sprang up increasingly and dramatically after World War II. The result was a more and more automobile-dependent society resulting in problems with which we must grapple today.

Prior to 1900 the parking of vehicles — wagons, carts, and so on — was not much of a problem in a rural and not densely populated nation. Along with the advent of the automobile came a dramatic increase in population and a shift from rural to urban lifestyles. By the end of World War I, the regulation of automobile traffic had begun with laws passed in a few places. Los Angeles reportedly had an early version of traffic gridlock by about 1919. Throughout the 1920s there was an increasing battle in city councils across America to get street parking under control. Store owners and employees regularly took the parking places early in the day and left their cars there all day. Yet those same owners complained the loudest when regulations were proposed, arguing that such laws would interfere with their customers' access to their stores. Nevertheless, by the end of the 1920s, most cities of any size had some type of regulations with respect to parking of autos in the downtown business streets during the day. Full bans were often advocated but rarely achieved due to intense lobbying pressure. As a trade-off, most cities put in place a street parking ban during the morning and evening rush hours.

Still, the problem grew worse. Other efforts were directed at creating more streets, widening existing streets, establishing one-way streets, and building parking lots and parking garages. More fanciful ideas emerged, including rooftop parking on existing and new buildings, and mechanized garage skyscrapers that would tower 30 and more stories into the air, wherein the car would never be touched by human hands; it was all to be done mechanically. More practical solutions that might have worked (such as a reduction in the number of cars entering the downtown cores) were only rarely mentioned and never considered seriously.

Parking meters, when they arrived in 1935, were quickly embraced by U.S. cities. They provided much needed cash for cities in the financially bleak Depression years and made the enforcement of parking time limits much easier and much more efficient. While there had been much discussion of the parking problem from the 1920s onward, by the early 1940s most observers agreed that it remained unsolved. With the boom times following World War II came an even greater embrace of the car culture. Any thoughts of a meaningful control of parking through a reduction of vehicles had even less chance than it had prior to the war. By that time the idea of pervasive parking had been accepted, it was felt that every American had a birthright of never having to walk more than 1,000 feet from his car to his destination.

Chapter 1

Banning Begins

In American and English law, the right of the state to keep its highways free for traffic movement was one of its most notable precedents and was contained in a judicial decision made in 1812 by the jurist Ellenborough, Lord Chief Justice of England. It was in the case of *Rex v. Cross*, in which the defendant was indicted for allowing his coaches to remain standing for an unreasonable time in the public street. The court said, "Every unauthorized obstruction of a highway to the annoyance of the king's subjects is a nuisance. The king's highway is not to be used as a stable yard." That authority was repeatedly quoted with approval in American courts early into the 20th century, including the New York case of *Cohen v. Mayor*, 113 N.Y. 532–535, in which Judge Peckham said, "The primary use of the highway is for the purpose of permitting the passing and repassing of the public, and it is entitled to unobstructed and unoccupied use of the entire width of the highway for that purpose, under temporary exceptions for deposits for building purposes and to load and unload wagons, and to receive and take away property for or in the interest of the owner of the adjoining premises, which it is not now necessary to more specifically enumerate."[1]

Retail stores of the late 1800s provided uprights and rails (hitching posts) at the curb for their customers to park their horses, with the number of such rails depending upon the number of customers. Churches and schools of the same period built sheds to accommodate the rigs in which their parishioners, teachers and pupils traveled. Once the automobile arrived, the parking problem got much worse. Over the 20 years from 1900 to 1920 the U.S. population increased by 30 million; there were one-third more people in America in 1920 than there were in 1900. Whereas in 1900 the U.S. population was split 60/40 in favor of rural over urban, in 1920 it was 51 percent in towns and 49 percent rural. Where there were 1,711,000 carriages and wagons made in 1904, cars and trucks were being manufactured at the rate of three million annually in the early 1920s.[2]

In the first two decades of the 20th century there was very little regulation of cars or drivers. But a rapidly increasing set of problems involving storage of cars, traffic flow, and so on, soon caused more and more rules and regulations to be imposed. A huge crowd assembled in Venice, California, for a day-long Fourth of July celebration in 1909. It was said to have been the largest crowd ever assembled in the area. Every rapid transit coach was pressed into service and cars were said to have turned out in record number. According to a news account, "Every available foot of parking space on the streets running down to the sea on the cross thoroughfares was utilized." Illustrated by the event were the growing presence of cars and the lack of regulations at the time.[3]

California District Attorney John D. Fredericks came up with a plan in 1913 to deal with the increasing number of auto thefts from parking places. Fredericks wanted to set up a centralized information bureau to deal with all aspects of auto theft, such as maintaining lists and statistics, sending out information to cars on patrol, and so forth. Reporter Bert C. Smith remarked, "Cars have been stolen from prominent corners, from well-known parking spaces, from in front of public buildings — in fact, from any place on the downtown streets. It is hard to stop thefts without a concentrated and consistent effort on the part of the right authorities."[4]

A year later, on July 15, 1914, Mayor Bell of Indianapolis signed Councilman Miller's traffic ordinance. In signing the measure he failed to heed the pleas of the many car owners who had asked him to veto it because the ordinance limited the time cars could be parked on the downtown streets to 90 minutes. Bell declared it was time to end the practice whereby motorists made "garages" out of city streets, especially in the congested business district. That time limit was in effect between 6:00 A.M. and 7:00 P.M.[5]

Increasingly, around the time of World War, I the growing number of cars was noted. On a Sunday in the summer of 1915 in Cranbury, New Jersey, the number of automobiles parked on the First Church lawn so surprised a party passing in a large touring car that members of the party stood up and tried to count them. What that suggested to the pastor was the idea that he should hold a special Automobile Day at his church, when all the members of the congregation owning automobiles might make a special effort to bring them to church, loaded with worshippers. And, while the people were worshipping God within the church, the cars outside would bear mute testimony to the power of the gospel and the influence of the church on community life. The pastor also decided he would deliver a sermon on the topic, "The Motor Age, Its Wonderful Possibilities, and Hidden Dangers."[6]

As late as 1916, Henry C. Wright, then a member of the Mitchel administration in New York City, was able to write, in a treatise on city government; "Cities of less than 200,000 population seldom have traffic congestion that requires regulation." But things were changing dramatically.[7]

Late in 1916, the question of what to do about car parking came before the common council of the city of Logansport, Indiana. Automobiles, it was reported, had become so commonplace in the town that they had absorbed much of the space on the downtown streets for parking purposes. Such a development was described as a peril to the city in times of fire, and a situation that interfered with business. A number of plans to solve the problem were put forward at council meetings, but all had critics. Mayor Guthrie said the most feasible plan presented to that point was the one in vogue then in Plymouth and one or two other cities in the state. That plan consisted of designating small parking spaces just large enough for one car by white or green lines running out from the gutter at an angle of 30 degrees. Between each parking space a small runway, four feet wide, was left for the ingress and egress of persons to and from the sidewalks. Another feature of the plan was that it mandated the backing of the auto into the parking space to avoid collisions (as opposed to driving in head first). However, if the plan was adopted by Logansport, only about half as many cars could be parked in the space of a block as was then the case.[8]

Writing in December of 1916, journalist Harvey Westgate declared there was not another city in the world where traffic conditions were as bad (meaning congested) as they were in Los Angeles. More than 70 men made up the Los Angeles Police Department traffic squad, compared to nine members at the end of 1908; 40,000 automobiles were owned by people who lived inside the Los Angeles city limits. Westgate argued several causes or conditions were responsible for that congestion: (1) the 40,000 cars; (2) narrower streets than were found in most cities; (3) downtown hills; (4) 175 hacks lining the streets in the business district and, allowing only 15 feet to each one, that meant the curbs for a distance of 2,625 feet were filled with vehicles allowed to stand there throughout the 24 hours if their owners so desired; (5) all business district streets contained a "swarm of jitneys"; (6) street car tracks; (7) ignorance on the part of drivers who, for example, did not know which streets to take to avoid congestion; (8)

inexperienced drivers; and (9) heavy trucks. With respect to his point about inexperienced drivers, Westgate said with amazement, "In some European cities every man and woman who wished to drive a car is compelled to apply, first of all, to the police department. An actual driving test is given, and if satisfactory the applicant is allowed to apply for a license" and "by law the driver is compelled to carry the license."[9]

Also on the Westgate list was parking: "Last, but not least, is the parking problem. Shoppers, quite naturally, wish to park their cars as closely as possible to the store where they are trading, but in this case, in order to save themselves a short walk, they are adding considerably to traffic congestion. In parking, where the driver has to back in, and jockey for position, and repeat the performance when he leaves, traffic is held up until the car is in line." He concluded the parking problem was urgent and Los Angeles had to solve it: "If parking space on top of skyscrapers is necessary, with elevators to carry cars to the roof, the plan will be adopted. If basement parking space is the only way out Los Angeles business men will see that it is forthcoming. Both of these plans have been adopted in Chicago and New York, and they are going a long way towards solving the problem."[10]

By April 1919, two more large cities, Cincinnati and Philadelphia, had joined the small but growing list of cities that prohibited street parking in their downtown business districts. The Cincinnati ban on daytime parking for passenger cars was put into effect after a two-month trial period showed it relieved traffic congestion. Such a ban made it possible for trucks to pull in next to the curb for loading and unloading without being forced to double park on narrow streets. Cincinnati had provided two large free parking lots at opposite ends of the business district to compensate for the loss of street parking. The city also provided a shuttle service from those lots to the business district, for a fare of five cents. In Philadelphia, following a 90-day trial, the city adopted an ordinance banning street car parking in the downtown business district between the hours of 8:00 A.M. and 6:30 P.M. After a survey indicated that less than three percent of the shoppers who drove to the business district parked at the curbs, it was said that city merchants supported the ban on parking. Philadelphia's city council also had appropriated the sum of $20,000 to be spent on a survey of off-street parking facilities in the affected area.[11]

Sentiment in favor of a ban on street parking by cars in the downtown district of Los Angeles began to crystallize in late 1919. At a November 29 luncheon meeting held at the city's Athletic Club, representatives of various interested groups — including members of the Business Men's Cooperative

Association, representatives of the Pacific Electric, Southern Pacific and Los Angeles railways (public transit systems) and all the members of the Los Angeles City Council — were in attendance. Reportedly, almost all seemed in favor of the plan. During the discussion the statement was made that local men had capital available for the construction of buildings capable of housing a "vast number" of automobiles, if parking on the congested streets was prohibited.[12]

In tackling city traffic congestion, the Los Angeles City Council held hearings on just one aspect — parking — and proceeded with a proposal to prohibit car parking downtown in the area between First and Tenth and Los Angeles and Figueroa Streets, with the exception of the hill section, where there was reportedly no traffic congestion. Some 25 business and civic groups had representatives at the hearing, and the general sentiment was again said to be in favor of such a ban. In attendance at the hearing were people from the Automobile Club of Southern California, Business Men's Cooperative Association, the Retail Dry Goods Merchants' Association, the Merchants' and Manufacturers' Association, the Co-operative Draymen's Association, and the American Express Company, among others. Spokesmen from a few groups wanted exemptions. Harry F. Wright, of the independent taxicab drivers, urged that his group be allowed to retain their cab stands in front of the hotels. Speaking for the undertakers, Fred E. Pearce wanted a provision made for the exemption of automobiles parked for funerals, and Dr. McNeil, speaking for the physicians, thought medical doctors answering emergency calls should also have exemptions.[13]

Late in 1919, using the streets listed above, the Los Angeles City Council created two zones in the area, a "congested" zone and a business zone, with no parking allowed in the former and one-hour parking (at most) in the latter. "The no parking" hours were from 9:00 A.M. to 6:30 P.M. The bylaw was expected to contain an emergency clause so that it would go into effect immediately after its passage, receiving the mayor's signature, and having one official publication. Thus, it was predicted the law would go into effect on January 1, 1920. Explaining the new law, a reporter declared, "After the first of the year it will not be permissible to stop any kind of a vehicle within the congested district, except for an emergency. A delivery truck may stop to deliver a parcel or take one away, but may not park, and a doctor can leave his machine standing for the length of time it takes him to make a call in that district, or an ambulance may hesitate there to pick up an accident victim, but a woman cannot leave her machine there and go into a store to exchange a spool of thread."[14]

However, things did not go as quickly or as smoothly as expected.

As the Los Angeles City Council pressed ahead on the new law, opposition increased. P. R. Greer (of the Greer-Robbins Company), who was not in favor of the proposed parking regulations, complained, "Why doesn't the Council try some experiments here before it turns the business life of the city topsy-turvy with the radical plan now proposed?" Greer was worried that the ordinance would simply drive business away from the downtown sections of the city to the outlying districts and undermine the value of the automobile for both commercial and pleasure purposes. "Under it there would be no chance of getting near town with a motor car. This plan has apparently been offered by the railways [public transit firms] and swallowed whole by the City Council." Ralph Hamlin, president of the Motor Car Dealers' Association thundered, "I think the proposed no-parking ordinance now before the City Council is entirely too drastic."[15]

Others who came forward to oppose the plan also thought it favored the railway companies and that they were probably behind it. Roy R. Meads, president of the Pacific Rubber Company commented, "I think this ordinance would be the absolute ruination of the efficiency of the automobile, as far as Los Angeles is concerned. Everyone wanting to get to town would have to walk several miles or take a street car. As a result, the congestion would be just as bad as ever but it would be street cars doing the blocking instead of automobiles." Said George Bentel, manager of the Ascot Speedway Association, "The no-parking ordinance as it now stands is an outrage and one of the worst blows ever aimed at the business section of Los Angeles." Believing the public would never accept such a measure he added, "What would be the use of owning an automobile, if it couldn't be operated in the city streets?" Jack Griffin, head of the J. G. Griffin Company, declared, "If this ordinance goes through Los Angeles might as well wave good-by to all out-of-town trade" and that few people "will be willing to park their cars a mile or two from the business section and walk the rest of the way. As the plan now stands it is certainly the last word in radicalism."[16]

Just before Christmas 1919, a five-man delegation from the Motor Car Dealers' Association lobbied Los Angeles City Council to postpone the implementation of the no-parking plan for 30 days so that they might reconsider it. That group declared the proposed measure was too severe, would cause property values to depreciate, exact great hardship on the merchants, and cause economic waste. It described the measure as "too revolutionary and too drastic, and altogether unnecessary." In its resolution the Motor Car Dealers' Association stated that many of the modern traffic regulations that had been found satisfactory in other large cities to ease traffic congestion had not been adopted in Los Angeles; this included (1) one-way traffic; (2) elimination of streetcars on certain streets; (3) elimination of streetcars turning at certain corners; and (4) regulations toward the elimination of loading and unloading of merchandise during certain hours of the day. The group also believed that the proposed ordinance "would make the street railway companies the sole beneficiaries."[17]

So much controversy and publicity swirled around the issue that the *Los Angeles Times* published an editorial against the proposal on December 24. According to the piece, the automobile, once regarded as a token of luxury, had fairly won its place in the industrial, business and social life of the American people. The fact that three million of them would be manufactured during 1920 (and that less than 10 percent of them would be of the luxury type) was deemed incontrovertible proof that the motor car was a prime necessity of American life. It had solved problems of transportation that, before the motor car was invented, were simply unsolvable. The editor argued that as an agent of progress the car had outstripped the steam engine and telegraphy and stood second only to the printing press. No other invention had adopted itself so quickly and so universally to the needs of a generation, and any city that endeavored to establish a blockade against the motor car by relegating it to back streets and suburban lanes was making a serious mistake.[18]

Acknowledging that traffic regulations in all big cities were necessary, the editor added, "but not of the kind of the no-parking ordinance which is now receiving the consideration of the Los Angeles City Council." Continuing on, he declared that to require a business man to park his car two miles from his place of business "is a manifest absurdity. It is equally absurd to compel a woman who comes downtown in her car to park it two miles from the place where she expects to trade. The inevitable result of such a decree would be to force stores to move outside the zone. It is equally unfair to drive the taxis from the streets.... Such an ordinance would turn back for fifty years, the hands of the clock of progress." Although he admitted relief was necessary, he held that it was not the kind the City Council proposed. And while he made that point several times in his piece, the editor never suggested a possible remedy. In his concluding remarks he said the ordinance would benefit a few to the detriment of the many. Since the streets belonged to all the people any ordinance restricting their use within narrow limits was an imposition. People had a right to own cars and businessmen had a right to ride to their offices in them, and to use them for transportation around the business district. "Owners of machines have a right to ride in them to any part of town that they desire; and it is blue-law legislation to require them to park their cars two or three miles from the place they need them," fumed the newspaperman. "The Council will do well to put that no parking ordinance back into the oven again for more baking; at present it is too raw."[19]

As December passed, more opposition to the ordinance was reported. M. G. Faulkner (of the M. G. Faulkner Company) grumbled, "This ordinance is literally unheard of in the traffic regulations of large cities. It is the most drastic piece of legislation against the motor-owning public that has ever been attempted. While the traffic situation is serious in downtown Los Angeles, there is no excuse for trying to put over anything like this." Western Motors manager Gilbert Woodill remarked, "Why we should deliberately take such a backward step as to virtually bar automobiles from our downtown streets is something that only a City Councilman can figure out.... It is an ordinance that cuts in half the value of every motor car in the city — and benefits no one but the street car company." Harold Tuttle, an executive with the Howard Auto Company, said, "It is a surprise to me that an ordinance of such radical tendencies would ever be considered." Another who expressed a similar sentiment was Robert S. Weaver, manager of S. F. Seager & Company, who stated, "To do away with the use of automobiles in the downtown section of the city is entirely too radical." Prominent musician Dr. Bruce Gordon Kingsley fumed, "It is an outrage to talk of passing the proposed no-parking ordinance. An auto owner coming downtown would be forced to leave his machine as far out as Fifteenth street. If the ordinance is adopted, my machine will be of no use for business purposes. I'll be a strap-hanger forever."[20]

In the opinion of J. Albertson, head of Albertson Motor Car Company, "The no-parking ordinance would work the greatest imaginable injustice to the motoring public — and the term motoring public means the public today ... it is unthinkable to virtually bar it from the business district of the city ... why try the most radical remedy imaginable first? It is as logical as amputating a leg to cure a corn." Simplicity Wheel Company manager F. K. Rockett suggested, "This ordinance threatens to deliver a blow that will question our modernity." Many critics of the proposed ordinance pointed out that other ways existed to lessen traffic congestion and that those methods were well known and well used in other cities. Yet virtually none of them ever mentioned what those remedies were.[21]

Physician Dr. Howard Moffatt authored a piece in the *Los Angeles Times* that was full of doom and gloom for doctors and their patients if the ordinance was enacted and went into effect. If a patient who lived in the zone called a doctor, for instance, the physician would have to park his car outside the zone and walk to see the patient, wasting valuable time. Explained Dr. Moffatt, "It is not the doctor's time that this foolish idea is wasting, it is the time of some other poor suffering or dying person, to whom the doctor is delayed in reaching. He is the one who suffers. How many patients do you think could be seen in a busy morning's work by this ancient method of locomotion [walking]?" By the time the doctor got to see his patient by a means other than driving, thought Moffatt, it might have been to late too help the patient: "No, none of us, the professional or business man as the case may be is ready for such drastic measures until we are better protected with other means of public parking.... If the professional man can't have his car with him, and it has become one of the greatest necessities of this profession, some one will have to lose out."[22]

Very early in 1920, commentator George Dunlop declared that the blame for traffic congestion was not always with the cars parked in the curb lane of the street. Sometimes they only interfered with traffic on narrow streets while not impeding traffic at all on the wider thoroughfares. For him, the real cause of traffic congestion came at intersections where more traffic arrived than could get through during each cycle. On the narrow streets there was no room between streetcars and automobiles parked at the curb, with moving autos having to follow streetcars in one line. Because streetcars stopped to discharge and take on passengers, cars would not pass, resulting in congestion. On wider streets there was room between for one full lane of automobiles and, thus, cars could move easily through the intersection.[23]

Late in January 1920, the ordinance was still on hold as the opposition continued to vigorously agitate. The Automobile Club of Southern California was described by a reporter as being "unalterably opposed" to the proposed measure. But eight out of nine members of the city council were said to be in favor of passing it, with perhaps some minor changes. David Faries, general counsel of the car club, declared that the ordinance was discriminatory because it prohibited parking in the congested district by passenger vehicles but allowed it by truck and delivery wagons, which he described as a "gross injustice." Faries maintained the club would oppose the ordinance in every way possible "to the extent of referendum and court proceedings if necessary."[24]

Finally, late in February, the Los Angeles City Council passed the controversial no-parking ordinance, to go into effect on April 10, 1920. In the view of the experts, the ordinance would work a "revolution" in the manner of the growth of Los Angeles. It was considered to be "inevitable" in that it would force the creation of new shopping districts outside the present congested area. Big stores were even then arranging to locate outlets on Hollywood Boulevard, on Wilshire Boulevard, and so on. Similarly, it was predicted that a second theater district would arise outside the no-parking area to cater to the matinee crowds who customarily left their cars downtown while attending the afternoon show. According to a reporter, the 30,000 autos that daily parked in the to-be-forbidden area represented 82,500 people who would be forced to do one of three things: stay at home; leave their cars outside the no-parking area and walk in or take the streetcars; or use the streetcars all the way from home. Reportedly, all that explained why 15,000 people had signed a referendum petition against the new law. One unnamed businessman had a four-acre Hollywood site and planned to put up a store on one acre, reserving the other three acres for parking spaces According to the *Los Angeles Times*, "It is his intention to maintain a regular auto-checking system. Customers can glide up in their cars, step out, and turn their machines over to experienced chauffeurs, who will remove them to the parking area, and drive them back to the store entrance upon call." Also, some relief was expected to come in the form of the construction of "gigantic storage" garages within the business district. During 1919, the first garage of that sort was erected at Fourth and Olive Streets; its four floors held 275 machines. A second was slated for the corner of Fifth and Grand, at a cost of $650,000. It would be 168 feet by 180 feet with eight floors for storing automobiles, with a capacity of 1,022 cars.[25]

Under the new Los Angeles law it was unlawful to permit any passenger vehicle to stand for a period of more than two minutes in the no-parking, or congested, district between 11:00 A.M. and 6:15 P.M. A stop of up to 15 minutes was permitted commercial vehicles for the purpose of loading or unloading, and that was allowed only when no alleys were available for the loading and unloading. That two-minute stop was also permitted passenger vehicles, but only for the purpose of discharging or taking on passengers. A motorist cold not stop to run into a shop for a quick purchase, even if it could be accomplished in less than two minutes. Roughly, the no-parking zone extended from First Street (north boundary) to Ninth Street (south), Los Angeles and Main Streets (east), and Figueroa and Hill Streets (west). As in the earlier draft of the provision, the hill section within that area was exempted from regulation. Also created under the new law was a "business district" that lay outside of and adjoined the "congested district," inside of which parking would be limited to two hours, from 10:30 A.M. to 6:15 P.M. That area extended from Sunset Boulevard (north), to Pico Street (south) to San Pedro Street and Central Avenue (east), and

Georgia, Bixel, and Boylston Streets (west). Outside of the business area there were no parking restrictions or regulations. Existing permits for cab stands within the no-parking area had expired and the city council did not intend to issue any new ones. That meant people in the congested district who wanted a cab had to phone for one or hail a passing taxi.[26]

On Saturday, April 10, the police arrested 1,500 people under the no-parking law. But two days later thousands of drivers left their cars outside the no-parking zone and walked into the city. On that day, at 6:00 P.M. (the 12th), Police Captain James McDowell reported that only about 200 of the little white "traffic violators" cards had been passed out by his men. None of those 200 arrested were taken into police court, but most of them appeared at Central Police Station and deposited bail. One arrest was made by prearrangement with police by a man who had announced he wanted a test case and would fight the law to the highest courts in the country. That was L. G. Thompson, an executive with the Earle C. Anthony firm, an automobile distribution company in downtown Los Angeles. Also on April 12th, many protests were voiced against the no-parking law at a regularly scheduled meeting of the Business Men's Cooperative Association by merchants whose business was said to have seriously suffered from the prohibition. However, it was decided at that meeting to give the new law a 30-day trial.[27]

More than 100 complaints charging violation of the Los Angeles no-parking measure were prepared on April 13 by the city prosecutor and the next day Police Judge Frederickson listened to the various excuses. But if the defendants appeared before court hours and deposited bail, said a reporter, "This they may forfeit and thus escape being taken into court." An early report from the city indicated pedestrian traffic in the congested district had already increased by 5 percent due to the new law. Extra police had to be sent to the area just north of First Street to deal with increased traffic jams as drivers sought to park there, just north of the congested zone.[28]

Another complaint about the measure was issued by the Los Angeles Chamber of Commerce's committee on entertainment, which declared that one of the principal functions of the chamber of commerce for the previous 30 years (providing hospitality) was nullified by the enforcement of the no-parking law. A request from the Shriners that the chamber of commerce be designated as the headquarters for entertaining their delegates brought out the fact that it would be impossible to have the chamber as headquarters under the no-parking law, as parties could not be taken either to or from the building in automobiles. E. H. Bagby, chairman of the entertainment committee, explained that every member of the committee was called upon to suggest a solution to the difficulty, but no one was able to offer any plan whereby it would be possible to assemble parties at the chamber or at the downtown hotels for entertainment functions. According to a reporter, "Usually the chief courtesy extended by the chamber is to take its distinguished visitors auto riding to points of interest. If this is to be done now it will be necessary to assemble the party in each case away from the chamber or from its hotel."[29]

Toward the end of April it was announced that, as a protest against the law, an automobile parade would take place on Saturday, April 24, with hundreds of cars expected to pass through the downtown streets that afternoon. A reporter went so far as to say, 5,000 cars were predicted, with practically every big establishment in the city represented in the parade by touring cars, trucks, and other vehicles. Each car was to carry a banner protesting the no-parking law, and demanding an immediate end to the measure. Reportedly, the idea for the protest parade originated with film actor Clara Kimball Young, who had called a meeting of merchants who pledged support. Behind the idea were groups such as the Merchants' and Manufacturers' Association and the chamber of commerce. Young was to be the parade's grand marshal, with 18 cars and nine trucks coming from her film studio, Garson. At least 200 letters of support were received by Young in the week before the parade, asserting they were unable to attend matinees at cinemas because of the ordinance and that they lived too far away to come downtown at night. Young received $2,000 from businessmen on April 21 to cover the cost of the protest (estimated at $5,000) and was said to be prepared to cover the rest of the cost from her own pocket, if necessary. Up until the day of the protest, Young and a committee of women drivers were still making visits to merchants to try and enlist even more support.[30]

Although the parade did take place as planned, it received only brief media coverage that gave little impression of the size of the protest except to say, "A long line of automobiles passed through the downtown streets yesterday afternoon."[31]

Meanwhile, the Los Angeles City Council met on April 23 for a three-hour public hearing attended by representatives of more than a dozen business organizations, all with complaints about the parking ban. After hearing all the complaints, the city council promised quick action to amend the ordinance. It was still awaiting a final report from its Engineering Department but hoped to have an amended law ready to go early in the following week. At that point it was reported that the business groups favored allowing 45-minute parking from 10:00 A.M. to 4:30 P.M. in place of the ban in the congested area.[32]

At the same time, the *Los Angeles Times* published a philosophical diatribe against the no-parking law. Declaring that the measure served once and for all to demonstrate the extent to which people in Los Angeles had come to regard the automobile as essential in their daily lives, the account went on to say that the measure was obviously a bad law, a fact recognized from the first day when businesses reported decreased sales, a trend said to have continued. "It didn't take Los Angeles twenty-four hours to realize that removing the automobile from the streets meant the same thing as cutting the throat of business," explained Gilbert Woodill, chairman of the committee of the Motor Car Dealers' Association, which led the protest from the time the measure was first framed by the city council. "I believe that there has never been any such demonstration of the extent to which the automobile has become a part of business life, as that brought on by the no-parking ordinance." Woodill added, "Simply because we were selling automobiles, the council seemed to believe that our protest was biased, but the truth is that the motor car dealers realized that the automobile is as essential to modern business as the street car, as electricity, as gas, as the telephone." All of the protesting had its effect on the Los Angeles City Council, he believed, and that people on that body "will think twice before they pass measures hampering the use of automobiles again. The no-parking experience of Los Angeles, while a costly one, for the merchants and most unpleasant from every standpoint will at least firmly fix the automobile in its rightful position as a real contributor to the prosperity of the city." As far as Woodill was concerned, "The automobile is an essential part of the business and the sooner the city, county and State authorities realize that the hampering of the use of the automobile is hampering the progress of civilization the better off we will all be."[33]

Even the national media picked up the story about the Los Angeles, ban on parking cars downtown. G. Gordon Whitnall, secretary of the Annexation and Consolidation Commission of the City of Los Angeles wrote a piece that appeared after the parking ban took effect but before it was amended. Traffic congestion in the downtown district, he wrote, had become such an acute problem that the result was akin to stagnation. Not only did the business district present an almost impenetrable barrier to motor vehicles, the resulting traffic jams played havoc with streetcar schedules to such an extent that the service on all lines entering the metropolitan district became "demoralized." That was especially the case during the rush-hour period in the late afternoon. Streetcars became uniformly overloaded, and yet, putting more streetcars into service only added to the problem as the real difficulty lay in getting the streetcars through the jams. Other problems in Los Angeles contributing to the congestion problem were that the city had the largest per capita ownership of automobiles of any large American city and a smaller percentage of street area to built-up area in the downtown section of any city in the U.S., except Columbus, Ohio.[34]

When the ordinance went into effect on April 10, said Whitnall, "The immediate effect was to produce the appearance of desertion on the downtown street during the busiest hours of the day. A perceptible improvement in street car service was apparent.... Proprietors of retail establishments within the restricted zone are about evenly divided in their opinions concerning the effect on business. Probably no authentic check on the true effect can be expected for a month." He concluded that local city planners had generally expressed the idea that the motor vehicle "is the expression of a new form of transportation that has many economic advantages over previous forms, notably the street car, and that legislation restricting its utility can have but one of two effects, either to retard the general development of those portions of the community affected, or to cause a spreading out of the commercial district of the city into sub-centers well distributed through the city."[35]

By unanimous vote on April 26, the Los Angeles City Council began the process of eliminating the parking ban. Amendments meant that no-parking hours in the congested district would be changed to run from 4:00 P.M. to 6:15 P.M. (every day except Sunday), with 45-minute parking permitted in that zone from 9:00 A.M. to 4:00 P.M. The vote by the city council was received with applause from the businessmen who were present. When told of the vote, Los Angeles Mayor Snyder said, "One thing is certain. If the amended plan is to be a success the business men must make good on their offer to hire or by cash contributions help the city hire special officers or extra policemen to patrol the congested district from 10 a.m. to 6 p.m. and enforce the 45-minute regulation. We have not enough policemen now to enforce the ordinance as it is to be amended." The Automobile Club of Southern California had formally offered that day to pay for the trial installation in the downtown district of a mechanical system of regulating traffic movement by means of electric lights at each street corner. Engineers for the city remained opposed to any change in the no-parking ordinance until at least a 30-day trial period had elapsed; but, in case the council should decide to amend the ordinance, the engineers recommended the no-parking hours be from 3:00 P.M. to 6:00 P.M. The idea behind the no-parking hours in the late afternoon was to allow street railway lines to better maintain their schedules. After telling of the improvement in streetcar service and of the reduction in the number of accidents, the engineers warned of a return to the previous chaos if parking was restored. Secretary Mitchell of the Automobile Club of Southern California insisted that the falling off in the number of accidents on the no-parking streets was not due entirely to the workings of the parking ban. Rather, he insisted that credit had to be given to the work of the Vigilance Committee of the club that was then conducting a campaign against reckless automobile drivers.[36]

Swiftly, the amended ordinance was signed by Los Angeles Mayor Snyder, published once, and went into effect on Thursday, April 29, 1920. On that first day, 15 violations of the measure were reported to the police, but cases of traffic congestion were said to be no more noticeable, according to checkers, under the 45-minute rule than under the no-parking measure. Mayor Meredith P. Snyder conferred on the 29th with members of the Business Men's Cooperative Association relative to the enforcement of the new traffic regulations. Doormen of the stores, according to association members, would assist police officers in enforcing the 45-minute limit. Also, thousands of handbills were distributed by the businessmen to drivers outlining the new regulations and asking that they be obeyed. Snyder said he was willing to give the educational play a trial but that, if it failed and the police department found it was unable to enforce the new regulations due to lack of manpower, the business community then would be called upon to make good on its promise to raise the money to hire additional police officers to enforce the law.[37]

In a proclamation on the subject of the new parking regulations issued by the mayor, Snyder said, "I call attention to the fact that heretofore it has been an unwise custom on the part of the many who think they are good law-abiding citizens to ask a preference on the execution of traffic laws, through enjoining or influencing police officers when in the performance of their duties, perhaps in some instances by giving them small tokens to create special favor toward them. Permit me to urge that such policies be discontinued: let the law fall upon all alike." He added, "I would also add a request that in order to help avoid a great congestion, as experienced recently and prior to the no-parking ordinance, every citizen should be unselfish and avoid bringing automobiles within the congested district, unless absolutely necessary, and in this manner manifest your loyalty with the city officials and your interest in the public good."[38]

Regulations governing the parking of cars in downtown Los Angeles were eased slightly on May 20, 1921, by the city council. Until the new ordinance was amended, the 45-minute limit in the congested area began at 9:00 A.M. but hereinafter it would not begin until 10:00 A.M. and continue until 4:00 P.M., followed by the existing ban until 6:15 P.M. After that time there was no regulation of parking. The Business Men's Cooperative Association had campaigned unsuccessfully to have the no-parking ban in effect only from 5:00 P.M. to 6:15 P.M.[39]

Later in 1921, a reporter observed the no-parking ordinance (from 4:00 to 6:15) had caused more discussion and dissatisfaction than any other municipal law of the previous ten years but had finally been accepted by the majority of car owners as a "necessary evil" and that the number of violations of the measure was steadily decreasing from month to month, according to the Los Angeles Police Department. Chief among the changed conditions that had enabled motorists to reconcile themselves with the law was said to be the fact that greatly increased parking garage facilities downtown had been provided since the no-parking ordinance became operative. At Fifth and Grand stood, according to one account, the "world's largest and most complete garage, the Grand Central, with accommodations for 1000 cars." Water, oil, and gas stations were available on each floor of the garage, and a motorist could drive out of the garage without waiting for any other car to move or be moved out of his way. "The big garage combines efficiency, convenience and economy to the last degree. It is frictionless, runs like a piece of well-oiled machinery. Visitors to Los Angeles are patronizing the Grand Central in ever-increasing numbers and give unstinted praise to the great establishment which is at once a show place and an asset to the fast-growing city."[40]

Visitors to Long Beach, California, who parked their cars on downtown streets in the summer of 1923 benefited from the repeal of a one-hour parking limit ordinance that had been in effect for a short time. Because it had resulted in the arrest of numerous tourists in the previous few months, the city council voted in June to repeal the regulation. The only remaining control of parking in Long Beach was between the hours of 1:00 A.M. and 6:00 A.M. and on certain parts of the main thoroughfare, Ocean Avenue. Drivers and visitors to Long Beach who were ignorant of the parking ordinance often found they had violated the law and for that reason the councilmen declared it a hardship.[41]

Yet the repeal in Long Beach lasted only a short time, less than six months. At the end of November 1923, the Long Beach City Council passed an ordinance that placed a one-hour parking limit on automobiles in the downtown streets.[42]

Also in November 1923, the Los Angeles City Council was preparing to ban the parking of cars on the downtown streets during the morning hours, from 7:00 A.M. until 10:00 A.M. The new morning regulations were recommended by the traffic commission so as to speed up the movement of street cars into the downtown district. Also, the traffic commission recommended that additional traffic officers be assigned to enforce the traffic regulations, including those prohibiting second-line [double] parking.[43]

That morning ban was passed on November 26 by the city council, signed the same day by Mayor Cryer and, due to the emergency clause it contained, went into effect on November 27.[44]

As more and more bans and regulations were placed on cars with respect to downtown streets, there was more and more complaining from merchants. In a lengthy pronouncement on the problems of retailers in general delivered by Roger W. Babson (entrepreneur and business theorist), he pointed out that the automobile had dramatically changed things as more and more people came to retailers in their cars rather than streetcars or by walking. Said Babson, "They have been coming in automobiles instead. But just now as they have formed the automobile habit, the authorities come around and forbid parking in front of the best retail stores. The police authorities cannot be blamed for making these rulings, but the effect on the retail trade in the congested districts is apt to be very harmful."[45]

Car parking on the streets in the downtown district of Ogden, Utah, was restricted to a maximum of two hours during the daytime hours, beginning in March 1924, when a new ordinance went into effect. The time limit was in effect between the hours of 9:00 A.M. and 6:00 P.M. each day except Sundays and holidays. Physicians were allowed to leave their cars in the congested zone for three hours. Some 2,000 copies of a booklet containing a map of the two-hour district and the complete ordinance were printed by the city of Ogden for free distribution to residents. White stall lines were painted along the curbing for the assistance of motorists, and traffic officers were instructed to monitor compliance with the law by making chalk marks on the tires of parked vehicles.[46]

Two months later, motorists in Ogden were still being hauled into court for violating the city's two-hour parking limit. On May 16, 1924, three more violators of the ordinance were given suspended sentences in court by Judge D. R. Roberts. One of them forfeited $5 bail. Traffic officers were to be set to watch certain automobiles, said Roberts, to see that they were not being moved a little to the next parking space just before the two-hour limit expired. Roberts emphasized that the law meant two hours in total per day, and added that as long as violators were not being brought before the court a second time for the same offense the policy of handing out a suspended sentence would continue.[47]

New police rules went into effect in New York City prohibiting car parking for more than 20 minutes (and even then only if the vehicle was engaged in receiving or discharging merchandise or passengers) on Broadway, Fifth Avenue, and several other main arteries. Those limits were in effect mostly from 8:00 A.M. to midnight, and in a few smaller Bowery, streets from 7:00 A.M. to 7:00 P.M., except Sundays.[48]

During the first week of September 1924, the Los Angeles City Council was ready to deal with a proposed new downtown parking ordinance, against which organized opposition had already started and a referendum threatened in case the measure was adopted and signed by the mayor. For months the council had received urgent pleas from citizens to do something to solve the traffic congestion problem and the councilmen and the engineers of the public utilities board agreed that the chief obstacle to the rapid movement of pedestrians, streetcars and vehicles was the parking of cars on downtown streets, many of them so that traffic jams ensued. In response to the complaints, the city council appointed a special parking survey committee headed by R. W. Pridham of the chamber of commerce as chairman, and having as its members representatives of the Automobile Club of Southern California, retail and wholesale merchants, the street railway companies, and other groups interested in the problem. A sum of $10,000 was appropriated by the city for the committee to study the congestion problem. Based on that committee's report, a new ordinance was proposed, to take effect on October 1. In brief, the new proposal provided that the parking of vehicles be prohibited entirely from 7:00 A.M. to 6:15 P.M. on the following downtown streets: San Pedro, Main, Hill, Figueroa, Second, Sixth, Eighth, Tenth, Pico, Sixteenth, and on downtown Sunset Boulevard. Also recommended was that the existing no-second-line parking (double) or standing law be rigidly enforced (it was mostly ignored then). The new proposal provided that on downtown through streets such as Broadway and Spring, where parking was not to be prohibited, the time limit for parking be reduced from 45 minutes to 30 minutes. A downtown association, which had just been organized to protect the interest of the business district, vigorously opposed the new ordinance as being an unjustified blow to the development and prosperity of the downtown business district.[49]

A couple of months later the Los Angeles City Council was considering yet another new and comprehensive traffic ordinance. Under, it the congested area and the business zone would be consolidated into one district to be known as the central traffic district and to be bounded by the following streets: Los Angeles, Pico, Figueroa, Fourth, Hill, and Sunset. Police would be empowered to impound vehicles that were left on the street in violation of the ordinance. Daytime parking in that central district (between 10:00 and 4:00) would be reduced to 30 minutes. A sliding scale of penalties was provided with maximum fines of $50, $100, and $500 for, respectively, first, second, and third offenses. Nothing came of either of these plans.[50]

Police heads of traffic departments of three cities — Los Angeles, San Francisco, and Portland (Oregon) — were the principal speakers in July 1925 at the convention of the Pacific Coast Claims Agents' Association. All three told the delegates that it was their opinion that car parking in busy downtown streets had to go. Captain Gleason of the San Francisco Police Department said that parking was one of the most perplexing problems of city traffic. As far as he was concerned, the elimination of that parking offered the best solution. In agreement with him were Captain Heath of Los Angeles and Captain Ervin of Portland.[51]

An ordinance to regulate the operation and parking of motor vehicles in the city of Panguitch, Utah, was passed by a vote of five to nothing on August 3, 1925, by the town council. According to section three of that measure, "All persons parking or stopping vehicles upon the streets of the City of Panguitch, shall park them with the right side to the curb, and at an angle of 45 degrees as near as may be, in the following named streets: Main Street from 1st West to 1st East and on Main Street running north and south through Panguitch City. On all other streets the vehicle shall be parked parallel with the curb and sufficiently close thereto so as to not obstruct travel in the street."[52]

Journalist George Britt reported, in April 1926, that traffic regulations the public regarded as "unreasonable and obnoxious" could not be enforced, no matter how many policemen there were on the street, at least according to Dr. John A. Harriss, who had been deputy police commissioner of New York City for eight years. "So long as the public regards traffic regulations as a sort of agreement for the benefit of all there will be enforcement," he explained. "Beyond that point, it serves no purpose to increase fines and give jail sentences. People will not abide by the traffic rules and will take pride in evading them." An example he gave related to two years earlier in New York, when the city had a 20-minute parking time limit and was issuing 1,100 summonses a day to motorists who violated that limit. When the parking limit was raised to 60 minutes there was, he said, no more traffic congestion than under the 20-minute limit. People were said to not park their vehicles any longer but the real benefit was, Harriss explained that "we virtually eliminated that source of summons, and of antagonism." He thought that in the city of Ogden, Utah, the saturation point for automobiles would be about twice the current number; that is, 40,000 cars over 20,000. In his view, the answer to the traffic problem for cities was expressways: "These must be developed into real super streets with lanes for local traffic and lanes for through traffic." Intersecting streets would go over or under the "super" streets.[53]

The two-hour car parking time limit on the streets of the downtown district of Ogden, Utah, would be limited to one-hour intervals in a new ordinance recommended by the area merchants. According to the account the Ogden Chamber of Commerce was to conduct a campaign to educate motorists with regard to parking rules. The area businessmen, professional men, and employees of firms, would need to keep their cars off the streets in the downtown commercial district during business hours in order that the space could be used by store customers.[54]

One of the most drastic moves yet made in a large American city to remedy the traffic situation was undertaken by the city of Philadelphia early in 1927. It took the form of an ordinance prohibiting all downtown parking of automobiles on the streets. An earlier, similar ordinance there had been erased in the face of protests. Philadelphia's forbidden zone was 1.5 miles long and 1.25 miles wide, with no parking in effect from 6:30 A.M. to 7:00 P.M. Merchants in the affected area were said to be about equally divided regarding the new measure.[55]

A sore spot with Los Angeles drivers and merchants was revived by the return of public interest in March 1927 in a proposed no-parking ordinance that would ban the parking of vehicles in the central business district (CBD) during the day time hours of 10:00 to 4:00. Interest was rekindled by the experiment being conducted by Philadelphia, where such an ordinance had been in effect for around two months. As was the case when the same regulations were in effect in Los Angeles (in 1924), a strong opposition had formed in Philadelphia against the law. That city's ban applied to the CBD streets with vehicles allowed to stop only long enough to load and unload passengers or merchandise. It was an ordinance that was put into effect one street at a time. According to the Philadelphia *Public Ledger* newspaper, "With the enforcement of the law throughout the entire area, traffic speeded up considerably, but business interests along the principle side streets were hard hit and immediately began organized action for the repeal of the measure." Although the law was only two months old, a once-strong backer of the measure — a councilman — was already wavering and suggesting that perhaps a one-hour parking limit should be allowed on those streets. E. E. East, chief engineer at the Automobile Club of Southern California, saw little chance of such a measure getting much support again in Los Angeles. One reporter noted, "Should parking be barred now in downtown streets there would be no sufficient area within reach in which to store machines. Parking stations are not numerous enough to be adequate. Some few buildings, but not many, provide parking space for patrons of the stores in the buildings. The streets must provide space for other vehicles."[56]

National traffic experts in the auto traffic field met in Chicago in April 1927 at a City Traffic Conference, under the auspices of the National Automobile Chamber of Commerce, which was attended by traffic authorities from a score of leading American cities. H. B. Peabody, treasurer of Detroit Garages, Inc., told of his personal experience with parking prohibitions in 11 of the largest cities, and recommended the building of "automobile hotels" in traffic-congested districts to relieve the problem. "To entirely forbid parking in business districts is like the prohibition law [the illegalization of alcohol under the Volstead Act]," he declared. "It is unpopular and it is not self-enforcing such as boulevard and through-street stop regulations."[57]

Further restrictions in auto-parking privileges in the midtown section of Manhattan and amendment of the building zoning law to permit the construction of ramp garages were urged in May 1927 as necessary to traffic relief. These were detailed in a statement by J. E. Harrington, chairman of the Traffic Committee of the Broadway Association. That group consisted of businessmen and merchants who conducted trade in and around Broadway. One of the new traffic regulations suggested by the business lobby group was to permit parking by cars on only one side of one-way streets. That would permit a third lane of cars to use the same street, increasing traffic flows. According to Harrington, Manhattan, south of Fifty-Ninth Street, had a continuous battery of cars parked nearly all day long at both curbs of the streets. Thus, comparatively few cars monopolized the street areas that should have been kept open for the free use of the greater majority of cars that entered the city. "A recent survey disclosed that many car owners parked their automobiles all day long several blocks away from their business," he added. "This is not a just practice nor fair to others."[58]

As of June 1928, cars were not allowed to park on the main streets of Price, Utah, for more than 45 minutes between the hours of 3:00 A.M. and

6:00 A.M. So it was decided after a long and acrimonious council debate with a final vote of three to two in favor of the limit. The measure was introduced by Councilman John H. Redd who did so because of the difficulty the city's street department was having in keeping its thoroughfares clean. It was said that the cars that were parked along the streets made it impossible for the street department to get all the dirt washed off the streets. Present at the council meeting was Harry Barrellas who presented a petition signed by 120 people against the measure. Following a pitch in favor of the bylaw by Redd at the meeting, various other suggestions were entertained by the council, such as establishing certain nights of the week for cleaning the streets. However, none met with the approval of the street commissioner, who felt that the city of Price was not obligated to furnish a garage for any class of people.[59]

Once again the issue of banning downtown street parking was raised in Los Angeles. In July 1928, Dr. Miller McClintock, traffic consultant of the Los Angeles Traffic Commission (a city agency) and director of the Erskine Bureau of Harvard University, declared that any advantages that might be gained through the prohibition of parking in the CBD would not balance the disadvantages that would result. He said he had studied the problem from all angles and, while he advocated prohibition for Chicago, conditions were different in Los Angeles. "The solution of the parking problem lies in a proper balance between the use of the streets for movement and their use for storage purposes," he explained. "Without movement there can be no intercommunication within the city, therefore no business activity. Without suitable terminal facilities for motor cars of all kinds, the utility of these vehicles is lessened." In Los Angeles, he added, the laws had been established to eliminate the long-time, all-day parker but permit the short-time use of the curb space, thus allowing liberal turnover. Complete prohibition of parking, he argued, would not cause as much reduction as commonly expected because the loading and unloading of merchandise trucks at the curb would still prevent the use of the additional traffic land. Many business blocks had no alleys, thus forcing loading and unloading to take place from the curb lanes.[60]

Robert Nau was secretary of the Street Traffic Committee, a part of the Chicago Association of Commerce. Reporting in 1929, he explained that a little over a year earlier — on January 10, 1928 — there began a trial of prohibited parking in the CBD of Chicago. Twice before in Chicago history such an ordinance was about to be passed but each time it was delayed — once in 1920 when the mayor of the city returned the ordinance to the city council for further consideration, and in December 1925, when the Street Traffic Committee of the Chicago Association of Commerce requested that action be postponed. On the latter occasion the city council asked the Chicago Association of Commerce to make a comprehensive study of the entire problem of traffic control. That survey was made in May 1926 and was conducted by a committee of 78 members under the supervision of Miller McClintock, director of the Erskine Bureau for Street Traffic Research at Harvard University. Included in the report was a look at existing ordinances and recommendations for a new set of regulations. One proposal was to prohibit parking in the CBD from 7:00 A.M. to 6:30 P.M. on all days except Sundays and legal holidays — with parking also permitted after 3:00 P.M. on Saturdays.[61]

During the course of that survey it was revealed that curb parking contributed a "negligible" amount of business and created much greater obstruction that would be indicated by casual observation under the traffic conditions of the area. In a one-day count of 96,082 shoppers it was found that only 1,505 (1.5 percent) used space at the curb to park. The count involved the patrons of 33 different retail establishments, including department stores, furniture outlets, shoe stores, book retailers, banks, and so on. In the same month the CBD attracted 846,750 persons daily between 7:00 A.M. and 7:00 P.M. Mass transit agencies carried in 80.8 percent of those people while the passenger auto brought in 19.2 percent. Curb parking caused a great deal of double parking and forced delivery vehicles to cruise around, hoping to find an empty space. Generally, though, they did not and found it necessary to double park, further increasing congestion. Those conditions led the Association to recommend in its report for an ordinance to prohibit car parking in the CBD. Such an ordinance was debated by the Chicago City Council for a year, but in due course it was passed. Chicago merchants agreed to a trial of the new ordinance, commencing on January 10, 1928. "Up to that time several cities had tried it, but panic-stricken merchants were successful in having the regulation discarded within a few days," said Nau. A court injunction was unsuccessfully sought by a businessman against the measure. During the first few weeks the law was in effect there was so much business opposition that the association promised it would repeat its May 1926 survey in May 1928 for comparison purposes. It was said that, prior to about 1925, the speed of auto traffic in the Chicago CBD was about four to five miles per hour. After left-hand turns were prohibited there in 1925 and after traffic lights were installed in 1926, the speed moved to eight to 10 miles per hour. The no-parking ordinance took speeds up to 12 to 14 miles an hour.[62]

Comparison of the second study to the first showed an increase in the number of cars entering the CBD. "It is apparent that the motor car, as a carrier of passengers into the central district, is the only agency which could have been affected unfavorably the application of the prohibited parking regulation," remarked Nau. "In view of the notable increases in automobile passenger traffic, the conclusion is fair that restricted parking has not destroyed the utility of this agency as a passenger and patron carrier." Passengers entering the CBD between 7:00 A.M. and 7:00 P.M. on a typical day in May 1926 and May 1928 were as follows, respectively: total passengers, 870,859–894,059 (an increase of 2.66 percent); by streetcar, 284,958–282,013 (down 1.03 percent); by elevated rail, 256,286–243,594 (down 4.95 percent); by automobile, 166,367–196,873 (up 18.33 percent); by steam railway, 118,857–124,107 (up 4.41 percent); by motor bus 44,391–47,472 (up 6.94 percent). Automobile registration for 1926 in Chicago was 317,459, while for 1928 it was 360,985, an increase of 13.7 percent.[63]

Nau observed the old 30-minute parking limit ordinance required a large number of policemen to enforce it, more than were actually available for such duty. Also, arrest slips for those parking violations in Chicago had to be served on the violator personally, as any ticket placed on the car alone had no standing in court. It was impossible for an officer to watch each and every vehicle in his area and, as a consequence, cars were parked for long periods of time. When he was ready to leave a shop, the driver of a car violating the parking time limit would await an opportunity to slip away unnoticed by the officer. The total ban on parking was much easier for police to enforce. When the May 1928 survey was made it was found that off-street storage facilities accommodated 14,571 cars, compared to 8,732 in 1926. As to whether the parking ban had been harmful to retail business, Nau believed it had not been and cited the fact that some of the oppositional interests had already opened additional places of business in the area. In conclusion, Nau said the association would continue to watch for negative effects, but "unless they develop unexpectedly, it is believed that the great majority of the business houses will continue to support the regulation. Business would not be satisfied to return to the old chaotic conditions of by-gone years." He added, "The early complaints by a very small and apprehensive minority have long since been forgotten — yet at the same it seemed their voices would block progress toward a new and better condition in the central business district."[64]

Late in 1929, an article in *Literary Digest* mentioned that nearly all cities had prohibited car parking on their main business streets, at least during morning and afternoon rush hours. Baltimore had such a rule for several years, but the difficulty had been in getting motorists to comply.

One car parked in a block that was supposed to be clear was just as congestion producing as if a dozen or more vehicles were all parked in the same block. Detroit and Pittsburgh both had an effective way of handling that problem. Each had tow trucks that patrolled the downtown streets and immediately towed away violators. "The article stated that the offending motorist then must claim his car at a police lot, and must pay a $5 towing charge. If he has left his brakes set, it is just too bad, for they will be burnt out."[65]

Charles Gaither, Baltimore police commissioner, commented in July 1929 that the ordinance restricting parking on downtown streets Fayette and Lexington had just completed a three-month trial period with "excellent results." Before the ordinance, two-hour parking had been permitted on both sides of Fayette in the ten-block downtown section, except between 7:30 A.M. and 9:00 A.M. and from 4:30 P.M. to 6:00 P.M. Under the ordinance, parking was banned between 7:30 A.M. and 6:00 P.M., except for loading and unloading merchandise and passengers. Similar rules were imposed on Lexington. Before the ban, explained Gaither, traffic moved on Fayette at a rate of 6.18 miles per hour from 3:00 P.M. to 6:00 P.M. on weekdays. After adoption of the ordinance, the speed of cars moved to 8.45 miles per hour, an increase of 36.7 percent. The same types of changes were observed on Lexington. Before the ordinance, streetcars traversed Fayette at an average rate of 5.11 miles per hour in the afternoon rush period but, immediately after the law went into effect, the speed moved to 5.73 miles per hour, or an increase of 12.13 percent in speed. Counts were made of individuals entering 15 representative retail outlets on Fayette between 9:00 A.M. and 6:00 P.M. for a full business week before the ordinance went into effect and for a two-week period after the ordinance was in force for ten days. An average increase of 25 percent in store patronage was observed. Said Gaither, "So far, little or no unfavorable criticism has been made of the effects of the ordinance.... The effect has also been to restore to full use the width of the highway, for which it was intended."[66]

One of the most drastic proposals came in May 1930 from John O. Walker, formerly director of public safety at Knoxville, Tennessee, who called for a complete and unequivocal prohibition on all parking. As Walker saw it there were only three solutions for the parking problem: (1) no limitation; (2) compromise; and (3) no parking at all. For him, compromise was the worst alternative, while with unrestricted parking the early arrivals got all the spots and left their cars all day. Thereafter there was no parking for anyone. Traffic, though, at least moved freely without constant interruption from automobiles pulling in and out from the curb. Compromise, or limited parking, he argued, was a great burden on the police and a source of favoritism and influence that settled nothing. "Limited parking, when it comes to results, produces the most hopeless muddle known to man," he added. No parking was best because roads were intended for movement. "Parking is at best not a right but a privilege. In a city of a million it removes 4,000,000 square feet of the most valuable land from use by movement. This is an unwarranted usurpation of public domain." His solution was the implementation of public parking garages, ones that charged only enough to cover their costs.[67]

Walter Lindersmith, executive secretary of the Los Angeles Traffic Association, declared at the end of 1930 that Los Angeles had proved, through "incontestable figures" that the prohibition of parking, or its severe restriction, not only had no adverse effect on the number of automobiles coming into the CBD, but that proper restriction encouraged the free movement of traffic and that greatly increased the number of cars bringing shoppers to the stores in the CBD. Those conclusions were based on a series of surveys made by the Los Angeles Traffic Association at intervals since 1924. He explained there was a time when Los Angeles merchants and businessmen simply would not admit that the banning of parking could mean anything but distinct losses to their trade. Every effort to prohibit parking by blocks was strongly opposed and eventually beaten. Lindersmith felt, that by 1930, the merchants were beginning to realize that their interests were not suffering as a result of parking restrictions and that, on the contrary, reasonable parking control was a distinct benefit to business: "Of late years, there has been no attempt to completely prohibit parking in the central business district of Los Angeles. Instead, legislators have been content to gradually increase the restrictions as they were needed to remedy conditions." At the time in the CBD all parking was prohibited from 4:30 P.M. to 6:00 P.M. and limited to 45 minutes from 7:00 A.M. to 4:30 P.M. Besides that, more than half of all curb area had various other restrictions in place ranging from a total ban to a 20-minute limit for loading and unloading.[68]

Yet with all those restrictions, noted Lindersmith, the total number of motor vehicles entering the CBD on normal days was increasing, according to surveys conducted in 1924, 1927, and 1930. Vehicle counts were 127,651 (1924), 149,307 (1927), and 166,959 (1930), despite the fact that in 1924 there had been practically no parking regulations in Los Angeles and nearly all of the curb space was available to automobiles. He said the increase in the number of cars entering the CBD corresponded closely with the increase in the number of cars registered over the period, although he gave no numbers to support his statement was. In 1927 there were 45,308 feet of restricted curb space and 63,844 feet available for parking, or accommodation for 3,547 cars at the same time. The 1930 survey revealed available curb space was down to 52,442 feet (capable of holding 2,913 cars). With the increase in cars entering the CBD and a decrease in curb space there developed a strong demand for off-street parking, in the form of lots, multi-story garages, and so on. Restricted curb space was broken down into several categories. Red zones (adjacent to street intersections and opposite streetcar safety zones) made up 45.7 percent of the restricted curb space. Yellow zones (20-minute maximum stopping for loading and unloading) accounted for 24.2 percent of the space; white zones (most of which were established in front of theaters or large hotels and restricted vehicles to a maximum three-minute stop to load and unload passengers) made up 4.4 percent. The rest of the restricted curb space was accounted for by fire hydrants, mid-block intersections, private alleys, and so forth.[69]

Fletcher Pratt wrote a gloomy article for *American Mercury* in October 1936, in which he declared the reason for traffic congestion in America was a very simple one. The 23 million car owners in the U.S. had taken over its streets and highways not for the purposes of transportation for which those thoroughfares were originally designed, but, "they have seized it, and are today using it, as restaurant, bedroom, business office, and bordello. Twenty-four hours a day these 23,000,000 drivers pre-empt space along what are euphemistically known as public highways — parking, parking, parking, for one hour, two hours, all night, a week, a month, as long as it suits them — to the end that it has become impossible for traffic to flow freely through any major thoroughfare in the United States." Pratt remarked that the attitude of the average car owner, after buying a $50 second-hand machine and paying another $10 for license plates is that "he has thereby purchased from the State a squatter's right to the possession of a certain section of road-room." He argued that the entire system of parking regulation was not working and needed to be scrapped. That meant one thing and only one thing to him — abolish all parking in the streets.[70]

Pratt then mentioned a 1929 example of parking abolition that had worked. With the New York theater district congested, Police Commissioner Grover Whalen called for a survey and then declared that the congestion was due to parking. Realizing an attempt to "abolish the evil" by ordinary methods would be fought by well-financed groups with much political influence and legal talent behind them, he tried something different. He called in newspaper reporters, made public his report, delivered a fiery speech about congested streets and announced that henceforth all parking in that district during theater hours was abolished. Reportedly, it worked, and while Whalen remained in office there was no change — no cars parked in Times Square. But the moment he resigned from office, restaurant and nightclub owners launched a drive against the regulation. Those protests succeeded in reducing the original ban, which extended from 7:45 P.M. to 11:15 P.M., into two periods, 8:00 to 9:00 P.M. and 10:00 to 11:00 P.M.; in narrowing the area from which parkers were barred; and in eliminating the effective method of towing violators' cars to the police garage where they were held until the owner paid the $5 automatic fine.[71]

One objection frequently made against abolition, said Pratt, was that it worked an unwarranted hardship on suburbanites. Yet the New York traffic squad made a compilation of the registration of cars that had been ticketed for overtime parking and found that of 9,300 summonses issued in the first six months of 1936, only 2 percent were for cars registered outside the city limits. It meant, argued Pratt, "That the cars that clutter the streets belong to local residents." He also argued that there was plenty of available off-street parking, in New York and other cities, but people resisted using such space, as long as they could park on the streets. "Every effort at parking moderation has broken down hopelessly. Attempts to limit parking to a shorter period than one hour always are wrecked by the opposition of merchants and restaurateurs. And even the one-hour period means, in practice, virtually unlimited parking, as it proves extremely difficult for an officer to present evidence that a parker has overstayed a one-hour halt. Moreover, a court fine appears to exercise no deterrent effect."[72]

Some 34 policemen of the New York traffic squad started out on January 1, 1936, to sweep parking violators from the limited section surrounding Grand Central and Pennsylvania Station. Within a few weeks of the campaign starting it became common knowledge that it was underway, yet the number of violators in the last month of a six-month period was greater (4,000 versus 3,000) than in January. Of the violations, more than half were for overtime parking and another one-sixth were for parking between signs, according to Pratt. Several of those ticketed went to court and secured acquittals on the grounds that the summonses had not been personally issued. Complained a police sergeant, "What can you do? If they get convicted, they draw a one- or two-dollar fine, and to catch them you have to keep an eight-dollar-a-day cop standing beside the car for maybe five hours. Then they come right back the next day." In conclusion, he urged that all street parking be abolished.[73]

Chapter 2

Other Measures

In its organ, the *Monthly Bulletin*, the Automobile Club of Philadelphia urged city officials in 1916 to impose more rules on automobiles. It mused, "Undoubtedly the time is very near when it will be illegal to park automobiles within two squares of the City Hall for any length of time, and all street users will welcome that day. We are looking anxiously for the ordinance or ordinances which will help the growing traffic of the city."[1]

During the month of June 1920, a record was broken in Judge Kryger's count in Eureka, Utah, with nearly 40 cases settled. Quite a number of those cases were said to be for violation of the automobile parking ordinance, with in most cases the fines amounting to $5 each.[2]

July 10, 1920, marked the beginning of a campaign in Los Angeles to arrest motorists for head-on (angle) parking in an area south of downtown (bounded by Pico and Seventh Streets and Main Street and Western Avenue), and known as Automobile Row. A warning to that effect was issued by the Automobile Club of Southern California, which noted that a number of arrests had already been made for violating the no head-on parking ordinance by officers from the Central Police Station, but a "wholesale raid" was slated to take place. That ordinance stated that all automobiles had to be parked with the two right-side wheels within a foot of the curb.[3]

A little over a year later, moved by hundreds of complaints filed with the traffic bureau of the police department and the Automobile Club of Southern California, the Los Angeles Police Department announced that a campaign would be waged against all drivers who stopped their vehicles in the second line of traffic (double parkers) in the congested downtown district, holding up traffic behind them for blocks and forcing all traffic onto the streetcar tracks. Worst offenders were said to be truck drivers and drivers of delivery vans; with such culprits to be arrested on the streets

33

and taken to police court immediately. Women shoppers and others who were also guilty of double parking were to be treated the same as commercial drivers. The same ordinance was violated by the double parkers and the head-on stoppers. That was the Los Angeles ordinance that made it unlawful to park or stop a vehicle unless the right-front wheel and the right-rear wheel were no more than one foot from the curb. Said LAPD Captain McDowell, head of the traffic squad, "Persons stopping their automobiles in the second line of traffic and by doing so blocking the traffic in the congested district has been reported to me so many times that I have reached the conclusion that it is becoming a general practice. This will have to be stopped." He added, "I have instructed all of the traffic officers and also the mounted men to enforce the curb parking law to the limit and will have all automobile drivers taken into court at once who are caught bringing their machines to a stop in the second line of traffic unless the traffic signal is set against them."[4]

El Monte, California, adopted center-of-the-street parking in 1923 on its crowded Main Street, a major thoroughfare through the area. It was said to be one of the busiest streets in the state, with over 5,000 cars an hour passing through the business section. Southern California towns that were troubled with speeders and a lack of space on their business streets were reportedly watching the El Monte experiment closely. A chief advantage of the plan, according to the locals, was the elimination of one line of parking, throwing open to view the El Monte store windows that had until then been blocked from view by parked cars. Another positive aspect of the plan was in the cutting down of speeding, as "the speeders fear the backing out of cars from the center of the street."[5]

Battles by motorists over parking spots were already breaking out in the early 1920s, before many cities had even gotten around to regulating the practice. In Indianapolis, Frank Hill was fined $11 and received a six-month sentence at the state penal farm. The sentence was imposed after Hill had demonstrated his manhood to his companion, Ruth Lawrence, by striking 82-year-old William Hayes, during a dispute with regard to a parking space on a street in the downtown district of Indianapolis. Lawrence was fined $100 and sentenced to ten days in jail by Police Judge Delbert O. Wilmeth for her part in the incident. "This will cost me but it will show you I am a man," Hill told Lawrence as he launched his attack, according to witnesses. Those witnesses also testified that Lawrence struck Maude Spech, a bystander, because she remarked that it "seemed such a shame for such a big man to be hitting that little old man."[6]

At the start of 1924, officials in Seattle were looking to buy 500 locks with which policemen were to secure automobiles wrongly parked along the streets. Motorists had gotten into the habit of paying no attention to the notices placed on their cars which demanded their appearance in court.[7]

Work began in Logan, Utah, in April 1924, on the removal of the parking area that ran for half a block on East Center Street. Property owners and businessmen had been lobbying city officials for the removal of the parking area. That area was a large strip of lawn between Main Street and East Second Street. However, it was found that traffic was impeded. Property owners had united in asking for its removal and had undertaken to pay for the paving of the area once the parking law was removed.[8]

Later in 1924, Police Judge Chambers in Los Angeles informed the LAPD traffic division that complaints charging minor violations of traffic ordinances would no longer be accepted in his court in cases where the violations were committed more than a week before the court appearance, nor would convictions follow in cases where officers were unable to make driver identifications. It meant the system whereby Los Angeles police officers tagged illegally parked cars was rendered almost worthless. According to LAPD Captain Cleveland Heath, "The only way to untangle the affair is to make some new laws. I am aware that my officers cannot identify the automobile drivers. I am also aware that the law requires identification of the defendant and that the ownership of an automobile is not enough to prove a case. Our officers tag thousands of automobiles every day. We are working at top speed in the division, but it takes too much time to get a violator into court and obtaining convictions is too uncertain." It then took about one month to get a parking violator into court, and identification was rarely made as the officer had originally ticketed an empty vehicle. Records showed that only about 15 percent of the people who arrived in police court charged with parking violations were convicted and paid fines. And of those, two-thirds pled guilty.[9]

Also in 1924, reporter William Ullman said various suggestions were being advanced in America with "a view to putting parking on a businesslike basis." He thought one of the worst problems was the all-day street parker — the man who moved his car every so often, getting around any time-limited parking rules. These were men who would rather take a chance on a fine, knowing that enforcement of parking regulations was lax or even nonexistent. One plan he mentioned was that a city would rent out parking concessions and would fix the parking rate according to the conditions with the parking fee varying by demand, more in high-demand spots. Another benefit of the idea was that "a number of men would be attracted into the business, and would thus serve as parking police for the city at no additional municipal expense." (Apparently, the plan envisioned those parking concessions to be on-street curb parking and not off-street lots.) For example, said Ullman, to park in the most congested area of a city might cost the driver 50 cents an hour over and above the base rate of five cents for the first hour and ten cents for the second, as against 25 cents an hour in a less congested area, also over and above the base rates.[10]

New York City Magistrate William McAdoo noted the persistent crowding in traffic court in 1924, and that to relieve it a second courtroom would soon be opened. At times, he said, as many as 2,000 people attempted to attend a morning session of that court. "Until the police began the thoroughly justifiable crusade against the dangerous practice of parking cars in the street, we had no great difficulty in handling the number of cases that came to this court," explained McAdoo.[11]

A month later, before New York City's Committee on Control of Street Traffic of the Merchants' Association, officials of the police department gave assurances that hardships inflicted on business establishments through the enforcement of the auto parking time-limit rules recently made effective would be eliminated to as great a degree as possible, consistent with the safety and convenience of the public. About 40 businessmen, mostly members of the association, attended the hearing. Representatives of the automobile industry also complained that the regulations were a blow to their businesses. One car dealer grumbled that he had lost 25 sales within the previous few weeks. Members of the Fifth Avenue Association and the Broadway Association (both groups of businesspeople) announced that, for the most part, their association approved the new regulations, but it was stated on behalf of the Broadway Association that an extension of the parking limit from 20 minutes to 60 minutes would be advisable.[12]

Under heavy pressure from business groups, car parking in Manhattan below 59th Street was extended from 20 minutes to 60 minutes early in December 1924, as a result of Mayor Hylan's directive letter to Acting Police Commissioner John A. Leach. In theory, the extension of the time limit was just for the upcoming Christmas holiday season but, reportedly, nobody involved was prepared to say it would revert back to 20 minutes after the holidays.[13]

In 1925, when the Motor Car Dealers' Association of Los Angeles appointed a committee to conduct a survey and then to eliminate all "waste" in downtown parking areas, it was said to have received immediate police cooperation. Almost immediately the police curb-painting squads at Lincoln Heights Station were instructed to change all yellow loading zones where they joined red "no standing" zones near street intersections, so that some parking space would be left open at those points for private cars. Police Sergeant Peyton explained the LAPD continually received letters from merchants, hotel men, theater men, and business concerns (both large and small), requesting more loading-zone space in front of their buildings. "The routine method is to send a man out to check up on all requests, and then grant as few of them as possible, in order that parking space may be kept open for the general public," he explained. It took three men all night to repaint 90 of the 30-foot loading zones. Each zone used a gallon of paint ($1 per gallon) and the requisite wages. Thus, it cost the city about $105 each night those maintenance operations were carried out. The bulk of the blame for squeezing out the privately owned car from curb spaces, according to the Motor Car Dealers' Association, rested with the businesspeople themselves and with the streetcar firms, all of whom wanted "generous" reservations for their curb zones.[14]

A few months later, complaints were still being made that there were too many loading zones in the business section of Los Angeles which might be utilized as parking spaces for people driving in to shop, according to a survey made by the LAPD. A study of the figures by Captain J. L. Butler, traffic consultant to the Downtown Business Men's Association, revealed that in the central district (out of a total of 2,822 checks made) the number of vehicles found in loading-zone spaces amounted to a maximum of 526. Since spaces were allotted for 751 vehicles, that meant an excess of at least 225 spaces that drivers could have occupied except for the zone restrictions. If that surplus were opened to the public, said Butler, it would "accommodate 3,375 passenger vehicles each business day or more than 1,000,000 per year." That survey had been conducted on six consecutive business days during the week of July 15, 1925.[15]

A complaint charging E. S. Olsen with parking a car on Washington Avenue in Ogden, Utah, in September 1927 in the rear of other cars lawfully parked at the curb was dismissed in city court. Olsen explained, he was a letter carrier and was engaged in making a collection from the mail boxes. He said he could not find a place to park, and stopped in the street for a minute. However, Horace Holey, a milkman, was fined $3 on a similar charge. Motorcycle Officer Clair Rasmussen said Holley's car was blocking traffic while the latter was delivering milk to a store. During the same court session, R. M. Rampton was given a five-day suspended sentence on a charge of parking his car against the curb on 27th Street instead of in the center of the street.[16]

In April 1929, New York City Police Commissioner Whalen said that he was putting into effect plans to have the Department of Street Cleaning trucks tow away cars that were violating parking regulations. Under an old ordinance that had not been used in recent years, the Street Cleaning Department was allowed to remove vehicles that were obstructing the streets and hold them, pending payment of a $10 penalty. That was the law that Whalen revived in his campaign against parking in the city's theatre zone. Whalen declared that he considered the eradication of the "overparking evil a business proposition" and added that it would be carried out in a "business-like manner." Heretofore, he said, various "chronic parkers" had left their vehicles for five and six hours and, even when summonses were issued, had accepted them with indifference knowing they would suffer no more than a small fine. His new campaign would be initially limited to the streets of Manhattan, but would be extended to Brooklyn later if it proved successful. Since the theater zone regulations went into effect a few months earlier, the street cleaning department had seized 1,198 automobiles, collecting $10 for each one. Parking regulations then in effect in New York imposed a one-hour limit in congested business sections from 7:00 A.M. to 7:00 P.M.; two hours otherwise, and three hours between midnight and 7:00 A.M. Parking was prohibited from 7:00 A.M. to 10:00 A.M. and from 5:00 P.M. to 7:00 P.M. in a number of areas south of 59th Street, Manhattan, daily, except Sundays and holidays. In Manhattan's theatre zone, parking was prohibited from 7:45 P.M. to 9:00 P.M. and from 10:30 to 11:30 P.M. daily, except Sundays, on certain named streets in the Times Square district.[17]

Whalen's tow-away plan was backed by the Eighth Avenue Association's board of directors who adopted a resolution favoring "reasonable limitations" on parking privileges "to meet the necessities of different localities." He declared that his crusade would be continued until car owners learned that the one-hour parking ordinance was meant for everybody and would be enforced.[18]

A storm of controversy arose in the spring of 1929 in Alhambra, California, with the divisive issue being whether to park the car at an angle or parallel on the two-mile length of the city's principal thoroughfare, Main Street. Until a few weeks earlier, angle parking was the official method of parking automobiles in business districts. The city commissioner had suddenly changed the rules to impose parallel parking, and new white lines were painted onto the street. According to a news account, the public (and that included merchants and shoppers, especially women shoppers) did not take kindly to the change. The retailers complained that parallel parking was driving away trade because "lady motorists said they just couldn't park their cars parallel." As a result, a protest meeting was called and presided over by C. H. Winchester, a furniture dealer. A day later businessmen staged a protest march to city hall and complained to officials. Petitions against the new rule were circulated and, after amassing 1,467 signatures, were presented to the Commissioners, asking that angle parking be restored. It was, and new white lines were painted on the street again as angle parking was restored.[19]

A 1929 proposal made in Los Angeles by J. L. Roche, manager of the Merchants Parking Company, called for tall skyscraper garages to be placed advantageously in downtown areas as a solution to traffic problems. Under Roche's plan (then in effect on a smaller scale, and which was said to be endorsed by downtown merchants), the company sold scrip to merchants. That scrip purchased by the merchant was given to the customers in an amount commensurate with the amount of their purchases and was acceptable at any one of the 16 centrally located parking garages operated by Roche's company. In that way, he explained, the downtown merchant provided a parking space for his customers without the expense of owning or maintaining a parking station of his own. Roche envisioned parking garages being 15 stories tall (five of those below street level) costing $1.75 million each, and capable of holding thousands of cars each.[20]

Police in Ogden, Utah, began a "crusade" in May 1929 against motorists who parked their cars out in the streets behind cars parked at the curb, as they were double parked. Several arrests were made on the first day with the crusade slated to continue until relief came in the forum of a new ordinance then being prepared. The practice of street parking had grown to such an extent that traffic was seriously impeded and there was an increased risk of accidents, according to Ogden Police Chief Curtis Allison. The ordinance being prepared was similar to one then in force in Salt Lake City and would make it unlawful for a car to be parked in the business district in one place for more than two hours in the daytime. An officer would use chalk marks on tires to ensure that the time limit was not exceeded. Chief Allison added, with respect to the current crusade, that he did not like to go to the extreme of arresting the offenders but he had found that cautioning drivers had proved to be of no avail and sterner action was necessary. The several drivers arrested for double parking on one day by traffic police were each compelled to deposit $2.50 bail to ensure their appearance in the city court a few days hence.[21]

A month later a large number of motor vehicle ordinance violators were handled in Ogden, Utah, city court by City Judge John A. Hendricks. Among those dealt with were Alonzo Jensen, who was fined $2 or a two-day jail sentence for parking a car not parallel to the curb, and Dick Jones, who had his $2 bail forfeited for parking in the rear of other cars.[22]

All but 14 of 67 cities, towns, and villages in New York State, which responded to a 1929 inquiry from the State Bureau of Municipal Information, reported that they limited the time during which autos could park in congested districts. The time limit in 30 of the places was one hour; in nine, 60 minutes; in eight, two hours; and in the others it ranged from 15 and 30 minutes to one and two hours, according to the congestion prevailing in the particular district. Auburn and Valley Stream reported that parking was not permitted at all in certain sections of the municipality. Nine of the 53 communities having a time limit on parking admitted that it was not strictly enforced by the police department, while several stated the police were lenient with visitors and tourists. Communities with no limits on parking included: Cortland, Long Beach, Norwich, Ogdensburg, Salamanca, Albio, Depew, East Rochester, Herkimer, Hudson Falls, Lancaster, North Tarryton, Solvay, and Walden. An "honor parking system" was in place in Cortland, where it evidently was the motorist's choice to formulate and observe his own parking time limits. Reportedly, 12 cities said they had difficulty enforcing their limits while 39 stated that they had little or no trouble. Practically all the communities in the survey reported that their time limits on parking had proven successful, with benefits including less congestion, more parking spaces available, and, thus, a stimulus to trade. Another benefit was a sharp reduction in all-day parking in front of shops by merchants and their employees. Said Ithaca officials: "From a survey of the parking situation in the congested area, it was found that violations by persons who park to do shopping are very few. The greatest problem has been with the merchants, lawyers, stenographers, clerks and the professional class in general, who are always using the streets for parking as long as they wish."[23]

Lewis Amis was assistant manager of the Broad Street Association in Newark, New Jersey. Inexpensive and convenient parking for shoppers was the primary objective of the Cooperative Customer Parking Plan, which had been put into operation by the group in 1929, in conjunction with 21 local merchants and 11 participating garages. The plan provided that merchants, garages, and shoppers shared the cost of shopper parking. It was formulated by the traffic committee of the association that concluded, after years of study, that the ultimate solution of the parking problem in all metropolitan centers lay in the more extensive use of pay parking places. An investigation of garage facilities in the Broad Street district disclosed that there was space for approximately 8,000 cars. Since not all of them were in use during shopping hours, the supply was considered adequate for the plan. The Cooperative Parking Plan was an extension of a pattern of arrangements that had existed between one or two stores and one or two garages. Each store signed up, or left, the plan individually so stores could come and go but not affect the overall structure and functioning of the plan. Shoppers using the plan paid 15 cents for parking at 25-cent parking stations, 20 cents at 35-cent stations, and 25 cents at 50-cent stations. Garages collected the difference from the stores. Leaflets, emblems at stores and garages, and so on, were used to publicize the plan. Also, some stores promoted the plan in their own newspaper ads. "Perhaps the plan's most far-reaching effect lies in the fact that it will tend to encourage the use of pay parking places by all motorists," concluded Amis. "The time has come when motorists must consider the cost of parking in the center of cities as a part of the cost of operating automobiles. Downtown parking charges must come to be accepted with the same equanimity that attends the purchase of five gallons of gasoline."[24]

In connection with the formulation of Newark's Cooperative Customer Parking Plan, the Broad Street Association collected data on parking restrictions (in vogue in 1929) in various cities and the reactions to them. St. Louis prohibited downtown parking from 7:00 to 9:30 A.M. and from 4:30 to 6:00 P.M. One-hour limits were in force from 9:30 to 4:30, with all those restrictions in effect for the previous two years. According to the St. Louis Safety Council, local merchants were very much in favor of the regulations, although they felt there could be stricter enforcement of the one-hour limit. In Cleveland, the chamber of commerce responded that parking was prohibited during the morning and evening rush hours on many streets extending several miles in the central part of the city and that no complaints about those rules had come from merchants. Chicago prohibited parking from 7:00 A.M. to 6:30 P.M. in the main business section and had done so since January 1928. Those restrictions were said to not have been harmful to retail business. In Philadelphia, the chamber of commerce declared parking was banned entirely on some of the downtown streets and that there was considerable division of opinion among the merchants.[25]

Boston's chamber of commerce explained that parking was banned from about 65 percent of the curb space in the CBD and also on many streets outside of that district. Where parking was allowed there was a one-hour limit. A majority sentiment among business interests appeared to accept the necessity of parking prohibitions, but the real problem was said to be enforcement. In Washington, D.C., rush-hour parking was barred on certain streets carrying traffic into and out of the CBD. That restriction was opposed by affected retail stores. Also, there were varying time limits on parking on all major streets, according to the amount of congestion. In Atlanta, there was a morning and evening rush-hour ban on parking in the streets in the CBD and time limits were imposed on all others (outside of rush-hours), ranging from 30 minutes to two hours. Kansas City prohibited parking on its three most congested north/south streets (Main, Walnut, and Grand) between 8:00 and 9:00 A.M. and from 5:00 to 6:00 P.M., with one-hour parking on those streets from 9:00 to 5:00. Other regulations prevailed on other streets in the CBD area, with merchants said to be generally in favor of those rules. Buffalo barred downtown parking from 7:30 to 9:30 A.M. and from 4:30 to 6:00 P.M. The chamber of commerce said merchants at first objected to those regulations, but after doing a survey showing a very small percentage of their customers came by car, changed their attitude and insisted the police enforce the regulations.[26]

The Indianapolis Chamber of Commerce responded that there was no rush-hour parking ban in its city and that such a measure was unnecessary. Besides, it added, any such provision would be met with strong objections from business interests and motorists. Baltimore had a ban on CBD parking from 7:30 to 9:30 A.M. and from 4:30 to 6:00 P.M., which had been in place for several years. However, in a recent referendum, Baltimore merchants voted against any further reduction of parking hours in the CBD. San Francisco had no parking ban in its downtown area in the rush hours but did forbid parking entirely on certain narrow streets. Cincinnati prohibited parking on some of its downtown streets from 7:00 to 9:00 A.M. and from 4:00 to 6:00 P.M., on one side of the street in the morning, and on the other in the afternoon. On a few other of its CBD streets parking was banned on both sides during both rush periods. Detroit also had a CBD parking ban in place for its morning and evening rush hours, with a one-hour time limit in place between those periods. Cars in violation were towed away, with a fee of $3 charged to the violator for the towing. Pittsburgh had a wide variety of parking restrictions in place in various parts of the city, all the way from no parking at any time to one-hour, two-hour, and three-hour limits. Commenting on the various rules, a spokesman for the Pittsburgh Chamber of Commerce remarked, "Each of the various restrictions was first received with more or less consternation, and predictions that the retail business of the downtown triangle would be driven into the suburbs. In the retail sections of the suburbs, however, it has been found necessary to install similar regulations. Latest reports on the business of department stores indicate a healthy increase."[27]

As of September 1930, the Dallas police had been aided by a city ordinance that allowed for cars parked illegally to be towed away. Mostly they were removed for overtime parking and for double parking. The towing charge was $2. On average, 900 automobiles per month were towed away.[28]

More than 123,000 cars were parked throughout every night in the streets of Manhattan, Brooklyn, and the Bronx, according to a survey conducted by the New York Board of Trade. W. Banham, president of the group, announced that a report of the survey would be submitted in a few days to Police Commissioner Mulrooney, with a request for action. He said the board would recommend a tag or poster system for warning car owners of parking violations. The survey was carried out by some 30 college students hired by the board of trade to make a triple check of all-night parking on every street of the three boroughs. Each area was checked twice, from midnight to 6:00 A.M., for three successive nights. Three months were needed to complete the survey. Results were as follows: Manhattan, 33,752 cars parked all night without lights on [a violation], 42,849 cars parked in total; Brooklyn, 40,229–48,068; and the Bronx, 28,698–32,543. Banham explained that auto parking was one of three factors of traffic congestion that caused a loss of around $1 million a day to businessmen of New York City. The other two were repairs in street areas by utility companies, and the storing of building materials on the sidewalks and streets. A survey of automobile parking in 32 other cities, included in the report, indicated that the system of warning car owners by tags or stickers attached to their automobiles had proved successful. And, added the article, the issuing of summonses in large quantities was considered "impractical and inadvisable."[29]

During the single day of November 25, 1932, more than 700 cases were disposed of in New York City Traffic Court by Magistrate Michael Ford. Most of the defendants, charged with illegal parking, were fined $5, with the alternative of a day in jail. A total of 59 could not pay the fine and went to jail.[30]

Meanwhile, in Los Angeles, a strengthened amendment to the ordinance that permitted police officers to ticket automobiles found parked illegally, in the absence of the owner, was adopted in May 1934 by the Los Angeles City Council. The amendment was modeled along the lines of other provisions of a Boston law that had been upheld by the Massachusetts Supreme Court.[31]

In 1935, a report was produced by the Highway Research Board's Subcommittee on Traffic Relations in Municipalities. With respect to the various parking problems confronting city officials, the report stated, "No other subject brings up so much argument with so many opinions," and "nothing is so full of trouble for local officials as discourteous or inconsiderate treatment of parking violators, particularly non-residents. Every inch of parking space on the streets must be made available with the fewest possible restrictions. At the same time there must be free movement for heavy volumes of through traffic with the least congestion and inconvenience to everyone concerned." According to the group's report restrictions to parking were of two forms — limitation or prohibition. Limitation was based on the business needs of a congested area to permit a greater number of motorists to enter the business area, stop at the curb, conduct their business and get away, or to stop all-day or all-night parking.[32]

Prohibition was based on the need to use the full street width to provide for free movement of vehicles, continued the report. Limitation most frequently used was that of one-hour. The report explained: "Probably the easiest limit to enforce is the one-hour. A single officer may then patrol three or four blocks and by observing license numbers or marking them with chalk can readily enforce the one-hour limit" On an average street, it was advised; the wheels of the parallel-parked cars should be not more than six inches from the curb. If placed thusly, the average vehicle would occupy a space about six feet wide and 15 feet in length. Vehicles parked parallel to the curb required a distance between them of about three feet. That meant that each parallel-parked car required around 18 feet of curb space. On the other hand, angle parking required a greater width of the street — about 15 feet and some additional footage to allow automobiles to enter and exit. As a final recommendation, the report noted, "No street upon which parking is limited or prohibited should be without at least two signs on each side of the street in every block, briefly stating the parking regulations."[33]

A new system of dealing with parking violators in which casual offenders would be let off with $1 fines while habitual ones would receive heavier penalties was begun in New York City in November 1935 by Jacob Gould Schurman, Jr., chief city magistrate. The plan was agreed upon at a meeting of the Board of City Magistrates. A casual violator was defined as one who had received fewer than four summonses for parking in one precinct. For each of the first three offenses he would be fined $1. Thereafter he was to be considered a habitual offender, although the penalties were not specified. Manhattan contained 34 precincts; 35 were located in Brooklyn, and 17 in the Bronx.[34]

Chapter 3

The General Problem and Solutions

An editorial in a small Utah newspaper in the summer of 1920 declared that there needed to be some definite rules established with respect to automobile parking and traffic regulations. The editor observed that many motorists followed the rules established in other cities by driving their cars into the curb at the proper angle, but some drivers, when there was no room at the curb at the particular place where they desired to stop, pulled up behind the parked cars and left their cars in the road, a "practice that is both annoying and dangerous." The editor concluded, "The automobile traffic in this community has reached such proportions now that well defined regulations are necessary and if the motoring public is made acquainted with the regulations there should be no trouble in avoiding all accidents and annoying experiences of all kinds."[1]

Sometime in 1920, Ernest P. Goodrich read a paper titled "The Urban Auto Problem" at a meeting of the National Conference on City Planning. He discussed some of the parking restrictions then in place in cities such as Detroit (prohibition on some streets and time limits on others) and mentioned other ways of dealing with the growing traffic congestion, such as increasing the use of one-way streets in American cities. Commercial vehicles were also placed under restrictions as to which streets they could use. Goodrich thought there would be a continued growth in street width, to accommodate the increasing number of vehicles. Experience from traffic counts had shown, he said, that one vehicle per foot of width of roadway per minute was the maximum under normal city conditions (creation of one-way streets was said to double that figure). He also believed it would be necessary to install automatic traffic signals at frequent intervals (then in use to a very limited extent). Goodrich declared, "The parking of vehicles is probably the most pressing question now before urban authorities in connection with automobile traffic problems." Regarding streets with heavy volumes of traffic he felt the needs of the general public had to take precedence over those of the individual would-be parkers. A vehicle owner who drove into the business district with the desire of visiting shops or offices could, in few instances, park his car immediately in front of the business because of the great number of people who wanted to do the same thing. "Under such circumstances the car is occupying space primarily for the driver's own convenience and generally only in a minute sense to the advantage of the adjacent property-owner. A marked tendency now exists toward doing away with this privilege," Goodrich wrote "A prophecy is hazarded that eventually no vehicles will be permitted to park except directly in front of property owned by those occupying the car or with whom they desire to do business, and then only for very short periods, depending upon the traffic needs of the streets in question."[2]

An extensive report on the Los Angeles traffic congestion situation was submitted to the Los Angeles City Council in August 1922 by the Automobile Club of Southern California. Included in the report was a remarkable aerial photograph of ten square miles of the central (and more congested) areas of Los Angeles. The photograph was 12 feet by four feet, on a scale of around 200 feet to the inch, and was taken from the air in more than 400 sections with the work being done on days when the light was favorable at the noon hour to avoid shadows. It was prepared under the supervision of J. B. Lippincott, the club's consulting engineer. That report took over a year to complete, with the actual work done by E. H. Richards (one of Lippincott's assistants) who himself had from two to 40 assistants for the report. It was described as an extreme report with extreme solutions recommended; one of which was to create 24 broad thoroughfares, in some cases by cutting new streets and in others by widening existing streets. And that was to be done even if it meant that, in some cases, existing buildings had to be destroyed. Other recommendations included the construction of new alleys in all blocks in the downtown areas that did not have them; synchronizing pedestrian with vehicular traffic; compelling public utilities to work 24 hours a day on construction work in congested areas; retention of existing no-parking laws; creation of more one-way streets; and "if traffic congestion continues after making the above changes remove all street cars from the downtown congested area and build a belt-line system or loop around it."[3]

According to the report, the cost of traffic congestion was estimated at $12,239.59 per day or $3,671,577 per year. Those figures were arrived at by computing the delays caused by congestion and assuming the earning power of streetcar patrons at $1 per day. Cost of delays was broken down as follows: to the streetcar company, $5,310 per day; to streetcar patrons, $2,500; to transfer companies, $2,184; to taxi firms, $646; and to passenger vehicles, $1,599.59. According to the club, the primary causes of congestion were a direct result of the fact that Los Angeles had the highest per capita ownership of cars of any U.S. city and also had one of the lowest percentages of street area of any large city. Unquestionably, the club contended, the percentage of street area had to be increased in the near future. The second primary cause was attributed to vehicular delays caused by jaywalking, which was described by the club "as the rank and file of pedestrians crossing and recrossing streets between and at street intersections without regard for the smooth flow of vehicular traffic." The third cause was a result of the utilization of street area for parking purposes, especially on the narrow east/west streets of the congested district. As well, the auto club felt that great improvements in traffic conditions would manifest themselves soon after the adoption of an ordinance regulating pedestrian traffic, which was expected in the near future. However, the group acknowledged the number of traffic officers needed in the congested area would have to perhaps be doubled for a time to deal with the regulation of the pedestrian public as it adjusted to the expected new regulation. "The officers now on duty along Broadway are authority for the statement that vehicular traffic could move much more easily if pedestrian traffic were under strict regulation."[4]

Hugh E. Young was an engineer with the Chicago Plan Commission, who also presented a paper at the National Conference on City Planning, in Baltimore on May 1, 1923. First, he presented a summary of the current parking conditions in business and residential districts of American cities, noting that traffic conditions had made it necessary to time regulate parking in business sections and that those rules were generally enforced. He felt that the enforcement of time limits met the situation fairly well with respect to public convenience, but the majority of business firms were not satisfied with the conditions resulting from those regulations, and the car owners were also not in favor of the parking time limit. Public areas, he argued, had not been made accessible for parking except on minor streets and occasionally public squares and open spaces. For such public parking no charge was made, except in a few instances, where a charge of 10 cents to 25 cents was imposed. On the other hand, public garages provided day storage in the central business districts, but there were not enough of them. The number that did exist were generally used to capacity but, said Young, levied charges that were "too high" to make them popular in a widespread way. Business firms maintained that adequate parking and storage facilities should be provided before cars were restricted from parking on the streets. Young argued that the parking of vehicles on streets in the CBD was economically unsound as it forced commercial vehicles to unload from the middle of the street, obstructing moving traffic.[5]

Young continued by observing, "A city thoroughfare is not a parking or storage yard. It is a public highway. The interests and convenience of automobile owners must give way to public necessity. The parking or storing of vehicles on any street when they interfere with moving traffic should not be tolerated" because the economic loss due to delay in the city's commerce caused by the parking and storage of vehicles was "excessive." In Chicago, he said, that economic loss was estimated to be $60 million per year. Since the parking of vehicles on streets slowed down traffic, vehicular movements resulting from cars "circling the block" looking for parking spots amounted to 30 percent of total vehicular movements, but was eliminated by a no-parking rule. "Statistics show that the majority of [car] owners will not pay a charge of 50 cents a day for storage," he added. Among the suggestions for improvement of traffic and storage conditions presented by Young was that parking should be prohibited on all streets in the CBD unless there was ample room for two moving lanes of traffic between the streetcar tracks and the curbs. When it could be permitted, Young wanted parking limited to 30 minutes. Also, he wanted to see many more multi-story parking garages built in the CBD districts. Young did a survey of 29 American cities with respect to parking facilities. One question was whether or not the parking of cars on business streets was restricted by time limits for specified districts or areas. All 29 cities responded that it was: Albany, Ashtabula, Baltimore, Boston, Birmingham, Cleveland, Cincinnati, Grand Rapids, Harrisburg, Hartford, Louisville, Milwaukee, Minneapolis, Memphis, New Orleans, Omaha, Providence, Richmond, Rochester, Seattle, St. Louis, St. Paul, Trenton, Chicago, Portland, Washington, Scranton, Los Angeles, Salt Lake City. In response to the question as to whether time limits were enforced, 86 percent of the cities said they were, with the non-enforcement cities being Boston, Harrisburg, St. Paul, and Chicago. Also, 86 percent of those cities had made public areas available for parking—Albany, Cleveland, Harrisburg, and Minneapolis did not. Of the 25 cities that did provide such space, 21 imposed no parking charges for use of such space; Baltimore and Portland charged 10 cents a day, while St. Louis and Chicago charged 25 cents a day.[6]

John Ihlder was manager of the Civic Development Department of the United States Chamber of Commerce. Writing in 1923, he remarked that a few years earlier people talked about the saturation point for cars in terms of the public's buying power. But, by 1923, the saturation point was coming to be the incapacity of streets in cities and even towns to hold more cars. As far as he was concerned, the most important part of the problem was not the regulating of moving traffic, but "to find out what to do with automobiles, not when they are moving, but when they are standing still." Ihlder thought officials had been making "tentative and superficial" efforts for sometime to answer that question, but results to that date had been unsatisfactory. "So recent is our realization of this problem that there are regulatory authorities who still approach it from the point of view that the automobile owner is more or less of a nuisance who should be thankful for whatever facilities are grudgingly granted him, and some traffic experts who maintain that inasmuch as two or three riders in an automobile take up more space in a city street than do several times that number in trolley cars or subway trains, therefore the answer is to limit more and more strictly the use of automobiles in downtown areas, perhaps confining it to taxicabs which being more constantly in use, serve a greater number of passengers and call for only a fraction of the parking space. Of course such a solution as this is no solution." he explained. However, he did not say why it was no solution. According to him, the first requisite was to approach the problem from the point of view that the passenger car was a necessity of modern life and "our purpose is to facilitate its use."[7]

Ihlder talked a little about time-limited street parking, but concluded that no matter how many time-limited expedients were devised, the streets in the CBD, and in many apartment house districts, were inadequate to contain all the automobiles whose owners wanted to park them there. Therefore, supplementary parking space had to be provided. He urged that, where vacant land still existed in the business sections, the municipality should acquire such spaces and maintain them for automobile parking. Either the city could charge car owners a small fee for the service on the principle it charged users of city water, or it could give the parking free on the ground that it permitted free use of the sewers to take care of what otherwise would become a public nuisance. But, he conceded, even if that were done it would not be sufficient and that left a large field for private enterprise to create parking garages, and so on. Still, even if that happened, Ihlder believed it would not be enough and the problem would remain. As evidence he cited Washington, D.C., where the streets were so wide that angle parking was allowed on both sides of the street but still found the parking problem as difficult as cities with many narrow streets: "The reason apparently is that the greater parking area results in a greater use of automobiles.... The fundamental evil in our urban centers is the crowding of people too close together."[8]

With respect to the curb in front of a residence, in Ihlder's philosophy that space belonged to the householder, but the same was not the case in business districts. "But if the curb in front of your house is constantly occupied by the cars of strangers, so that you cannot drive up to your own front door and so that your visitors have to leave their cars at a distance, if the starting of motors and the smell of gas constantly wreck your quiet and peace of mind, you have legitimate cause for complaint," he said. He argued it should be the rule that all-night parking of cars on public streets, even in residential areas, should be forbidden. Even if the householder did not have a garage and could not afford to build one he should at least drive his vehicle onto his own lot. If he lived in a row house on a lot so small that it left no space for a car, or if he lived in an apartment house without storage facilities for its tenants' cars, then the owner of the vehicle "is under the necessity of renting garage space somewhere else." Pointing to himself as a practical man, he observed that he made no suggestion in his article for automobile subways, double-decked sidewalks, or for sidewalks raised a story above the roadway, as had been seriously suggested in some quarters. He dismissed all such ideas as too costly and/or impracticable. Ihlder did suggest that on main streets in retail business districts the roadway should be wide enough for a line of cars on each side, parked at an angle of 45 degrees, for a line of traffic in each direction, and for two trolley car lines. Regarding secondary business streets, he argued that the width should permit two lines of cars parked parallel with the curb, while in apartment-house districts, streets should be wide enough for parking at an angle. "In one-family house districts there should be no need of providing for continuous lines of parked cars. Unnecessary width of roadway means unnecessary cost for the home. It is cheaper to park one's car in the yard."[9]

When an Ogden, Utah, newspaper reporter looked for a solution to the automobile parking problem in 1923, he recommended the adoption of overhead streetcars in large cities. Cited as an example was a torpedo-shaped car recently invented by Los Angeles resident Fletcher Pelts, a private detective by trade. Reportedly, the invention had been approved by that city's police department and that California railroad companies were studying the plans of the proposed system.[10]

At the same time the editor of that newspaper offered the thought that one misconception motorists had throughout the U.S. concerned their parking privileges: "Many a driver has run into an argument with a traffic officer because he misinterpreted his privilege to park on a crowded street, as a right. He is set back a bit when he is told parking is only a privilege, and comes second to the right of moving vehicles." Traffic officials and safety advocates were then trying to instill that idea into the minds of motorists, he added. Once advised of that fact, those officials felt motorists would first see that their parked cars did not interfere with traffic before they left their machines at the curbs. He predicted, after noting a few helpful possibilities such as the growth of parking garages, "Eventually the parking problem will resolve itself to more strict control of downtown traffic, with permission for short interval parking only to those who need their automobiles in their work."[11]

At the end of 1923, city planner E. E. East argued that the automobile parking problem was not limited just to the big cities but that every city, town, village, and hamlet within the reach of the car was fast coming to realize that it, too, had a parking problem that sooner or later had to be met squarely and solved in an intelligent manner. In general, preliminary studies on all sides, declared East, had become convinced there was a problem to be solved. "The parking problem is the direct result of the widespread ownership and use of the automobile, resulting to an appreciable extent in the substitution of individual for mass units of transportation," said East. "Parking is an essential function of the efficient use of the automobile." According to his figures, the average car was driven 10,000 miles a year, or 27.5 miles a day. With an average speed of 15 miles per hour that meant driving took up only two hours a day, and for the other 22 hours of each day the automobile had to be parked. East argued that city streets were designed to serve the transportation needs of a time when mass transportation units served the individual and were designed for the use of such units and the transportation of merchandise from wholesaler to retailer and from the retailer to consumer. However, the units employed in mass transportation ordinarily allotted from three to four square feet per person, while the individual transportation by automobile required about 75 square feet per person. East believed it was pointless to argue that individual transportation was much more expensive than mass transportation since the car was here to stay. It was estimated, then, that California had one million cars for its 3.5 million people — an automobile for every 3.5 people. As East figured it, there were three "outstanding" solutions to the parking problem. One was the restricting of the use of automobiles as individual units of transportation through something such as the imposition of a tax upon the ownership and/or operation of a vehicle.

A second solution was the decentralization of population, businesses, and places of recreation, something he said that was then being carried out to some extent. Third on his list was the apparently "simple" solution of providing ample parking facilities through and adjacent to business centers.[12]

The scope of the parking problems in Washington, D C., was outlined in a February 1924 account in which it was observed that the city had 105,680 vehicles, as compared to 85,425 the previous year, an increase of 23.7 percent. According to a survey made by Colonel Sherrill, chief military aid to U.S. President Calvin Coolidge and superintendent of public buildings and grounds, 11,000 cars were parked every morning in the congested area of the nation's capital. In addition to his other duties, it was Sherrill's responsibility to find parking space within walking distance of their offices for all those thousands of motorists. At the time the United States had a total of 15,221,183 registered cars and trucks, almost 90 percent of the total world registration of motor vehicles. In 1924, there was one car for every seven people in the United States; in 1914 there had been one automobile for every 70 inhabitants.[13]

According to Edward S. Jordan, president of the Jordan Motor Car Company, speaking in January of 1924, a few fundamental facts would make the movement of traffic impossible in the business sections of 50 American cities within five years' time, unless the problems were addressed. One was the growing number of cars—the four million being added to the ten million in use one year earlier were to be augmented by the production of another four million in 1924. "Retail merchants will soon wake up to the fact that their front doors are barricaded by six or eight automobiles, the property of six or eight owners, while sixty or seventy customers are roaming around the streets looking for a place to park," warned Jordan. He added, "Every old fashioned bulky car owned and driven by Father will be replaced by at least three motor cars adding two for Mother and the children." Taxpayers would wake up to the fact that the cost of parking spaces outside of the congested area, and wider streets, would double, then triple, then quadruple. Millions of dollars could be saved by a city, he reasoned, that took the first step. And the step was that "no motor cars will be parked at the curb. Most streets will be one way streets. Taxicabs will be as thick as mosquitoes on a July night."[14]

Speaking at around the same time was Dr. Thomas A. Jagger, director of the U.S. government's Hawaiian volcano observatory, who had studied the impact of the Tokyo earthquake in September 1923, and linked its destructiveness to the parking problem. He said that cars had so jammed up some narrow streets that firefighting equipment could not get through and that hundreds of gasoline stations and gasoline in automobile tanks provided fuel for the innumerable fires that broke out after the earthquake. More generally he predicted, "I consider it only a question of time when, due to the increasing problem of automobile traffic, all large cities will provide special parking areas or buildings for automobiles and never allow any machine to stand in the streets without a driver at the wheel. It is one of the lessons we shall have to learn from this calamity." Jagger acknowledged the threat of earthquakes and subsequent fires on the Atlantic seaboard was fairly remote, but he pointed to cities such as Seattle and Los Angeles as areas where it could happen.[15]

Fanciful ideas for solving the parking problem were regularly raised in the first half of the 1920s. Reporter Jefferson Bell remarked that parking spaces in the air and underground were among the proposals under consideration in New York City in 1924, particularly in the borough of Manhattan. The idea for subterranean garages under some of the parks and for parking spaces on the roofs of buildings originated with the New York City Police Department. Still another expedient under consideration was the multi-story parking garage, of perhaps five stories, that would be available to store cars day and night, for a nominal fee. Police officials were also said to be in conference with professional drivers such as truck and taxi drivers, looking for solutions. The most radical step advocated was to bar passenger cars from certain commercial sections in the same way that trucks were barred from certain streets in the shopping districts. Bell said there were then, in Manhattan, 24 public parking areas set aside by the police where automobiles could be left without charge by their owners for a "reasonable time." With a range of from ten to 200 vehicles, those areas had a combined capacity of 1,380 cars. Apparently, though, the public was unaware of their existence because few of those lots were utilized to capacity.[16]

Few people realized it but, under an old law, said Bell, it was illegal to leave a car parked anywhere in the streets of New York, at any time. However, it was never enforced. Any motorist who left his car unattended at the curb violated Sec. 152, Chapter 23, Article 13 of the Code of Ordinances. It specifically stated that "vehicles must not be left in the street." According to NYPD Inspector William T. Davis, head of the traffic division, that law was written before the streets were "cluttered" up with motor cars. Abiding by the letter of the law, said Davis, "We could seize every automobile left standing at the curb longer than ten minutes, impound it and hold it until the owner paid $10 for the release of the motor car. I'm not advocating that the ordinance be enforced with such rigidity. The police are reasonable men, and take into consideration every possible condition which must govern the parking of automobiles." He added, "We have no complaint to make of the man who parks his car, when he does not obstruct traffic, for a reasonable time while he transacts his business, but we do object to men driving their cars in front of their places of business and parking them there for more than three hours or for the whole day, thus converting the city's streets into public garages."[17]

Besides municipal lots for cars, observed Bell, there were a number of private garages in New York City. One, on West 30th Street between Sixth and Seventh Avenues, charged ten cents an hour or 50 cents a day. That place was said never to be full, even though the nearby 32nd, 33rd, and 34th Streets were "choked" with vehicles. "Motor cars are parked, especially during holidays, two abreast on each side of Thirty-fourth Street. Often an automobile next to the curb is marooned for a long time because drivers of the cars on the outside leave their cars and the inside automobile has to wait until they return and move their cars.... Yet they choose to encounter difficulties of that kind rather than park their cars for a nominal fee in a private parking space or send their cars several blocks away to a parking space set aside by the Police Department," he said. Davis, of the NYPD, had strong feelings on the parking problem and declared that any person who deliberately blocked traffic by parking his automobile at a point of congestion should have his license revoked. The suggestion for a parking area on top of the Pennsylvania Railroad Station was laid before the officials of the railroad by the NYPD. As evidence that such a plan was feasible, it was observed that the Fiat auto factory in Italy had a testing track on the plant roof that was reached by a ramp. While the Fiat factory was a low building, the police argued that Pennsylvania Station was only a five-story building and that a parking garage on top of it would be readily accessible by means of a ramp.[18]

At the start of 1924, the Los Angeles City Council appropriated $10,000 for the use of a special committee of businessmen and traffic experts, which was investigating the street parking problem and was to make recommendations to the city council later that year for new ordinances or changes in existing ones. Those recommendations were to be based on engineering checks on the extent of the use of the streets for vehicle parking and for determining the exact amount of interference with the flow of traffic resulting from that street parking. When a confused oil company advertisement misinterpreted and announced that the Los Angeles City Council had offered a prize of $10,000 for a solution to the city's traffic problem, letters poured in at the rate of 150 a week despite the best efforts of the city to point out it was all a mistake. Suggestions ranged from using one man's patented but not-all-bugs-worked-out collapsible automobile, to a ban on all passenger vehicles and streetcars in the downtown area so people would have to walk and, thus, would be made healthier.[19]

When *Literary Digest* surveyed the parking situation in February 1924 it reported that in a number of cities parking was entirely prohibited in parts of the business section, with others putting time limits on parking. Still, the publication declared: "But these prohibitions are not sufficient." Among the other leading ways of providing for downtown off-street parking were: (1) parking in basements of office buildings; (2) parking garages; (3) open lots; and (4) space in public parks. The closest approach to the old hitching post idea was said to have been found in the provision in a building of parking space for its tenants. One example cited was the Pacific Mutual Building in Los Angeles, with the two lower floors of the building (each being 350 feet by 60 feet and underground) devoted to parking with room for 140 automobiles. As the building was occupied by 200 firms with 2,000 employees working in the structure, it was only a partial solution. A rental charge there for parking ranging from $17.50 to $20 per car per month was said to be a "limiting factor." A more popular strategy was the use of the parking garage. Cheap land in cities was increasingly taken up as a site for that type of structure. The Seventh Street Garage in Pittsburgh was one of the largest examples of the type — located within a few blocks of the city's business center, it had room for 450 vehicles with the average charge being $20 a month. Many downtown garages — that is, the standard ones selling gas and oil and doing repairs were being pressed into service for parking purposes. In Louisville, Kentucky, such spaces rented for $10 per month; in South Bend, Indiana, it was also $10 a month. In Portland, Oregon, the parking charge was 50 cents a day and in Oakland, California, day storage of cars could be had for from $5 to $7.50 per month.[20]

Literary Digest thought it was appropriate that municipalities stepped in to relieve the problem, by providing parking on vacant land. Baltimore condemned a rundown residential section near the downtown area in 1920, making the space available for car parking. Hugh Young proposed a plan for Chicago whereby 7,000 cars would be parked in subterranean garages under Grant Park, and the remaining 24,000 automobiles that entered Chicago daily would be stored in regional garages. Young's plan had been costed out at $43.5 million but, reportedly, all expenses of the project could be met by a parking charge of just 25 cents per car per day. John A. Harris, special deputy police commissioner in New York City, in charge of traffic, had a plan to provide for 30,000 vehicles under Central Park and 4,000 under Bryant Park. Included in the project was an electrical system that allowed owners of chauffeur-driven cars to summon their vehicles from department stores or theaters. With respect to open lots taken over by cities for parking, many levied no charge but some made a charge because, in some cases, protection against thieves and vandals required some supervision and that involved cost. But the open-lot strategy had limitations that were quickly met; every time a new office building was constructed on a former open parking lot, not only did it remove those parking spaces but it also created a need for still more. "Merchants are opposed to the prohibition of curb-parking, as it hurts their sales," Said the reporter. "Yet in many areas both the street and the garages are inadequate for the cars of shoppers and business men. Many communities are finding, accordingly, that if a city is overcrowded, the logical course is to decentralize. This is perhaps the most hopeful remedy of all." As a result, the suburbs were building up rapidly, becoming retail trade as well as residential centers.[21]

Miller McClintock, Sheldon Fellow at Harvard University, was another who looked at the general parking problem in 1924. In an attempt to solve the problem of street congestion in their business districts, he noted, practically all cities had by then placed limits on the length of time that vehicles could park on the street, with limits ranging from ten minutes to six hours. The tendency had been to shorten the time with the increase of the problem. "In actual practice, however, they have but little effect, for they cannot be enforced," he concluded. Boston, Buffalo, Chicago, Cleveland, Washington, Kansas City, New Orleans, Philadelphia, Seattle, and Portland (Oregon) had already prohibited parking in certain limited localities. Those and other cities had contemplated an extension of the prohibition to the entire business district. But when such proposals were made they had always met with strenuous opposition. When an extensive prohibition was put into effect in Los Angeles and Washington, D.C., "The merchants were successful in bringing about an abolition of the rule within a few days."[22]

McClintock argued that the principle involved in prohibiting parking was simple and one that cities would be forced to accept in the near future, "The streets were dedicated for the purpose of travel and for acts incident thereto. Thus travel and the loading and unloading of goods and passengers are proper acts in the street. The storage of cars on the street, however, is an act not immediately connected with the purpose for which the streets were created. The fact that such a use of the street has been permitted in the past is no reason why it should be continued." Double-parking, he argued, was an indication of super saturation and was the most threatening aspect of the traffic problem. The principle that should guide cities in that respect was: "When the use of the street for storage purposes impairs the use of the street for purposes of transportation or for acts directly connected with transportation, the former use must be prohibited." He felt the actual effect of prohibited parking on business had never been determined. Shops that catered to the poorer classes would not be affected, he reasoned, as their patrons did not usually shop from their cars. Shops catering to the rich would also be little affected since their patrons came chiefly in chauffeur-driven cars that did not have to park. The extent to which shops catering to middle-class customers would suffer depended on a number of factors such as the availability of paid storage spaces in close proximity, frequency of pubic transit, and so on. McClintock argued: "That prohibited parking will keep some small per cent of the population from the accustomed markets in the center of the city is probable. This patronage, however, will not be lost to the city, but will be absorbed by the local neighborhood stores, thus bringing about a decentralization of interests, which is greatly to be desired." He also thought it unfair for the city to hold onto vacant lots for parking with a property value as high as $25,000 "for the storage of cars which are not of sufficient utility to owners to warrant their paying from 25 to 50 cents for their housing."[23]

Wondering if adequate storage could be provided for those drivers who were willing to pay for the storage of their cars, McClintock declared that in any case no city had such facilities. In Boston, for example, it was estimated that 10,000 cars would be turned out of the streets by a parking prohibition, while public and private garage facilities had a capacity of only a fraction of that number. For that reason he suggested a gradual prohibition should be undertaken, starting with the most congested streets. Experience was said to have shown that public and private storage facilities would be built when demand was sufficiently great. In Cleveland, a publicly owned plot of land in the center of the city had been converted into a parking square. Although it only imposed a "nominal" charge for parking, "substantial" revenue was realized by the city. Officials in Chicago had turned a portion of Grant Park into a parking lot that held 3,000 cars and charged 25 cents per day per car. McClintock concluded that private facilities held out the greatest hope to cities for relief from the traffic problem.[24]

So much a part of the national psyche had the parking problem become that a two-reel Hal Roach film comedy (starring humorist Will Rogers) was released in June 1924, titled, *Don't Park There!* Playing a small-town farmer, Rogers is crowded off the road by an automobile while driving a horse and wagon, so he buys a car. But in looking for a place to park it long enough to make a few purchases he finds he has to drive farther and farther away from his Los Angles home, finally ending up parking in Seattle. Said Rogers, "The national question of finding a space where the family limousine can be cased while shopping has become more acute than the nation's debt or the soldiers' bonus." He added, "Since parking of automobiles has become such a problem, the collecting of traffic tickets has put foreign postage stamps, old coins and cigar coupons to shame."[25]

When J. N. Shannahan, president of the American Electric Railway Association, addressed his organization at their 1925 convention in Washington, D.C., he issued a call to the nation's 43 million daily electric railway riders to rise up and demand traffic congestion relief. He declared that the failure to limit parking and to restrict traffic to specific lanes had played havoc with electric railway and bus schedules. Describing traffic congestion as "unspeakable," he said that while mass transit vehicles should be able to average from ten to 12 miles per hour, in some cities in the downtown sections it was impossible to do better than two miles per hour.

According to Shannahan there were two major steps to take that would help enormously. As a first step he advocated the stopping of all street parking in the downtown areas, declaring the streets should not be used for storage purposes: "They are built to be used as passageways, and not as garages. Some people will of course resent not being permitted to store their cars all day long in the streets, but do not forget that when you offend one person by enforcing a no parking regulation, you please several hundred others whose ride has been accelerated by it." His second point was to unscramble traffic and create specific channels. For example, let streetcars move unimpeded in their own lane, give buses the right of way on certain streets, and set aside certain streets for trucks and other heavy vehicles.[26]

J. L. Butler, managing director of the Los Angeles Downtown Business Men's Association and a former Los Angeles police chief, returned to Los Angeles late in 1925 after completing a traffic survey he had undertaken in 20 of the larger eastern cities. He said the merchants there were fast coming to the realization that the downtown parking and traffic problems were their own even more than that of the municipalities, which was evidenced by the fact that downtown merchants in a great many of the cites in the East were erecting parking garages that cost $300,000 to $400,000 to build and $30,000 annually to maintain. One of the big merchants in Boston told Butler, "Unless the merchants in the important cities of the country realize at once the traffic problem is their own, the downtown districts, within fifteen years, will disintegrate with shopping centers established in the outlying and suburban districts more accessible to the automobile shopper." Butler claimed statistics showed that 30 percent of the trade of any large downtown store was from the automobile shopper. Of those Eastern merchants, declared Butler, "They realize that customers who own automobiles like to drive them and that when they are unable to drive them to the shopping center they will tour to other localities where there are more facilities for parking their automobiles. In view of this, much of the trade has gone to the store equipped to care for the autoshopper." Many merchants were said to maintain parking spaces for their customers. One store in Newark, New Jersey, maintained a parking lot ten blocks distant from its store. It operated a bus from the lot to the store. Still other merchants paid a part of the cost of customer parking in privately owned lots or garages.[27]

Other merchants, continued Butler, felt the cars had to be catered to but that municipalities should look after it. And many had done so. St. Louis, Missouri, at a cost of $1,500,000 had erected a garage building covering an entire block with a market occupying the first floor. The second floor was devoted to transient parking at a rate of 15 cents for two hours, with the third and fourth floors used for all-day parking, at a rate of 35 cents per car per day. Located at the edge of the shopping district, this garage had a capacity of 750 cars. In addition, three large stores in St. Louis supplied parking space for their patrons. After Chicago threw open a portion of Grant Park south of Monroe Street to free parking there was agitation for excavating under Grant Park just east of Michigan Avenue and establishing a parking garage. Buffalo, New York, provided parking on the waterfront at ten cents per day; Cleveland also provided space for parking along the waterfront. Another thing noted by Butler on his trip to the East was that buses were coming into prominence in that area. He said the sentiment in the East was that the bus would eventually replace the streetcar.[28]

Edward S. Jordan, president of the Jordan Motor Car Company, predicted in March 1926, "Cities of the future will increase in population and prosperity in proportion to the amount of space provided for the movement of traffic." He pointed out that there were then 20 million cars and trucks in the U.S. and over four million would be added during 1926. What was needed, he argued, was a variety of things such as wider streets, more one-way thoroughfares, and greater speed. Parking at the curb would gradually be prohibited, he predicted, as merchants discovered that the six or eight customers parked outside their doors were keeping away ten times as many.

"Department stores will maintain parking accommodations for their customers, and will tend to spread out into the suburbs," said Jordan. "The day is surely coming when we will drive in from the suburbs to within a mile or so of the business district, park our cars in municipal garages and go the rest of the way in fast, small taxicabs that will never stop except to pick up and discharge passengers."[29]

Writing in *Scientific American* in 1926, H. W. Slauson pointed to the growing traffic and parking problems. As an example, he cited an importer who brought goods from a German supplier in Hamburg and had them freighted by boat to the Port of New York and from there by truck the four miles to his Manhattan warehouse. When all the freight and trucking bills were paid, said Slauson, the customer found the four-mile land transportation cost exceeded that of the 3,000 miles of ocean shipment, due to delays, congestion, and so forth. When a new office building was constructed in Manhattan, he added, perhaps 30 to 40 old brownstones were torn down to make room for a building that took up a whole block. Maybe 150 residents lived in those brownstones while the new office building could house 5,000 employees, with no extra parking space added to the block. Slauson proposed that all such new buildings be required to devote part of their space to parking areas. Those structures already devoted part of their otherwise rentable space to vertical transportation for its tenants — that is, elevators: "The owner of a modern building should be glad to devote at least five percent of its profitable space to the temporary storage of vehicles which the business or social activity of the occupants of that building brings to its immediate vicinity." Basement parking space struck Slauson as the most likely way to provide that space. For him, the solution to the parking problem lay within the building itself.[30]

A 1926 study by the Domestic Commerce Division of the United States Bureau of Foreign and Domestic Commerce looked at expressions of opinions on traffic problems from representative merchants in more than 800 American cities and towns. Most of those merchants reported that their business was interfered with because of traffic conditions. The largest problem revealed was the belief that regulations were not enforced. A lack of parking facilities was given as the next-greatest cause of producing congestion, while narrow streets ranked third as a cause. More than one merchant reported, with respect to shoppers, "They go where they can park," but lack of parking facilities was seen as only one part of the whole problem of traffic congestion. A total of 7,621 questionnaires were mailed to merchants representing the following lines of merchandise: dry goods, men's and women's clothing, hardware, furniture, jewelry, shoes, groceries, and drugs. A total of 1,426 useable surveys (18 percent) were returned. Noted was the rise of the "subcenter" shopping district that was rapidly becoming a complete shopping district differing from downtown centers only in size and number of shops, as a trend to decentralization proceeded. In some cities downtown merchants had sensed the trend and were establishing branch stores in the subcenters. Trade was foreseen as gravitating permanently to subcenter districts with ample parking facilities. Still, there was a worry that the traffic congestion of the downtowns might simply repeat itself in those newly arising business centers. According to reports from the National Conference on Street and Highway Safety, detailed traffic tallies in a city of more than 175,000 in population indicated that congestion was costing the community $35,000 a day. In another city with about twice that population estimates were that congestion cost $100,000 a day. In the vast majority of cities, however, parking was permitted on business streets, at least some of the time. The length of time that parking was allowed seemed to be the debatable issue.[31]

From the survey noted above, it was found that the average shopping time varied by the size of the city. In cities with a population of over 200,000, 52 percent of the shoppers took less than 30 minutes; 29 percent took 30 to 60 minutes; 11 percent one hour; 4 percent one to two hours; and 4 percent took two hours or more. With cities having a population of 50,000 to 200,000 the percentages were, respectively, 53, 37, 9, 0, 1; in municipalities of 10,000 to 50,000 the numbers were, 69, 27, 3, 0.5, 0.5. Finally, in the smallest communities surveyed (population 2,500 to 10,000) the percentages were, 82, 16, 1.5, 0, and 0.5. A different survey, made in the CBD of one city where the parking limit was 45 minutes, found that the average car was parked for 29.5 minutes.[32]

Again, from the U.S. government survey, in the largest cities it was found that 86 percent of them had parking time limits (11 percent, 10–20 minutes; 22 percent, 30–45 minutes; 52 percent, 60 minutes; 15 percent, over one hour), 5 percent of the cities allowed unlimited parking, and 9 percent permitted no parking at all. Going down in population the next group had 89 percent of the cities with limited parking (11 percent, 36 percent, 38 percent, 15 percent), 7 percent with unlimited parking and 4 percent with no parking. In towns with 10,000 to 50,000 in population 53 percent imposed limits (7 percent, 27 percent, 42 percent, 24 percent) with 46 percent having unlimited parking and 1 percent allowing no parking. Just 10 percent of the municipalities with the smallest populations imposed limits (24 percent, 18 percent, 25 percent, 33 percent). In those centers 89 percent permitted unlimited parking, and 1 percent allowed no parking at all. Efforts on the part of merchants, who responded to the survey, to adjust store service to meet the need for parking space had taken the form of garage service, outdoor area service, bus service and chauffeur service. An estimated 80 of those services were reported to the government's survey. Indications were that area services offered by merchants removed from the streets more than a million cars annually. A reporter commenting on the report observed that if the problem of providing day storage for automobiles was a municipal one, as many believed, then municipal garages were a logical way of approaching the problem of a lack of parking facilities. However, he acknowledged that the cost of such facilities to a city could be considerable. He concluded, "The most important part of any city plan is said to be the traffic plan. This part of the city plan has been until recently much neglected, although it appears to be especially important for all cities contemplating expansion."[33]

A report by a firm of engineers and consultants, The Buler Organization, prepared for the Belmoy Corporation of New York, in 1926, said the growing traffic congestion in CBDs made possible a new type of shopping center in suburban communities. According to the report, the growing traffic congestion in cities is making it increasingly difficult for the suburban customers of city stores to reach these stores and shop in leisure and comfort. Surveys show that these people are reducing the number of their shopping trips to the stores in the congested centers, and are shopping in a more hurried manner, and many are forced to reach the stores by congested transit facilities when they prefer to use their automobiles. A larger and larger proportion of their buying is being done in stores within their own suburban area." After noting that subcenters had developed in many American cities, the Buler report showed that they had followed the old conventional lines and as they grew their usefulness was throttled by traffic congestion. As far as the report was concerned, "The modern center must be planned to suit modern conditions, chief among which is the apparent determination of people to shop by automobile." Surveys showed a larger proportion of shoppers wanted to shop by car, but were unable to do so because of traffic congestion.[34]

As new business centers developed, noted the Buler report, the desire of people to shop by car could not be ignored. The modern business center was told it had to provide off-street parking or garage space for the vehicles of its customers and employees. Suburban centers then developing in the more open spaces where property values were relatively low were said to have an exceptional opportunity for building to conform to modern conditions. Suburban stores could provide adequate area space within their grounds for all those cars at reasonable cost. As the study declared: "Customers can then reach the shopping floors easily and can shop leisurely and in comfort without fear that their cars may be stolen or that some parking restrictions may be violated. Nor will they be forced to negotiate blocks of congested streets on their return trips home. "Ample parking space on the store's own grounds, where customers' cars could be left in safety, is so unusual and so desirable in this day that it offers a convincing advertising feature."[35]

According to a comprehensive parking survey completed by the Los Angeles Traffic Commission in the summer of 1926, three of every four cars using the central business district each day were parked in private garages or parking lots. That survey was conducted in the district bounded by First, Ninth, Main, and Figueroa Streets and disclosed that there was storage space in garages and on lots for 135,888 cars. Within the same area there was room to park 3,875 cars at curbs. Because the 45-minute curb limit allowed the use of a curb space 12 times each business day, 46,500 vehicles could be accommodated through street parking. A recent count made by the traffic commission indicated slightly more than 210,000 cars entered the CBD each business day. Reportedly, the difference between that number and the parking space available for 182,388 vehicles could be accounted for by the fact that some motorists used parking facilities and/or curb space immediately adjacent to the CBD, and that some people drove through the downtown streets without parking. Approximately one-third of all curb space in the Los Angeles CBD was restricted from parking, taken up by red and yellow zones, fire hydrants, driveways, alleys, and entrances to garages and gas stations. In the CBD was a total of 97,485 feet of curb space (about 18.4 miles). Restricted curb space amounted to 39,354 feet: yellow loading zones, 13,003 feet; red safety zones, 20,909 feet; abandoned driveways, 269 feet; alley entrances, 1,318 feet; garages and parking lot entrances, 3,765 feet. That left 58,151 feet of curb for parking space, with each space taking an estimated 15 feet. Most restricted block was the west side of Hill Street between Second and Third Streets; out of a total of 590 feet of curb space, 524 feet were restricted, leaving just 66 feet for parking. Least restricted was the west side of Hope Street, between Eighth and Ninth Streets — of 580 feet in the block just 67 feet were restricted leaving 513 feet available for parking.[36]

Dr. Miller McClintock, consultant to the Los Angeles Traffic Commission and its survey, said the city had more private parking space for cars within its CBD than the average American city, thanks mainly to a dramatic increase in the number of parking garages in the recent past, while the amount of curb space for parking had remained practically unchanged. At the same time the number of parking lots was decreasing as more and more new office buildings and retail space were constructed. Net gain in parking spaces over the previous two years had been more than 6,000, he said. McClintock observed that while there were 47 parking garages with total floor space of more than one million square feet in the CBD, "The city must look to the continued construction of these storage garages as the solution of the downtown parking problem." Curb space was free but accommodated only 25 percent of the number of cars using the CBD. Parking in garages then cost an average of 46 cents per car per day, while the use of a parking lot cost the motorist an average of 26 cents per car per day. Most of the garages and lots used each space more than once a day as Los Angeles motorists spent $8,047 a day for the storage of automobiles, or almost $3 million a year. In addition to public lots and garages there was a growing number of office buildings that were providing parking space in their basements — the new City Hall had such room to park 500 cars. Discussing the parking situation, McClintock said the parking of cars was imperative, as a privately owned vehicle had no value as a transportation unit unless it could be stopped and left in close proximity to the owner's destination. "Every responsible automobile owner provides a garage near his home but too little thought has been given to the establishment of equally satisfactory terminal facilities at the other end of the run," he declared.[37]

The editor of *American City* formulated a statement of principles, applicable to all cites for the parking and storage of autos and the facilitation of street traffic, in the October 1926 issue of that publication. Reportedly, that editorial stance was drawn after he collaborated with a dozen or so experts. Catalyst for the stance was the editor's rhetorical question: "Can our progressive business men no longer build big retail shops, theaters and other structures where the crowds congregate, with reasonable expectation that the city will somehow make it possible for their customers to continue to arrive — and park — by automobile?" Principles in his stance included: (1) that streets were primarily provided for general public use as lines of communication for pedestrians and for the transportation of persons and merchandise and that the rights of the different classes of traffic to unlimited use of the streets, including the right to park, were subject to the public and civic welfare; (2) that unlimited parking be allowed at all times in all business districts where it did not cost the traveling public more than it saved those who parked, nor interfered with the expeditious movement and safety of street traffic, and with reasonable access of vehicles to the curb. Another of his principles was that the right to move a car was superior to the right to store a car on the public ways, and that when parking caused a net economic loss to the public through hindrance to safe and convenient travel, there should be limitation — or in extreme cases, at certain hours, total abolition — of parking, both commercial and private and that in some cities the complete prohibition during certain hours of private vehicles from congested CBDs was to be regarded as an "ultimate possibility."[38]

Also, the editor argued all future department stores, theaters, "tall" office buildings, and other business structures catering to large numbers of customers or tenants should be built only with a knowledge by the owner that he had to either provide parking space himself for the storage of his customers' and employees' cars, and for the unloading and loading of merchandise or depend on the trade and services of people who traveled by foot or public transit, or establish branch shops outside of the congested centers in areas with ample parking space. As a general conclusion the editor declared, "In the public interest, every city must consider a deliberate policy of decentralization and the adoption of a plan for major street and transit developments with a fair division of cost between the city and the benefited property." Commenting on the editor's principles, Walter Jackson, a transit consultant from Mount Vernon, New York, observed, "The personal machine uses up so much of the street area in proportion to its passengers that those who simply must enjoy such exclusiveness ought to pay for it in the form of garage fees. Merchants who encourage parking are surely shortsighted. Not more than two or three autos bringing hardly six customers will block off the view of their shop windows from pedestrians on the opposite side and from persons riding by." On the other hand, added Jackson, one streetcar would deposit 20 customers at a shop's door every few minutes and not linger a second longer than necessary to unload its passengers: "Only the public utility transport vehicle leaves the merchant's curbs free for loading and unloading his goods."[39]

Automobile parking in Asbury Park, New Jersey, in 1926 had grown to be such a serious problem — in keeping customers from stores — that businessmen of the area took matters into their own hands and devised an "honor system" of parking. Signs were placed along the town's main street, Cookman Avenue, appealing to the public to refrain from parking cars any longer than necessary. Merchants hoped that system would work, although they admitted an existing ordinance that limited parking on Cookman to no more than 20 minutes had failed to keep the street clear. According to the businessmen, cars had been left standing for as long as

30 hours, with the result that Cookman had become so congested shoppers had to leave their cars several blocks from the business street and walk to the shops. One group who endorsed the honor system plan was the employees of the Seacoast Trust Company, located on Cookman. They voluntarily agreed to park their cars hereafter on other streets. Edward Marsh, secretary of the local chamber of commerce said that if any car owner failed to enter into the spirit of the new scheme, their license number would be recorded. Following that, the Chamber would first telephone the owner, then, if that failed to work, the car owner would receive a diplomatically worded letter. If the owner still paid no heed to those cautions and persisted in parking overtime, he would be prosecuted. Asbury Park Police Commissioner Harry White said the police would stand behind the businessmen in their plan and that he thought the honor plan was a "fine thing" because putting people on their honor worked a much greater compulsion than did a law, and thus should be much more effective.[40]

Morgan A. Collins, general superintendent of police of the city of Chicago, told a radio audience in May 1926 over Chicago station WBBM that parking spaces in city streets were doomed to go the way of city cow pastures of some 30 to 40 years earlier. "We read funny accounts in the papers about pigs running about in the streets a generation ago, but these stories will not seem any more comic fifteen or twenty years hence than the stories about automobiles parked on the streets," he explained. "Congestion, retarding and jamming traffic has doomed this practice."[41]

In a 1926 article that discussed the efficiency and cheapness of the streetcar, the writer noted that if all 31 passengers on a given streetcar had taken their cars instead, it would have likely meant 31 more vehicles on the roads. If all had ridden downtown in cabs, two to a taxi, the fares would have totaled $17, with those 15 cabs occupying a line in the street of about 200 feet. If they had all ridden down in their own autos, the investment in cars would have been about $30,000, yet the streetcar did the entire job for $1.80, for all the passengers, and took up no more room in the street than did two automobiles.[42]

Dr. Miller McClintock, director of the Albert Russel Erskine Bureau for Street Traffic Research, stated in 1926 that the tremendous increase in the use of automobiles in the past decade had made it evident that cities would have to make some provision for their parking. "The streets cannot care for the great volume of moving traffic and at the same time afford convenient or sufficient storage space," he explained. A survey just completed by the Erskine bureau (in conjunction with the National Association of Building Owners and Managers) revealed that in 17 cities a total of

1,424,600 cars entered the central business district every day and that in those districts there was available only a total curb space sufficient to park 85,424 cars. Additionally, the study showed that parking garages and parking lots in those same cities afforded space for 147,081 more automobiles. Those cities contained 341 parking garages that were said to be well patronized by the public and were financially successful. Frequently merchants, realizing the advantages that would come from a parking space for their customers, said had assisted in the building and operation of garages, according to McClintock. A very large retail store in Chicago had just started a service whereby customers could drive up to the store, have their autos taken by a driver to a garage, and returned by the driver when their shopping was over. McClintock argued that public officials could often assist in the storage of cars by making available for parking purposes pieces of public land that would otherwise be idle. Businessmen who were constructing stores, theaters, and other establishments that drew large numbers of people "should seriously consider incorporating in their plans provision for the storage of automobiles," he admonished. In Los Angeles, for example, it was said to have become almost standard practice by then to build garages in the basements and sub-basements of new office buildings. Concluded McClintock, "Business men in all cities should adopt the new slogan of 'a convenient parking place for every automobile.'"[43]

When a visitor came to the town of Gunnison, Utah, in 1926 he complained to a reporter that Main Street was in a state of disorganization because cars were parked every which way. Checking out the complaint, the journalist found it to be true. On both sides of Main Street automobiles were parked without regard to a system. Of the 50 or more cars parked along the main business block, only a few were conforming to the regulation of the 45-degree system of parking (head-in on an angle). Trucks were parked parallel to the sidewalk, some cars were parked at an angle in the wrong direction, while some autos were parked facing each other.[44]

Late in 1926, Dr. Miller McClintock made the news again when he declared that the development of additional off-street storage facilities for automobiles to overcome the acute shortage of parking space in the business districts of American cities was a factor of major importance in the relief of traffic congestion. "There is no city in the country that possesses curb space in the central business district capable of accommodating the parked cars of more than a small fraction of the motorists who enter the district daily," said McClintock. As an example he cited Chicago's Loop district where, if the curb space was used to full capacity and had a 100 percent turnover every half hour, it could accommodate no more than 15 percent of the actual number of cars that daily entered the district. It was also discovered that in the off-street facilities for parking there was room for only 3,000 vehicles, compared with the 122,000 vehicles that daily entered the Loop area. "There is no more important improvement that can be undertaken to encourage the use of the automobile as a standard and daily means of personal transportation than for cities to encourage, either by public construction or by private means, the construction of storage space for automobiles near the center of the business district," McClintock stated. "There should be accommodation for every motor car that is brought into the city in some safe, off-street storage space."[45]

Another detailed parking survey was completed by the Los Angeles Traffic Commission in the summer of 1927, under the direction of its traffic consultant, Dr. Miller McClintock. From its results was declared the fact that violators of the 45-minute CBD parking limit kept more than 30,000 automobiles, carrying nearly 60,000 persons who wanted to conduct business or shop, from parking at the curb in the central business district. Of a total of 21,682 cars parked at the CBD curbs during an average business day, 5,413 violations for overstaying the parking limit were reported by the Commission's checkers, equaling 25 percent. If the regulations were obeyed, 5,000 more cars could be parked downtown each day, or 30,000 a week. More than 12 percent of all parked cars (2,679) remained parked for the full 45-minute period; 592 autos parked for three 45-minute periods; 27 vehicles were parked at the curb at 9:00 A.M. and were still there, untouched, at 4:30 P.M. Said McClintock, "Failure of many Los Angeles motorists to obey parking restrictions, included in the traffic ordinance for the public good, greatly inconveniences thousands of other motorists, who are denied their right to use the curb while conducting their business affairs or shopping. There is no question, too, but that business men throughout the central business district suffer distinct losses through the failure of the parking law to function properly." It was due to a lack of manpower that the LAPD did not enforce the parking laws to any great extent. Repeated requests had been made by the LAPD for more officers, but such requests had always been denied. It meant that, with over 200,000 cars entering the CBD each business day, only about 10 percent could be accommodated at the curb. The other 90 percent had to pay to park in garages or lots, or park at curbs on streets outside of the CBD.[46]

An editorial on the above survey, in the *Los Angeles Times*, declared it was manifestly unfair to the law-abiding motorist that space he might otherwise have used for parking was usurped by drivers willing to take the slight risk of being fined because they had found by experience that there were too few policemen to monitor the vehicles parked at the curb. Concluded the editor, "The traffic problem is a big one, and in many respects it is admirably handled, but in one of its chief phases — that of this parking business — a great and grievous abuse had developed, and it calls for immediate correction."[47]

In 1927 Austin Macdonald, of the University of Pennsylvania, wrote an article that looked at parking outside of the CBD and to some extent, within it. (He argued that prohibiting or restricting parking on CBD streets left motorists with just three options: (1) leave the car at home and find another transportation option; (2) find a suitable storage space near the motorist's destination; or (3) drive the car to the edge of the CBD, park it in a convenient space, and make use of some other conveyance — usually the streetcar — to complete the journey. Whether the third option was to be much used, thought Macdonald, depended largely on the nature of the facilities provided at the edge of the congested area. He argued that little had been done up to that time to encourage drivers to park outside the CBD. Most cities had directed their efforts instead to the negative task of discouraging motorists from entering the district. However, he cited a few cities that had established parking spaces on city-owned property; some of those spaces were within the CBD and some were at its border. Pittsburgh provided space for 900 cars near the river's edge and levied a daily charge of 10 cents per car. In Akron, Ohio, the charge was 25 cents while in Michigan City, Indiana, the 25-cent fee was collected only on certain days when the traffic was likely to be heavy. Many cities provided free parking spaces but usually no attempt was made to establish those parking facilities at points where they will be of the greatest value to motorists. Rather, their sites were determined instead by the changing location of vacant city land.[48]

More significant, believed Macdonald, was the experience of street railway companies. A number of them had hit upon the plan of providing ample parking space at their suburban terminals, making it an easy matter for drivers to transfer from the private to the public conveyance. "Park with Us And Ride with Us" was the slogan of the Philadelphia Rapid Transit Company, which used the method more extensively and with more success than any other street railway operator. It established three large parking areas in different parts of the city, along the edge of the CBD — together the three lots held 870 cars but, reportedly, were scarcely ever filled to capacity. During summer months about 600 motorists made daily use of the facilities, but in winter the number was considerably less. A fee of 25 cents was charged, which included two streetcar tokens worth 15 cents, so the actual fee for parking was ten cents for all day. An additional fee was charged only if a vehicle was left standing for more than 24 hours. Attendants were on duty most of the day and night, and at two of the lots regular gas station services (such as gas, oil, air, and so on) were available. Several other streetcar companies made similar arrangements but on a smaller scale. The United Railways and Electric Company of Baltimore had a lot designed to hold about 300 cars and also charged 25 cents for parking and two streetcar rides. Unlike the Philadelphia utility, it did not directly control the parking facility but leased the land to a private oil company that operated the filling station and collected the parking fee. The Boston Elevated Railway had a small lot at the end of one of its lines, also operated by an oil company under a rental agreement. Some firms in other cities had tried such a plan, but without much success. In at least two cities, Pittsburgh and Poughkeepsie, the park-and-ride plan had been abandoned because of lack of patronage. A parking lot maintained by a streetcar company on the outskirts of Fort Worth held 50 cars but usually contained just ten to 20 vehicles. No charge was made, but there was also no attendant on duty, nor were there any service facilities provided. The Chicago North Shore and Milwaukee Railroad had parking lots at 15 stations along its line, but the average number of vehicles that could be accommodated was only slightly more than 20.[49]

Macdonald concluded, "From this hasty sketch it is clear that the establishment of parking spaces outside the congested area has not served, except in very small measure, to relieve the pressure on the center of the city. Automobilists have not made extensive use of the facilities provided." The most successful plan, Philadelphia's, had only succeeded in keeping a maximum of 600 cars out of its CBD, assuming all the motorists that used the lots would have driven downtown (not necessarily true), while Baltimore's experiment kept out a maximum of 200 automobiles. The Pittsburgh Railway Company gave its plan a trial of less than three weeks before discarding it. Macdonald wondered if the park-and-ride plan was inherently weak and could not be made to appeal to car owners; that motorists could not be induced to park outside the traffic zone: "But no such conclusion is warranted from the experiments thus far made. Nowhere has the plan been given a fair trial. In some cities parking sites have been selected without sufficient regard for the character of the surrounding territory intended to feed them. In others the undertaking has received little publicity, and a considerable portion of the motoring public has never fully understood the experiment. The parking fee has in several instances been too high."[50]

Suggestions from Macdonald, if the public were to use park-and-ride lots more frequently, was that the parking fee should be very small, no more than ten cents, and preferably abolished altogether. Such outlying facilities had to be looked at as primarily for the purpose of relieving congestion and not of producing revenue, if they were to succeed. The difference between the outlying and CBD parking charges should, he felt, be considerably more than the price of two streetcar fares. Because the outlying lots had to be operated without much regard to revenues, private capital would not step it and, thus, such lots had to be operated by the city or the local street railway company. Whenever, possible parking spaces in such facilities should be covered to protect cars from the elements; attendants should be on duty a minimum of 18 hours a day (for security); and service station facilities (such as gas and oil) should be provided at every such facility. Also, such park-and-ride lots should be well publicized. Given the degree of congestion in the larger cities and the sometimes-drastic parking restrictions imposed on CBD streets Macdonald concluded, "Under such circumstances it would seem wise to experiment more widely than in the past with parking facilities outside the heavy traffic zone. These facilities, if properly operated and widely advertised, should make a strong appeal to the suburban motorist. And if the suburban motorist can be induced to keep his car out of the central business district, traffic congestion will be a far less serious matter."[51]

Harold Buttenheim, editor of *American City* observed in 1927 that the idea that buildings should provide parking within their property line was then under discussion in various cities. Pittsburgh was considering such an ordinance, but Burton W. Marsh, Pittsburgh traffic engineer, admitted it was hard to tell at what point such a law should kick in — how large should the building be, what percentage of expected parking should it contain, and so forth. West Palm Beach, Florida, passed such an ordinance on October 31, 1926, which required that, under certain conditions, commercial establishments had to provide on their own land for parking in connection with their own business.[52]

Buttenheim also touted the virtues of decentralization. Not only would a decentralized city afford greater comfort and safety to most of its inhabitants, he believed, but the majority of real estate owners would profit by a spreading out of values, compared to "excessive values" for the benefit of a few in a highly congested center. He added, "Automobile manufacturers, dealers, and service stations, for example, have a very definite financial interest in the parking problem and in the prevention of too intensive use of the land by skyscrapers and apartment houses. There will obviously be a much larger market for automobiles if there is not too great congestion in the streets of our cities."[53]

In 1927, according to R. B. Stoeckel, motor vehicle commissioner at Hartford, Connecticut, the time was coming when there would be no automobile parking in the streets. Merchants, he said, would find it to their advantage if space in front of their stores was free for prospective customers to travel on instead of being blocked by parked cars.[54]

Also in 1927, St. Louis and New York City were both reported to be planning to relieve traffic congestion by the construction of elevated streets. Chicago already had a double-decked street in use — Wacker Drive, to the extent of three-quarters of a mile in length. Planners in St. Louis wanted a three-mile, two-layer roadway with, in addition, an elevated plaza for the parking of 6,000 automobiles. New York City residents were then purchasing cars at the rate of 30,000 a month, seven miles of automobiles.[55]

When a 1928 survey was made by the Traffic Committee of the Rochester (New York) Engineering Society, it was made in connection with the committee's recommendation that street parking be prohibited in Rochester during the afternoon rush hours (4:30 to 6:00) without inconveniencing shoppers. To conduct the survey, about 200 Boy Scouts were stationed at the doorways of department stores and other retail establishments and approached people with a questionnaire. Of 48,700 shoppers approached by the boys, 34,233 (70 percent) answered the questions. Less than 2 percent (621) of the 34,233 shoppers interviewed during that one day parked their cars on the streets between 4:30 and 6:00 P.M. Those Rochester shoppers got to the stores as follows: by street car, 16,572; by walking, 8,029; cars parked in private facilities, 4,719; cars parking in the street, 3,798; street railroad, 614; bus, 501. That total of 48,700 shoppers entered Rochester stores between 9:00 A.M. and 6:00 P.M., with the peak half hour being 12:30 to 1:00 P.M. (4,159) while the slackest half-hour period was from 9:00 A.M. to 9:30 (1,360).[56]

After it conducted a 1928 survey of the parking problem, the United States Chamber of Commerce concluded that the problem was one for which there was no universal solution. Conditions in all cities varied so greatly that each city had to work out its own solution. While traffic regulations could be made uniform, the questions of where, when and for how long motorists could park their autos were ones for which rules and practices had to be evolved that would best serve the community affected.[57]

John A. Miller, Jr., was the editor of the trade publication *Aera* and the associate editor of *Electric Railway Journal*. He said that traffic delays caused by the street congestion in greater New York in 1928 resulted in an annual loss estimated at more than $540 million, a sum that was $28 million more than the budget of the city for 1927. Some firms were solving the problem by moving out of the CBD to less-congested districts, and that it was happening in large cities all over America. A bellwether for the growth of outlying commercial centers could be found, he argued, by the location of banks. For example, in a certain large Eastern city there were 37 banks of deposit in the city and its suburbs in 1914. In 1928, there were twice that number, but during that period only seven of the new banks opened in the downtown section of the city, while 30 had been established more than a mile away from the CBD. He noted that many plans for relief of traffic congestion were based on the general theory of providing more roadway such as widening streets, and creating new streets, or more expensive options such as putting streetcar lines underground. And, in any case, said Miller, "Experience has shown in a number of instances that new streets cut through to relieve overcrowding on older streets downtown soon become congested themselves without any marked diminution of traffic on the other streets." It was, he felt, a problem that should be approached, from the point of view of the more efficient use of streets, and that allowing street parking was the greatest hindrance to expeditious street flow.[58]

According to Miller, the elimination of car parking would increase the effective width of existing streets from 30 percent to 200 percent. Often parking was allowed on both sides of streets having a width of 60 feet or less between building lines. Deducting two 12-foot sidewalks left 36 feet of roadway. But a row of parked automobiles took up eight feet on each side, leaving 20 feet, or one lane for moving traffic in each direction. "Such use of the public streets is obviously selfish, because many are inconvenienced and only a few are accommodated," he concluded. Nor did he accept the argument that elimination of parking would not create an additional traffic lane because a certain number of vehicles would always be stopping in the curb lane to pick up or discharge. He argued that, with a parking lane allowed, vehicles which could not find curb space double parked for those brief stops, therefore a new lane would be created with parking prohibited. Traffic counts made in various large cities showed that public transportation vehicles carried upward of 75 percent of the total traffic, although they constituted only about 15 percent of the total number of vehicles. Miller said the retailers' fear that restrictions on parking would injure their trade were unfounded. Checks made at 76 leading stores in New York, Chicago, Detroit, Cleveland, Los Angeles, Baltimore, and other large cities, showed that of 444,1333 customers, only 66,454 (15 percent) came in private cars, with the ratios being about the same in all the cities where counts were made. Thus, the restriction on auto parking was not much of a menace to retailers. Said R. C. Haldeman, president of the Pennsylvania Motor Federation, "The present-day habit of using our streets as a public garage is one of the greatest evils tending to increase congestion in the business districts of our municipalities. It is both a selfish and a time-wasting habit of the motor-car owner. The individual apparently gives no thought to the inconvenience that his action places on the many."[59]

As to the suggestions that the private car not be allowed to enter congested districts at all, Miller dismissed these as impractical. Another proposal then making the rounds was for half the private cars to be permitted to enter the CBD on one day, the other half the next day—based on odd/even-numbered license plates. Miller favored more lots, more garages, and more underground parking provided by buildings. All of which, he argued, had to have the cost borne by the users: "This would not be popular with motorists, but after all, no good reason exists why storage space for private automobiles should be provided at public expense."[60]

William J. Pedrick, executive vice-president of the Fifth Avenue Association, declared at the end of 1928 that automobile parking on Fifth Avenue in Manhattan was essential to the development and maintenance of that thoroughfare. That conclusion was stated on the release of a report after a two-year study of the parking situation on Fifth Avenue, under the direction of that group, from the merchants' viewpoint and from the standpoint of traffic congestion in the Fifth Avenue district. A restriction then in force on the street allowed a one-hour parking maximum for a car between 10:00 A.M. and 5:00 P.M. and reportedly was observed by 94 percent of the cars parked there daily. Of that 94 percent, more than 60 percent did not use the entire hour. An estimated 65 percent of the Fifth Avenue stores had doormen, which helped to control the parking of customers' cars. Also, 89.9 percent of the stores queried as part of the survey declared the parking privilege was essential to continued prosperity and development. According to the report, automobiles brought 30 percent of the shopping trade to the district, furnished 51 percent of the daily business of 215 Fifth Avenue stores, and that a great part of that trade would be lost if a no-parking ban was enforced.[61]

Studies of Fifth Avenue were made between 19th and 50th Streets, with the Fifth Avenue Association finding that more than 50 percent of the checked cars parked 15 minutes or less, and 75 percent parked for 30 minutes or less. Results from those studies, declared Pedrick, certainly "justifies the stand taken by the association that a reasonable parking period is essential during the business day for all the streets in midtown Manhattan and that the parking privilege, when strictly enforced, does not work a hardship upon traffic." As far as he was concerned, the entire argument of the no-parking advocates was based on an obsolete generalization that streets were laid out for moving traffic. "That generalization is open to challenge. From the day of the first hitching post on Main Street to Fifth Avenue today, parking has been accepted as a necessary adjunct to a street system." Concluded the report, "New York can find some other way to solve its traffic ills without betraying the great business institutions that have contributed to its growth throughout the last quarter-century." Instead of any more restrictions on parking, the report recommended the use of elevated highways, boulevards, bridges, tunnels, and the curtailment of taxis.[62]

In late 1929, an editor with the *Columbia Missourian* newspaper pointed to the steadily increasing number of automobiles in all parts of the country and remarked that nearly every city was confronted by a problem of proper parking facilities, including his own. He said the chief problem was the arrangement of parking space on Broadway, Columbia's main business street. Broadway had a "center zone" system of parking and, in his mind, presented the typical quandary in which a city often found itself. "It seems as if we should take some action on the matter to remedy the existing parking evil. Other cities have met the identical problem and have satisfactorily disposed of it. Why cannot we do the same thing?"[63]

R. J. Dorsey, engineer with the Los Angeles Street Traffic Engineering Department, remarked in 1932 that of all traffic problems none was more difficult than that of providing a proper balance in the use of streets in business sections for moving and stationary automobiles. Merchants opposed giving up curb parking in the vicinity of their stores. Not only did they want parking, but in many cases, ample parking as well. "When streets are very wide, or the volume of traffic is comparatively light, those in charge of traffic regulations usually hesitate to interfere with free curb parking but as congestion increased, regulatory measures often became necessary," said Dorsey. Los Angeles then banned parking in the CBD between 4:30 and 6:00 P.M. and limited it to 45 minutes during the remainder of the business day. In addition, parking was prohibited in certain zones at all times. Those restrictions were not entirely satisfactory on a number of east-west streets, which were not only narrower, but carried considerably more traffic than the north/south arteries. "Consequently, considerable effort has been made to have parking prohibited on these streets," he explained. "This has been consistently opposed by landowners and merchants, who have contended that it would make serious inroads into the volume of retail trade."[64]

Thus, Dorsey's department did a street parking survey of those east-west streets. Each driver of every parked car was approached and the following data obtained: type of car, license number, time parked, time departed, number of occupants, number of occupants discharged, destination of discharged occupants, purchases (if any), type of purchase, and amount spent. In all, 4,498 cars were parked in the area with full information being obtained from 4,200 (94 percent). It was found that each curb-parked car spent on average $2.15, although 68 percent of these cars made no purchases whatsoever. Also, the average car was parked for 31.3 minutes, but 20 percent overstayed the 45-minute parking limit, generally only by a few minutes. Each parked car, on average, carried 1.4 persons with 1.2 people being discharged; the remainder stayed in the car. While the 4,200 cars contacted represented total purchases of $9,032.73, the merchants with frontage exclusively on the streets surveyed obtained only $1,443.89 (16 percent) in trade with the balance going to businesses on the longer north/south blocks. The four largest department stores alone got 22 percent of the total amount spent; restaurants got $116.11 in trade and drugstores received $92.69. Dividing the money spent on the east-west streets equally among the 597 business establishments located thereon, it was found that the average merchant could expect only a little over $2.00. In an attempt to determine the possible loss in business to merchants due to prohibition of parking, the department checked the availability of off-street parking space within 300 feet of the blocks under study. Total off-street parking capacity was found to be 8,436 cars, with an unused capacity for at least 2,814 vehicles during the hours of maximum parking. As there was room at the curb for only 383 automobiles at any one time, it meant that available off-street parking space was approximately seven times the curb parking capacity. That indicated to Dorsey and his department that a parking prohibition on the CBD streets for the full business day would result in no loss of trade, providing the drivers were willing to pay a small off-street parking fee; it seldom exceeded 25 cents for a period equivalent to the street time limit and, in many cases was only ten cents.[65]

John Miller returned with a 1936 doom and gloom article in which he fretted that people were not declaring parking as the real problem and were not dealing with it. Traffic congestion had been estimated by the National Conference on Street and Highway Safety to cost the people of America more than $2 billion annually. That was about $15 per inhabitant per year, or about seven times the per capita fire loss. For a city of 500,000 people, it amounted to $7.5 million a year. Said Miller, "No deep mystery exists concerning the most effective way to relieve this congestion. The first important step to be taken is recognized by everyone who has studied the subject, but nothing is done about it, because they are all afraid to mention it.... The essence of the street traffic problem is parking." Clark S. Hobbs wrote in the Baltimore *Sun* that no matter how the problem was approached one eventually came face to face with the fact that the movement of traffic was limited by the amount of available pavement. When that was reduced 50 percent by parked vehicles, discussion of more rules and regulations and newer and fancier traffic signals became "disingenuous piffle. Traffic engineers know that. Even the politicians and the 'important citizens' may be said to know it. Nevertheless, they have suppressed that knowledge up to this time, because the giving or withholding of the parking privilege always arouses political passions." The curb lanes of a 500-foot city block, explained Miller, provided space to park not more than 50 vehicles — 25 cars on each side of the street. If the street was of average width and moderately busy, at least 1,000 vehicles would pass through the block in an hour's time, all forced to move in the two center lanes because the two curb lanes were being used for storage instead of movement. Thus, 20 vehicles were inconvenienced for every one accommodated as a parked vehicle.[66]

Rhetorically, Miller wondered why there should be any hesitancy about abolishing parking where it interfered with traffic movement. One reason, he said, was that many retail merchants were bitterly opposed to restrictions on parking around their stores. They feared it would injure their "carriage trade." As an executive of a prominent New York store once expressed it, "We are more interested in a single customer who comes to our store by automobile than in 10,000 other people who merely pass by in the street." Yet, said Miller, a check made at the entrances of the very store whose executive expressed such concern for his carriage trade, showed less than 2 percent of the people entering the store to have come from private cars parked on the adjacent streets. Overall, he said, "Nowhere does the number of private automobile customers constitute a large portion of the total patrons of a big store." Concluded Miller, "Any way you look at it the mathematical argument runs strongly against parking. The trouble is that questions of this kind are seldom settled on the basis of mathematics. Psychology enters the situation and plays a larger part than figures."[67]

Parking was a difficult problem psychologically, argued Miller, because "the average free-born American feels that he has an inherent right, guaranteed by the Constitution, you might almost say, to park his automobile wherever he wants to, whenever he wants to. Legally there is no basis for this idea. That parking is a privilege, not a right, has been established in law for more than a hundred years." Despite the lack of a legal basis for the idea that parking was a right, he believed most people continued to regard it that way and set up a "fearful outcry" if any suggestion was made to abolish it. And that was why city officials were so easily persuaded to support costly schemes for widening streets, building elevated highways, and so forth. Miller continued: "Such improvements cost millions, and do far less to relieve congestion than could be done at no cost at all by eliminating parking, but they don't deprive anyone of what he considers to be his rights." As far as he was concerned, only one city in America had ever dared tacked the parking problem "frankly and fearlessly." Chicago abolished all parking in its CBD on January 10, 1928, and had refused to retreat from that stand in spite of agitation to have the ordinance modified. The movement of traffic in the downtown area had been greatly facilitated by the elimination of parking, he said, and the merchants had not suffered any noticeable loss of business. "As yet, however, no other city has had the courage to follow Chicago's example in a convincing way. Such steps as have been taken elsewhere to abolish parking have been timid and faltering. Some, even, have been retracted almost as soon as they were taken."[68]

Physically, Miller saw no problem in removing parked autos from streets as he felt there was an adequate supply of off-street parking everywhere, although he conceded that some of those facilities were shoddy and sometimes too pricey. However, he was opposed to the idea that municipalities should provide that off-street parking, feeling that the provision was simply an "ordinary commercial undertaking." Nor was he in favor of the use of parking meters on the streets — they had just debuted in Oklahoma City. With respect to meters he observed, "This is probably the most paradoxical of many parking paradoxes. The city, in effect, sells to a limited few of its citizens the roadway space that rightfully belongs to all of its citizens. In any event, the parking meter does nothing to relieve congestion. It is little more than an automatic check on the observance of parking time limits — and these time limits are of no particular help to traffic movement." For Miller, those devices failed to accomplish what was really needed, and that was the restoration of the curb lanes to the use of moving vehicles, "Without that the roadway space on busy streets will continue to be inadequate to meet the demands upon it."[69]

Writing in *American City* in November 1936, Willard Chevalier wondered why the parking of cars on streets was allowed and why it continued:

"With all the effort for more efficient municipal administration, it is interesting to observe how little progress is made with the wasteful parking nuisance. It is not entirely clear why private individuals should be permitted to use the public streets for the storage of their cars at any time. And when the street areas thus preempted are so urgently needed for their intended purposes, the mystery is deeper." An example he used was certain big streets in New York City that had been made one-way, to lower congestion. But from morning to night both sides of the streets were lined with parked cars, cutting the effective width of those streets from four lanes to two. Although the people of New York had provided for four lanes because they needed four lanes, he argued that " a handful of individuals are permitted to preempt 50 per cent of that costly real estate in order to avoid a 50-cent parking lot fee, while the cost to thousands of them, in lost time, excessive fuel usage, loss of access and danger to life and limb is wholly ignored." And those conditions were repeated in other American cities. "And not the least interesting aspect of it all is the success with which the beneficiaries seem to ward off any move toward curbing the abuse. To be a public nuisance seems to have become a vested right of the few that the many are bound to respect," he added. Chevalier believed that until the public demanded an end to the nuisance little would be done about it and "meanwhile the wonder remains that city dwellers will continue to put up with so flagrant an imposition on their patience and pocketbooks."[70]

Late in 1936, New York City was trying to get some congestion relief by extending its one-side-of-the-street-only parking regulations. As reporter E. L. Yordan explained, "The presence of too many parked cars is a menace in fire fighting, delaying the passage of apparatus through streets and hampering activities at the scene of the blaze." In dealing with the overall problem, he said the NYPD had followed a policy of compromise between the ideal and the practical. From a 1930 traffic survey by Police Commissioner Whalen of more than 150,000 cars parked on the streets below 61st Street, it was revealed that 35 percent exceeded the one-hour limit, with 7 percent parked from three to nine hours. Whalen estimated that less than 40,000 parked cars were responsible for the delays and inconveniences that parking caused in the area studied. He put the loss to commercial and business interests at $1 million daily as a result of such congestion. A more recent survey done by WPA workers showed 10,000 cars, trucks, and taxis parked at the curb on an average day in the section between 14th and 72nd Streets and Second and Eleventh Avenues. About 25 percent of those parked for longer than the legal limit of one hour while less than 2 percent were parked long enough to warrant the epithet "all-day" parker.[71]

T. T. McCrosky, planning director on the city planning board of Yonkers, New York, remarked at the start of 1938 that a total of 1,113 cars parked in the CBD of Yonkers during a typical business day, from 8:00 A.M. to 6:00, P.M. with 216 of them (19 percent) remaining longer than the 60 minute limit legally allowed. The average time of legal parkers was 21 minutes, whereas illegal parkers stayed an average of one hour and 46 minutes. No substantial change had occurred in the parking situation since 1932, when the same percentage of cars violated the 60-minute limit for the same average amount of time. In the opinion of the planning board, enforcement of the law so as to give space for 2.25 times as many legally parked cars would provide all the short-term curb-parking space needed. It would take care of 1,100 additional cars in the CBD, which had curb-parking space for 600 automobiles. Added to that were off-street free public parking space for 350 cars, private pay-lots holding 300 autos and garages with a combined capacity to hold 200 vehicles. No attempt was made to ascertain the ownership of cars parked longer than the legal limits, but members of the city staff assigned to the survey reported informally that many of the violators were local merchants and businessmen who preempted curb space despite the fact that by doing so they were preventing their own customers from reaching their stores.[72]

Also at the start of 1938, the *New York Times* presented a round-up article on the parking problem in a number of large American cities, a nationwide problem that was described by a reporter as being "out of control" in many areas. New York City was in the process of launching a new attack with ten east-west streets between 17th and 54th Streets and Third and Ninth Avenues to have street parking entirely prohibited. In addition, fines for parking violations — which had increased from 167,000 to 400,000 in the previous three years — had been raised from $1 to $2. Officials in Miami declared the elimination of parking from downtown streets would probably be implemented soon. In curb space that accommodated 2,000 cars a strictly enforced hourly turnover would accommodate 20,000 vehicles a day. The Miami Police Department was encouraging the owners of vacant lots to open their land to parkers. While there were no municipal lots in Miami, it was hoped that "such conveniences would be arranged for." For the previous ten years a Chicago ordinance had banned all CBD street parking between 7:00 A.M. and 6:30 P.M. According to Robert H. Nau, chairman of the Chicago Association of Commerce Traffic Committee that regulation — protested by merchants in the beginning — had proven to be beneficial. Located within the 3.75 square miles of downtown Chicago were 152 privately operated parking lots with accommodation for nearly 4,000 cars. Also in the CBD were 26 first-floor or basement garages with a capacity of 18,000 cars, and 34 multiple-story garages with space for 10,000 cars. A publicly owned lot in Grant Park, close to the CBD, had 3,200 stalls that rented for 25 cents a day and nearly 500 stalls for which there was no charge. And there was also free parking for 10,000 cars at Soldier Field, within a mile of the CBD. More than 2,000 cars were parked free of charge each business day on the lower level of the city's two-decked streets, Wacker Drive and Michigan Avenue.[73]

In Washington, D.C., brick homes were said to stretch mile after mile that had been divided and subdivided into smaller and still smaller apartments over the years, none of which had any parking. Said a reporter, "Except in spots where parking is forbidden at all times, every parking place seems to be filled from early morning until far into the night. Boys earn many quarters and dimes by arranging with car owners to move vehicles once around the block or a few feet or to the other side of the street to avoid parking ordinances that limit the time of parking." Philadelphia had also been grappling with the problem for more than ten years. At least two new office buildings that were erected in the CBD provided space under their structures for tenant parking. One proposal then under consideration was to find space for lots or garages outside of the CBD with a shuttle bus service to the downtown area. Some years earlier, Philadelphia had abolished street parking in the downtown area but found the results "unsatisfactory." Detroit's parking problem grew more acute as up to 1,000 extra cars were added each week to those entering the CBD. Officials were considering the building of large city-owned parking lots to be double or triple deckers and to charge a parking fee of just ten cents a day. A census of parking lots in Detroit revealed a total of 969 with a total capacity of 48,500 cars. Police in Detroit were said to be unable to handle the parking problem because of the ever-increasing number of vehicles and the inadequate number of traffic officers. Signs in the city that read "No Parking" were "disregarded." When two trans-bay bridges were opened, the city of San Francisco experienced a dramatic increase in traffic congestion. The only relief was an ordinance that restricted parking in the CBD to off-peak hours.[74]

Arthur Pound produced a lengthy article for *Atlantic Monthly* in March 1938, one he described as a "layman's" attempt to examine the parking problem in relation to the city trading areas. He felt the public was sadly inconvenienced by the immobile automobile, but the existence of great stores was actually threatened by it. The trend to concentration in the form of the huge retail establishments found in the CBDs of all American cities of any size was continued as long as streets in and near the shopping districts could hold the parked vehicles of retail customers without blocking the essential movement of merchandise in and out of the area. When that point of blockage was reached, the benefits of concentration began to fade with those large stores taking the first hesitant steps in a retreat toward the country. Some of the department stores established branches in residential districts. Pound explained "New department stores began to arise in the suburbs, where cheap land provided more parking space. The great mail-order houses, holding their hand until sure that streetcars were vanishing as automobiles increased, put millions into peripheral emporia, with ample parking spaces of their own roundabout. "Decentralization of merchandising is society's defeatist answer to automobiles abandoned [parked] in shoals by their owners." A traffic count in most cities revealed that about 80 percent of all persons passing the enumeration point were traveling in cars and only 20 percent in streetcars and on foot. And some of those on foot were likely heading for their cars.[75]

Pound argued that automobiles without drivers constituted a parking problem that daily became more acute and depressing. On its solution depended the shape "and perhaps even the fate of the city of the future." He felt dynamic traffic was easier to control than static traffic. Anyone at the wheel was better than no one at the wheel. A combination of public money, engineering skill, and traffic police could cope with automobiles in motion, but not those in suspended motion, "The moment a motorist leaves his machine, it becomes a bulky nuisance." He worried about the long-term effect of decentralization as he understood that as trade was lost from the CBDs and retailers relocated to outlying areas, the tax base of the city, from those rich CBD blocks, was eroded, which caused problems for the cities and led to more erosion in the core as a vicious circle was established.[76]

In 1938, an account in *The New Republic* observed that the Depression had reduced the number of cars on the road and had thus relieved but not solved the parking problem. The piece argued that the most popular immediate remedy seemed to be the parking meter. More than 50 cities in all parts of America had by then installed the devices and only about ten had subsequently removed them, in most cases because of court decisions that they were illegal and not because the authorities found that they did not work. Of course, the parking meter only solved the problem by making it expensive to park a car and, thus, discouraged its use. A more direct attack, said the story, consisted of providing additional facilities such as off-street lots and garages. However, more attention was devoted to the eye-catching novelties that were doomed to failure. It was reported that in Chicago and Pittsburgh, parking machines were employed, roughly similar to the Ferris wheel as found in any carnival. A motorist drove his car onto a platform and, with the rotation of the wheel, it was hoisted into the air until it was again desired. In the far West it was said shops were being built only one or two stories high, where the customer could drive a vehicle up to the roof and leave it there while he did his shopping. A recent ordinance enacted in Bronxville, New York, required that every apartment house built thereafter had to provide off-street parking for at least one car to each family.[77]

In a late 1939 an article in *American City*, after noting that every city had numerous groups involved in the problem of traffic and parking, declared, "If the solution of congestion were at all obvious and logical, things would have been done locally long ago." This observer divided parking into several parts: (1) short-term; (2) two to three hours; (3) for the business day; (4) overnight and by the week or month. He also divided parking lots into types based on ownership: (a) municipally run; (b) run by transit companies; (c) privately run. He argued that the first two parts of the problem could be greatly simplified by the installation of parking meters, permitting short-term parking on heavily traveled roads and longer-term parking on adjacent streets. As a first step meters should be installed. Then it was possible that any secondary congestion in streets adjacent to the metered streets could be due to the business interests of those streets. If that was found to be the case, then those business interests should themselves devise an all-day parking plan to take care of their cars. For example, in California the Oakland Downtown Merchants Parking Association was organized in 1929 and a decade later accommodated more than one million cars a year in six stations, with the cost averaging 3.6 cents per car parked. If such was done, he argued, "It may then be found that nothing else needs to be done, or that the volume of automobile traffic is so great that piecemeal solution is inadequate, and wholesale solution by the provision of a parking terminal just outside the present congested district, and permitting no parking within the district is the logical course to pursue." Continuing with a somewhat simplistic view of the situation he concluded, "The most volatile elements appear to be curb parking and business men's parking. The elimination of the difficulties connected with these two elements is likely to result in a practical solution of the remainder of the problem, and therefore of the entire parking problem."[78]

A seven-day detailed traffic survey of Murray City, Utah, was submitted to the city commission in December 1940 by R. Whitney Groo, superintendent of the state highway patrol, and Ezra C. Knowlton, chief engineer of the state road commission. Murray City was the fifth-largest city in Utah, with a population of 5,172 (in 1930), an area of 8.16 square miles and had 32.1 miles of city streets and state highways. A parking survey was held on one day, November 22, and of the 1,291 vehicles observed during the period between 10:00 A.M. and 6:00 P.M. on both sides of State Street and 48th Street South, 1,045 (81 percent) parked for a period of one hour or less. According to the survey, adequate off-street parking areas were available on either side of State Street in the rear of the buildings and, with a little improvement by the business owners, they could be made desirable for parking lots to be used by motorists intending to park for more than one hour.[79]

Chapter 4

Garages

W. J. Joscelyn was the proprietor of a large automobile garage in New York City in 1913 when he raised the rate of car storage by $5 a month. At the same time he declared: "Storage must be the backbone of the garage business," contending that to derive all one's profit from storage was the only means by which the business "can be placed anywhere near where it belongs." As far as he was concerned the garage business was largely an outgrowth of the stable business and had brought with it the old stable charges, but with increased expenses. Joscelyn had graduated from the business of stabling horses into the garage field. In the beginning of the trade, he explained, the first garages in New York, and doubtless in other cites, were opened by a dealer in cars who wished to care for those who bought cars from him, customers who had no place for a vehicle. Thus, the dealer rented a building and charged a price that was as small as could be, just enough to cover expenses. And that was the beginning of the then-current storage fees. The dealer made his money on sales, with making profits on storing the cars not being his intention. Because of that, a storage fee schedule evolved that would not permit a profit to the man who wished to run a garage as a separate stand-alone business. Then there was the garage that sprang from the repair shop, and that was what Joscelyn termed the second step in the development of the garage. His profits came from his repair work and, if he could persuade a man to store his automobile in a vacant part of this building, he was fairly sure of getting practically all of the repair work, which in the early years of the auto industry was no small item. Therefore there sprang up from this source — as in the first case — a low storage rate.[1]

At the time Joscelyn converted from stabling horses to storing cars he had been charging $35 a month for a horse and generally two carriages (he had to feed the horses as part of that fee). So when he converted his operation in 1909, he charged $35 a month to store one car, assuming he would likely double his profits. But expenses turned out to be much higher than anticipated. Whereas his stable needed a superintendent and a bookkeeper in the office, in the garage he needed, additionally, a night superintendent, stockman, two telephone operators, a checker, and an engineer. In the stable he had employed two or three washers ($16 a week each) who took care of the 220 to 230 wagons on hand, but in the garage ten or 12 washers (each paid $20 a week each) were required to keep the cars in shape. Heating the stable cost $50 a month while heating the garage cost $500 a month. Average monthly expenses for the busiest months of the year (November and December) were $3,157 in the stable and $4,345 in the garage. Income for the stable was derived from 112 horses (it had a capacity of 115) with which went generally two wagons for each horse, at $35 a month for a total of $3,920, which left a profit of $763 a month. On the other hand, the garage (with a capacity of 120 cars) stored 107 "live" and nine "dead" automobiles — the latter brought in $10 a month each while the former averaged $37.50 a month, with about half of them being open cars stored for $35 and half being closed vehicles stored at $40 a month. That produced an income of $4,102 per month, and a net loss of $243 a month. As to how Joscelyn kept in business, it was said he did so on the sale of gasoline — buying gas at nine cents a gallon and selling it at 20 cents. Each of his parked cars consumed about 100 gallons a month, most of which was purchased from him at the garage. That meant a gross profit of 11 cents a gallon on 10,700 gallons, which amounted to $1,177. Deducting his loss from storage alone left the garage with a $934 profit, which was $171, or 22 percent better than that from the stable. Then gasoline started to go up in price and cut into his profits, so Joscelyn changed his policy and pegged his charge for gasoline to the wholesale price (his cost plus three cents) and raised his storage fee by $5 a month.[2]

Scientific American presented a line drawing of a large (16 or 17 stories), round skyscraper parking garage with a spiral access in the middle of the structure, in its September 13, 1919, issue. As background the article pointed out that the problem of parking motorcars was growing increasingly serious. The more densely populated the city, the more businessmen there were who wanted to go back and forth in their vehicles, but the less space there was to accommodate their cars. Parking areas grew smaller and smaller (buildings going up on vacant lots) while the number of cars was steadily increasing. Also, the laws regulating the parking of cars were growing constantly more stringent and "motor car thieves are becoming more and more bold, so that it seems as if something of a radical nature must be done soon to solve the problem of caring for cars." And one of those radical plans had been proposed by Eugene Higgins of Jackson, Michigan, who proposed to build a garage in the form of a tower right in the middle of a city's business section. The ascending driveway had a 3 percent grade and the descending driveway a 7 percent grade. Elevators were provided for the car's occupants. According to the story, "Each stall may be locked so that the driver of the car after he runs his machine into the stall, may feel sure that it will not in any way be molested during his absence."[3]

In 1921, Robert G. Skerrett wrote an equally fanciful piece for the same publication in which he stated that the car was going to function more efficiently as it took on the role of elevator as well. All of this occurred during America's post–World War I fad for the power of science and its ability to solve every problem. Skerrett argued that the great majority of owners of cars and trucks had not awakened to the full potentialities of those vehicles as carriers of good. In industrial and business circles, for instance, it had occurred to comparatively few that it was entirely practicable to utilize the hill-climbing powers of the truck and car to link directly the floors of shops, factories, warehouses, garages, and so on, with the public highways, and "thus to avoid dependence upon the elevator as an intermediate agency." With respect to conventional freight elevators in buildings, he continued, the mind instinctively pictured the series of handlings necessary to deal with outbound or arriving goods so "why not make it practicable for trucks and delivery cars to climb directly to any floor of a business or industrial establishment, there to load or unload as the case may be? This can be done." Inspiration for that plan came from the ramp system then in use in parking garages. "This means of ingress and egress has been adopted for a goodly number of garages, and has served to obviate the installation of elevators. While a step in the right direction, these ramps have compelled sacrifices in revenue — making space that has minimized the economics promised by the abandonment of the lift. Let us make this clear," he wrote. Ramps did take up quite a bit of space, as their gradients could not be too steep. That issue was said to have been solved by the invention of a new ramp system that took up much less space, the invention of an American engineer named Fernand E. d'Humy. "What applies to the garage is equally true of the factory, the warehouse, the great department store, etc.," Skerrett declared. Drawing a more general conclusion Skerrett wrote, "Finally, let it be said that the immediate future of the automotive industry is dependent upon the prompt providing of ample garage facilities in our principal cities. Many a prospective car owner is hesitating because he cannot be sure of a convenient place in which to house such a vehicle; and it is likewise vital that these accommodations be offered at prices that will be in keeping with the average purse."[4]

Streets of busy cities could no longer be used for automobile parking, according to J. T. Hurst of Los Angeles, who gave the main address at the Pacific Southwest conference of Building Owners and Managers in 1925 at Fresno, California. Hurst stressed the need to include garage construction as part of hotel buildings, business buildings, or as stand-alone downtown parking facilities. As an example he cited the double-deck garage beneath the 15-story Pacific Southwest Bank building in Fresno. Hurst predicted the day when cities would be forced to obtain, through municipal ownership or private enterprise, an adequate system of downtown garage structures of more than one floor each.[5]

Manhattan's private business lobby group, the Broadway Association, passed a resolution in the spring of 1927 favoring an amendment to the building zoning law to permit the construction of modern ramp garages. Pointed out was the fact that ramp garages had been successful in such places as Buffalo, Cleveland, Detroit, San Francisco, Washington, D.C., and other cities. Broadway Association executive J. E. Harrington said it was accepted by many that New York was losing nearly $400 million a year in trade on account of its mid-town congestion. To those who had given the subject of traffic congestion careful thought, he added, the relief was seen in placing those cars in conveniently located ramp garages when not in operation and allowing the streets to remain free for the movement of traffic in all directions.[6]

A little later, in 1927, it was revealed that undercover parking spaces for more than 15,000 autos would be available in downtown buildings in Los Angeles by early in 1928, according to a survey just completed by Alfred T. Pelton, president of the Interstate Mortgage and Investment Company. His survey was limited to off-street undercover parking facilities. At the time of the survey, Pelton said downtown garages and office buildings with basement parking space could accommodate 11,000 cars, and new undercover space for 4,000 more automobiles was scheduled to be available by the spring of 1928 when construction on several new buildings was completed. Pelton explained that a new trend in office building design was started when the Board of Trade Building was opened in Los Angeles about two years earlier — it held 150 cars in the basement and the reception was favorable. Others had followed suit, such as the Pacific Finance Building with room for 150 vehicles, and the Roosevelt Building (200). Then came more such buildings, including the Title Insurance Building (200), Los

Angeles City Hall (a basement garage held more than 500 cars), and the May Company garage (500).[7]

Hawley S. Simpson was the traffic engineer for Essex County, New Jersey, and in 1927 he wrote of the traffic problem, the "parking evil" that was not an evil but a necessity becoming an evil only through the abuse of privilege. He argued, "Terminals are necessary to the operation of a motor vehicle, generally furnished by the individual at his residence in off street space, but by custom and precedent — inherited from the day of the hitching post — provided in the business district by the municipality." He also felt street space was too valuable in the CBDs to allow any portion of it to be preempted for vehicle storage — which he defined as a vehicle left standing for longer than a "reasonable" period. Simpson felt the best type of garage was the ramp style, multi-story, to ensure absolute freedom from interruption of service. If garages were then not used to capacity — and they were not — it was due to high fees: "Modern garages charging up to $20.00 per month for storage can not be patronized by all of the employed persons in a business district who have occasion to use motor vehicles in going to and from work. Centrally located garages are the rule with the high land value contributing materially to high storage rates." He recommended the construction of garages in a belt circling a CBD, as that would involve cheaper land prices, and presumably lower parking rates. However, he recognized that if such facilities lacked a good transit connection between themselves and the CBD their usage would be lessened, so he recommended having buses going back and forth from the CBD to the rim, or outlying, garages to solve that problem. Private capital should be encouraged to build those garages, he declared, and cities should refrain from entering a field in which there appeared "no logical reasons" for municipal operation. Even the operation of underground parking structures (another idea he favored) beneath public property (such as parks) was to him not necessarily a municipal function. Rather, the city could lease space beneath a park for garage purposes for a consideration only sufficient to legalize the transaction. After the facility was built and the private investment had been amortized, the underground structure would revert to the municipality, which then leased it out to the highest bidder.[8]

One recent trend Simpson commented on was that many downtown stores had undertaken to provide storage for customers' vehicles while they were shopping, either at a much-reduced rate or at no cost to the shopper, in a garage solely or cooperatively owned, or in a public garage by previous arrangement — that is, the provision by merchants of some form of subsidized parking to their patrons. It would appear, he explained, that such concerns should be commended for attempting to help in the solution of a troublesome problem, but further consideration led him to believe such efforts were not well directed: "Storage furnished free to the shopper increases the cost of merchandising and is eventually met by the shopper.... And rather than assisting in solving the street traffic problem it may very probably have the opposite effect of inducing a large amount of unnecessary vehicle usage. Free storage is an economic fallacy readily realized if consideration were given to the law of the conservation of energy." With a public believing it was receiving something for nothing from low-cost or free parking provided by merchants, it "is inclined to revolt against paying regular garage storage charges in the business district when not on a shopping tour. Free storage of any sort severely limits legitimate storage garages and militates against their fullest use. Motorists must be educated that if they desire the advantages of private transportation they must meet all its obligations." Simpson concluded that off-street parking was essential. As far as he was concerned the fact that the public did not utilize parking garages to their full capacity did not mean the public did not desire their services. Rather, it meant the service was too costly for many and he optimistically predicted increasing usage would lead to more garages and lower charges. He reiterated that "free storage offered to shoppers by merchandising interests is an economic error and acts as a boomerang not only to the merchant, but to regular storage garage enterprises."[9]

As of early in 1928, the largest garage in Los Angeles was said to be able to accommodate 1,000 cars. But there was a much larger one in Boston. Said to be the world's largest parking garage, the Motor Mart had space for 2,500 automobiles.[10]

Lee J. Eastman was president of both the Packard Motor Car Company of New York, and the Broadway Association of New York in 1929 when he commented that there was hardly a municipal problem anywhere that was receiving more attention than the work of traffic relief. After a certain amount of vagueness in discussing the issue and in pointing out that no one single solution fit all cities, he allowed that he liked the development of the parking garage and waxed somewhat ecstatic over that item. He called the new Fisher Brothers Building in Detroit the best example of the modern type of hotel garage. Practically under the same roof with a theater seating 3,000 people, had been erected an 11-story, twin-ramp garage with a capacity of 1,200 cars; it housed anywhere from 500 to 700 autos nightly. Eastman also mentioned one near the CBD of Richmond, Virginia, that reportedly was operating profitably at a charge of only 25 cents for three hours of day parking, or for theater parking from 7:00 P.M.

to midnight. Special rates were available by the month and the facility provided such services as car washing and brake testing. Also mentioned was a new type of ramp design with a separate driveway from the basement to the roof, one for ascending traffic and the other for descending vehicles. The grade was a uniform 13 percent and the radius was constant. With a car speed of ten miles per hour, five seconds were required to ascend one story.[11]

In George Horace Lorimer's editorial for the February 16, 1929, *Saturday Evening Post*, he started by remarking, "When Vice President Marshall issued his famous edict that the country's greatest need was a good five-cent cigar, he probably was unable to foresee the massed squadrons of harassed motorists looking for a place to park, or he might have coined an entirely different phrase. In all seriousness, the parking problem seems to be the most difficult of that vast array of riddles and complexities which are known under one collective term as traffic." American cities, he said, had street parking space for only 6 percent of the cars that entered their CBDs daily. While the problem was acknowledged by the editor to be many-sided he nonetheless reduced it to a debate between those who believed in the total abolition of all parking in the most congested urban areas and those who greatly feared such a move: "Obviously, parking for limited periods of time is a rather unsatisfactory compromise, both because of the abuse of the privilege and the difficulty of police enforcement."[12]

Lorimer cited an example of a case of a request in a city for an appropriation for a street widening, at a cost of $25,000. Upon investigation, it was discovered that if 20 cars belonging to employees of a nearby establishment were not parked along one side of the street all day, the street would have been wide enough for all traffic needs. In other words, he explained, the taxpayers were asked to subsidize each of those private vehicles to the tune of $1,250. It was to be feared, fretted the editor, that despite all the inconvenience involved, nothing but the gradual forced abolition of parking would pave the way for the development of adequate storage or so-called hotel garages that were needed for a solution to the parking problem. "As long as the motorist feels that by cruising around he can find a free curb parking place, he is loath to pay for storage," wrote Lorimer. Fortunately, he predicted, the skyscraper garage was coming into style. He concluded, "The only point which is certain is that garage facilities on a scale now undreamed of must be developed.... The force of necessity, the very logic of events points to the gradual abolition of curb parking and the storage of cars in structures erected for that specific purpose."[13]

Literary Digest discussed the parking problem as well in 1929. It began by noting that the fire department in an unnamed city was on the scene of a blaze quickly but the building burned down nevertheless. It seemed the firemen could not work efficiently because the curb lane was blocked by parked cars. "Incidents of this sort becoming more and more common, are one of the more spectacular reasons why city officials all over the country are trying to devise ways of keeping the streets clear of automobiles not in use." However, no details were provided. Various articles mentioned the "problem" caused to fire departments by parked vehicles on the street but none ever gave any details, nor was any city or fire department ever identified by name. Most of the article was about cities turning to parking garage, usually skyscrapers, to solve the problem. Noting that parking garages had been in operation for some time, the reporter said that until recently the growth of those facilities to the tremendous dimensions that were needed had been blocked by the time required by the garages in handling large numbers of automobiles during rush hours. The type of elevators that had been in use in the ordinary garages for some years were entirely too slow to handle a rush of cars, while "the two-way ramp system has been little better." Both of those methods worked less effectively as the garages got taller.[14]

However, according to the *Literary Digest* article, those sticking points were being eliminated. Refinements in ramp design had led to the double ramp (one for up and one for down), taking up no more usable space than a single ramp. Around the same time there came into use the fast elevator, and it was in that field where the most progress was said to be occurring in the swift handling of vehicles. First experiments made with those units in New York, Chicago and other cities found a heavy influx of cars handled in "good order" but always there was loss of time at the various floors when an attendant had to start the car's motors and run them off, shifting them about to fit the space. During the afternoon rush hour, too, loss of time was experienced in moving machines around in order to get one particular car out of those parked on an upper storage floor. The latest and most efficient of the new garages had just opened in New York and its owners promised any car in the building would be delivered to the owner (waiting at the ground-floor entrance) in three minutes, without being touched by human hand. It was parked and retrieved in the same mechanical manner.[15]

Located on 43rd and 44th Streets just east of Third Avenue on a 50-foot by 140-foot lot (the size of two home lots) in Manhattan was a mechanized parking garage that could accommodate 1,000 cars. It used three high-speed elevators that traveled at a speed of one floor per second. But the big attention-getting detail was its fully automatic system of parking, using lifts under cars that jacked them up and then moved them around. The elevator was operated by an attendant with a system of lights that told him what floor to stop at to drop off a vehicle, and what floor to stop at to retrieve one. A variation of that design was then in operation in a building on Wacker Drive in Chicago. The Pure Oil Building there was an office building with a garage as its core that ran all the way up the 550-foot-tall building. Unseen by the public, the parking section handled from 500 to 700 cars a day. To the naked eye it appeared to be only a large, modern office building. All offices had the benefit of daylight since they were arranged around the garage that formed the center of the building all the way to the top. While it used a somewhat different system from the one in the New York garage it accomplished the same end — parking and retrieving vehicles without the touch of a human hand, with the use of guide rails, tilting platforms, and so on. The publication enthusiastically announced that in comparison with those mechanized systems the pioneer parking garages of several years ago seemed clumsy and inefficient, although they filled for some cities a very definite need: "Detroit, Cleveland and Cincinnati were among the leaders in the movement to erect specialized parking buildings whereby the pressure of curb parking might be relieved. They set the precedent of structures built only for automobile parking, with floors like shelves which were reached, in most cases, by the double ramp idea that was accepted first as an efficient means of handling automobiles in volume," said the reporter. "But in spite of the large number of cars that these buildings hold, they take up a great deal of ground space, because they were spread out and were not built to very great heights."[16]

At the 22nd annual meeting of the National Association of Building Owners and Managers in June 1929, M. W. McIntyre of Cincinnati told the delegates the most important problem then confronting owners of central business district property was the provision of a terminus for autos. Pointing out that in most large cities throughout America parking restrictions were becoming more stringent, he argued the solution lay in the construction of skyscraper garages that he recommended go as high as ten stories. "The increased use of automobiles for business purposes makes it imperative that the office building owners and managers take full recognition of the fact that a garage connection is essential to the successful management of the office buildings," he said.[17]

Another who favored the garage was Miller McClintock, director of the Erskine Bureau for Street Traffic Research at Harvard University. In a report to the American Institute of Architects he observed the 25 million mark in the U.S. registration of cars had just been passed in 1929, and he expected that number to double in 25 or 30 years. In typical cities, he added, motorcars carried in the central business districts anywhere from 25 percent to 75 percent of the total number of people who came into the downtown area. Declaring parking facilities to be as important as the thoroughfares, he felt the CBD garage offered a solution. However, he said there appeared to be a definite antipathy on the part of zoning officials, on the part of many builders, and on the part of many merchants who owned property in central districts, against the garage. McClintock explained, "Many of them think of the garage as the converted livery stable, which was, of course, an undesirable neighbor. A modern garage can be constructed in such a way that it is not only a very presentable neighbor from the standpoint of artistic appearance, but likewise a very desirable neighbor from the standpoint of the operations which are carried on within it." As an example, McClintock mentioned the largest garage in America, in the heart of an exclusive section of Boston and neighbor to one of the city's best hotels: "Assuredly no one conducting business or anyone interested in the preservation of the beauty of the city could object to such a structure.... Yet many of our zoning regulations, many building laws, are such that it is financially impossible or legally impossible at the present time to construct adequate garage facilities in the central parts of our cities." He pointed out that; "one not unoccasionally finds a firm of a character which must of necessity depend to a considerable extent upon the convenience of automobile traffic for its very existence opposing desperately the location of a garage in its vicinity."[18]

Another of the fanciful automated car parking structures surfaced late in 1929 when the Westinghouse Electric & Manufacturing Company announced they had developed something that seemed to be a modular car parking garage. Entering the device, the motorist drove his car onto a platform, pulled a lever and obtained a check and the car was automatically whisked upward out of sight. The device immediately placed another empty platform at ground level, ready for another car. When he was ready to retrieve his vehicle, the motorist pushed a button corresponding to his check number and his car was delivered to him at ground level "almost immediately." That device was said to occupy a ground space equal to that of only a small private double garage and, said Westinghouse, "it can be built for any capacity into old or new buildings, or alone. The machine consists of two endless chains passing over wheels at the top and bottom. Platforms are suspended between these chains. Each platform provides space for one automobile. The housing for the machine is unique because it has no floors. The automobile remains parked on the machine until called for."[19]

According to H. D. James, the Westinghouse engineer in charge of the project, "With such devices built into office buildings, hotels, theater and public buildings, and set up at convenient locations on vacant lots, downtown streets could be kept clear of parked cars and made safer for moving traffic." Explaining that the time was soon coming when each building would have to care for the cars of its tenants, he went on to say, "The building of parking machines into apartment houses would solve the garage problem in congested apartment house districts. They could also be erected at frequent intervals in residential neighborhoods. A battery of automobile parking machines built into a theatre or store building would permit motorists to drive from their homes directly into the theatre or store and park their cars without exposing themselves to the weather." A reporter remarked on still another feature of the device: "It can be equipped to operate by placing a coin in a slot thereby doing away with the necessity for attendants."[20]

Enthusiasm greeted Westinghouse's modular device in many quarters. *Scientific American* explained at the start of 1930 about the development of automatic machines in general and that development had come to parking as well: "This has recently been accomplished by the design of an automatic parking machine, resembling an elongated Ferris wheel, which can be installed in hotels, apartment houses, theaters, department stores and office buildings as well as garages." The part of the building in which the device was located had no floors and could be merely an enclosure surrounding the machine or it could be a portion of a building used for other purposes. According to the account, "The arrangement enables ordinary passenger cars to be placed eight feet apart in the vertical position. A building 100 feet high will provide for a 24-car machine, which occupies a ground area of approximately 16 feet by 24 feet; this is about the same space that is occupied by an ordinary two-car garage." Reportedly, there was no particular limit to the vertical height of the machine as that would usually be determined by the building limitations as well as" by the time required to bring the car from the top of the building to the driveway level. The machines which have been constructed have had a chain speed of 100 feet per minute which would bring the car from the top to the bottom of a 100-foot building in one minute. Higher speeds can be used where the conditions make it desirable to do so."[21]

A year later it was reported that one of the Westinghouse modular machines had been in successful operation for several months at the Westinghouse East Pittsburgh plant, and that it was fully occupied by employees' cars. Said a reporter, "The machine is entirely automatic, no attendant being required for its operation. It may be operated either by key, by pushbutton or by coin, all three methods using the same control, but having different types of master switches." Engineer H. D. James, who remained in charge of the project, said "that in designing the machine, every element of personal danger had been taken into account and provided against." He added that the problem of ventilation and fire hazard (often a feature of parking garages) had been virtually eliminated by the fact that the automobile was not operated under its own power after it was driven onto the device. Also touted as an advantage was that cars were not handled by anyone but their owners, which prevented unauthorized persons from tampering with the vehicle or removing any property or accessories from it. Since each car occupied its own cage, it could not be scraped or bumped by another. "We have directed the first application of parking machines toward the relief of the traffic problem, because we believe that is one of the most critical situations confronting the American public to-day," James explained. "We are convinced that we have developed something that will go a long way toward solving that problem, and solving it economically. We believe further that the idea has unlimited possibilities in many other lines of human activity, and that it will perform an important function in the evolution of vertical expansion." One of these machines that held 24 cars occupied a space 16 feet by 24 feet and was 100 feet high.[22]

But, of course, there were problems with James's machine. Initially, the control board had a sort of switchboard with 24 separate locks and a master lock. A patron put his key in the corresponding lock and gave it a quarter turn to cause the mechanism to go into action. "The annoyance of finding the right keyhole on a large panel has been eliminated in a new parking machine control-unit. It is now possible to get the same individual service for twenty-four customers with only one lock and twenty-four different keys." The first experimental model had been installed in the East Pittsburgh works two years earlier, in 1930. Improved machines followed and had been housing cars for a year. A recent installation of one of these machines was said to have been made in the downtown Loop district of Chicago and "numerous" other installations were under consideration in several cities. However, no details were provided.[23]

A few months later James commented, "Just as elevators gave us the vertical transportation that solved the pedestrian problems in the business districts of our cities by making super-skyscrapers possible, so will vertical parking go a long way toward the solution of our worst traffic problem in those areas where further horizontal expansion has become impossible." After that, little more was heard of James and his automatic modular parking machine.[24]

Franklin Hugh Ellison, engineer and architect of New York City, submitted plans in 1932 for a proposed super steel tower more than a mile high, to be erected at the Chicago World's Fair, to open in 1933. The structure, 6,500 feet high, was planned to have 48 floors, one dedicated to each state in the union. As well, there was to be an observation platform more than a mile above ground, and a 350-foot airplane landing platform on top. Supposedly, the edifice would house two or three dozen planes, 50,000 cars a day, and two dirigibles simultaneously. Ellison said the fees for automobile parking space alone would be more than enough to pay the $7.5 million estimated construction cost.[25]

Several years later, in 1936, when reporter E. L. Yordan discussed the menace and problems of parking, he mentioned that one solution put forward by engineers was the building of parking towers or vertical parking machines. He then described the Westinghouse system, although he did not use the name of the company or the engineer. After that, he mentioned another fanciful idea whose time had never really come, with the odd exception — the building style with parking at the core. "Another suggestion entails buildings designed to all appearances as ordinary office or store structures, but having inside several roadways on which automobiles and trucks would be parked," he explained. "These roadways would run around the entire inside of the building on all sides flanked by sidewalks for pedestrians, and show windows and stores on each floor, very much the same as we find on the street level today. There would be separate ramps for vehicles going up or down, and the roof of the building would be used for additional parking."[26]

In 1940, C. T. MacGavin, of the Bureau for Street Traffic Research, Yale University, declared that bold, well-directed action was necessary to solve the parking problem. Car ownership had moved from four vehicles in 1885 to 27 million that year and had sparked a revolution. "The automobile revolution has given new flexibility to locations of homes and places of doing business," he said. Studies showed that urban population distribution was shifting outward from the city center. Other reports indicated that people with the highest buying power were moving out to the periphery of the city: "The trade which comes from the population living at the periphery of the city is most lucrative. It is the first to abandon its formerly established buying habits.... Speedy parking is vital." MacGavin commented that Samuel Eliot created the first "cage" parking structure in 1934 (commonly called the "wall-less" garage). At the time, he said, people did not realize that autos could be left in anything but a closed garage. It was also assumed that commercial garages had to have plumbing, lobby space, sprinkler systems, elevators, and window treatments. The wall-less garage structure cut building costs by more than half. Other revolutionary garage designs included that of Joseph Breuning of Kansas City, whose design eliminated the space loss resulting from the use of ramps or elevators as a means of inter-floor travel. His system used a sloping floor for direct access from street to storage floor. The "rote-floor" design used elevators in conjunction with a rotating platform. That platform acted as a storage space and also as a selector rig to shuttle the cars to a radial stall on the storage floor. MacGavin concluded, "While there are hopeful signs of growing recognition of the deep significance of problems related to parking, it is still a question of whether it comes too late to prevent losses from over-rapid decentralization of business."[27]

Philadelphia had a parking lot and garage industry estimated to be worth $2 million per year in 1941. Two new parking garages (for 1,250 cars) had just been built right in the middle of the CBD shopping district. The larger of the two occupied the third and fourth floors of a block-long structure on Chestnut Street, between 11th and 12th. Retail outlets occupied the first two levels. To reduce pedestrian interference, motorists entered the structure from the rear, with attendants storing the cars. At 8th and Chestnut Streets was a new open-deck Thrift parking garage, a few yards from Gimbel Brothers department store. Construction of ramps and bays provided nine levels for 450 cars in a single line, eliminating shifting. Even the roof, then a parking space, could in the future become another floor as the design allowed for more stories to be added as desired. "The garage has rest and check rooms but not a chauffeur's club room, swank features of the bigger rival, operated by the Sley system," related the account.[28]

Chapter 5

Parking Lots

As of the middle of May 1916, the municipal car parking lot at the corner of Apple Street and Meadow Lane in Connellsville, Pennsylvania, had been open almost two weeks, but so far as was known only one car had been parked there. The Business and Professional Men's Association of that city had cleared the lot of debris and laid a foundation of ashes. It was set up so car owners would have a handy place to park and not leave their vehicles standing all day along the city's business streets. That only one car had so far used the lot was said to be "discouraging" to the civic association.[1]

In responding to the parking problem, some companies took the initiative. For example, in 1924 the C. C. Bet Tractor Company of San Leandro, California, purchased property adjacent to its plant and constructed a private parking lot for the exclusive use of its employees. The area of 35,000 square feet accommodated 150 vehicles. Stalls for 80 cars had been erected, as were wash-racks where employees could clean their automobiles. An attendant was in charge of the station for the purpose of directing motorists to their proper stalls and protecting machines from possible car thieves. It was estimated that the lot would save from $50 to $100 per year for each car owner, as annual depreciation on autos standing out-of-doors in all kinds of weather was said to range between those amounts. Prior to the lot being open, employee cars had been parked on both sides of streets surrounding the plant, adding to congestion and making ingress and egress from the factory more difficult.[2]

Reportedly, in May 1927, the largest outdoor parking lot in the world was in Chicago and stretched between Michigan Avenue's row of skyscrapers and Lake Michigan. In that tract of lowland hidden mostly from view by the Illinois Central suburban tracks, downtown workers parked from 4,000 to 5,000 automobiles each day. Yet that huge space held only half the cars parked for all day, six days a week, in the downtown district and city planners were urging that open-air parking space be provided in Grant Park for at least 15,000 cars. Also, those planners predicted the day was near when all parking in the business streets would be forbidden.[3]

Around the same time the city of Washington, D.C., had gotten down to the work of beautifying the downtown section, parts of which had been for years described as an eyesore. In the block adjoining the post office department building, an entire city block occupied by stores and other business houses had been razed. When the brickwork and other debris was removed, the area was found to be so smooth that it was immediately pre-empted by motorists as a place where automobiles might be left indefinitely without the dread of finding them ticketed for parking too long.[4]

And vandalism of cars in parking lots was a problem, even in those early years. Because of the large number of complaints made in 1929 to the members of the Los Angeles Fire Commission by patrons of parking lots who said their cars were not protected in the manner they expected after paying to park their machines, the commission came under pressure to formulate new rules and regulations for the operation of parking lots and garages; these were conducted under permits granted by the fire commission. As a first response, the commission struck a committee to investigate the various patron complaints. One case, for example, involved Irwin Steinberg, who owned a lot in downtown Los Angeles. A complaint was registered by G. W. Cazier who said his car had been damaged on the lot, with the owner refusing responsibility. Another complaint against the same lot was made by B. Forbes who said he parked his car on the lot for a day, having paid in advance. While in Steinberg's keeping, the engine had been raced and damaged to the extent of $419.51. Forbes told the committee he obtained a judgment in Judge Pope's Municipal Court, but upon Steinberg's refusal to pay the judgment, Forbes was compelled to attach his bank account and later had to attach the business to satisfy the judgment.[5]

A week after being struck and hearing complaints, the Los Angeles Fire Commission committee told the commission that the city council should be requested to amend an ordinance to more clearly define the powers and duties of the commission on that subject and also on the matter of changing parking prices on short notice for different periods of the day. The Los Angeles City Attorney's office had informed the committee that the existing ordinance did not provide for the fire commission regulating the lots (except from the standpoint of public safety) and that the most it could then do would be to reprimand operators for the practices complained of by patrons. Thus, the fire commission planned to ask the city council for the passage of an amendment to the car parking-lot ordinance giving it the power to regulate the handling of cars and the prices charged for parking. However, it was also decided that Irwin Steinberg, against whom two judgments had been obtained in court for damage to cars on his lot, had been "sufficiently punished" and dropped the case against him, with a reprimand.[6]

Owners of parking lots and garages were required to exercise only ordinary care for the protection and safety of goods entrusted to them, as it was held by the Superior Court of Los Angeles, in February 1933, when it reversed a judgment against R. E. Garner, who operated a service station and parking lot in downtown Los Angeles at the corner of Ninth and Flower Streets. John J. Burby, a physician, obtained a $220 judgment against Garner in municipal court for the loss of his machine for a month, the car having been taken from the lot on March 1, to be returned to him by the police on May 5. The court concluded that an examination of the findings failed to disclose any negligent act on the part of the defendant declaring that "a bailee for hire is not an insurer against the loss of anything bailed."[7]

A piece in *American City* in 1936 argued in favor of more free municipal parking lots. According to a survey, the chambers of commerce of 48 New England cities had been queried and it was revealed that 24 of them operated free municipal parking space. Bar Harbor, Maine, provided space for 150 to 200 cars at a cost of $15,000 to the city per year. Woonsocket, Rhode Island, had two lots (one of which cost $75,000 to acquire) and was planning another space that would hold 500 automobiles. Brattleboro, Vermont, parked 100 cars for no fee at a cost of $20,000, while the municipalities of Waltham and Quincy were considering lots that would cost them $125,000 or more to accommodate 1,200 and 2,000 cars, respectively. One problem mentioned with respect to the municipal lots was that they were not always found in the handiest spots, nor were they always scientifically selected.[8]

Cars stolen from parking lots proved to be an escalating problem in Los Angeles. For the three-week period July 1 to July 21, 1936, a total of 380 vehicles were stolen from parking lots, compared to 278 machines in the same period a year earlier. Of the 380 cars stolen, 80.2 percent had been recovered by the police. Most were said to have been taken by youths for joy-riding purposes, or by bandits and hold-up men. That increase caused the police to urge the Los Angeles City Council to pass an ordinance making it mandatory for parking lot operators to have an attendant on duty every moment a car was on their premises.[9]

Less than a month later, owners of parking lots and their representatives protested the provisions of a proposed Los Angeles ordinance for regulating parking lots in the interest of car owners, at a hearing on the measure before the police commission. Chief of Detectives Seager, in favor of the measure, told the hearing that hundreds of cars were being stolen from the lots, and that the number was increasing monthly. Seager said the police were investigating reports that parking lot attendants were in collusion with thieves and declared that criminals stole the cars from lots in order to commit more serious crimes. Under the proposal all such lots were to be fenced, an attendant had to be on duty for each entrance of a lot, a requirement that keys for the vehicles left on lots after closing had to be placed in safekeeping and a requirement that all attendants had to obtain permits from the police department carrying their fingerprints and photographs.[10]

A few months later a draft of a proposed ordinance to regulate parking lots was prepared by Los Angeles Fire Chief Scott with the assistance of the city attorney's office and submitted to Fire Commissioner Adams for a report. Under the measure, parking lot attendants would be required to obtain certificates from the fire commissioner as to their "character and ability." To obtain such certificates, attendants would have to submit their photographs and fingerprints to the police for checking. Parking lots would be required to have a "secondary dyke or low wall" to enclose the cars and metal gates, which would have to be kept locked when the attendant was absent. At least one attendant would have to be on duty when a gate was left open. Receipts given car owners had to contain the license number of the vehicle along with notice of where the key to the gate could be obtained in case the lot was closed.[11]

By the end of 1937, Los Angeles had over 1,250 licensed outdoor parking lots with about 450 of them situated in the central business district of the city. Those downtown lots had a total estimated capacity of some 40,000 vehicles at one time, but due to turnover, accommodated several thousands more each day. During 1937, at least half a dozen new parking lots were created in the heart of the downtown district following the demolition of obsolete structures. Of course, that was a trend fueled by the Depression, as new buildings were much less likely to be constructed. Overall, the Depression worked to slow the growth of the parking and traffic problems with the large decline in economic activity.[12]

Journalist E. L. Yordan observed in March 1937 that New York City

Mayor Fiorello La Guardia had "officially" endorsed the open-air parking lot and thus he felt it would attain a new respectability. La Guardia had just told a committee studying traffic in Manhattan that New York City needed more parking facilities before cars could be barred from the streets, and he urged the establishment of more lots and parking garages at points of congestion. "Time was when the open-air automobile lot had to hide as an outcast behind tall buildings, and was tolerated only as a nuisance in sections jealous of their high-class residential or business heritage," said Yordan. "Today, though, it takes its place in the shadow of Rockefeller Center." Real estate men were said to describe the parking lot boom as "truly amazing." Just eight or nine years earlier there were scarcely enough parking lots in most cities to be worth counting, argued the reporter. But in 1937, according to the U.S. Bureau of the Census, 4,341 parking lots were doing business in America, grossing $18 million annually. New York City was home to 255 lots; Philadelphia had 156; Chicago, 129; Washington, D.C., 78; San Francisco, 52; and 43 were located in Boston. "In almost every case the figures represent sizable gains; they include only the privately owned places, not the hundreds of other municipally operated in scores of communities," remarked Yordan.[13]

One of the more remarkable booms in parking lots was reported to have taken place in Detroit. Whereas ten years earlier there were 110 privately owned lots holding 7,700 vehicles, that number had moved to 265 lots in 1933 with room for 17,250 cars and by 1937, the total lot capacity was close to 30,000 automobiles. Milwaukee had open-air parking lots capable of holding 3,000 vehicles in 1927, and more than 9,000 cars in 1937. All over America there had been a "wholesale" razing of buildings to make room for parking. In Detroit in 1931, the city tore down buildings having a total assessed value of $594,000 to create parking lots; the following year it removed 53 buildings valued at $473,000; and the year after that (1933), 32 more buildings worth $462,000 were razed to make way for lots. Many realtors believed that the use of high-priced land in crowded cities for parking was non-economic and that any widespread upswing in building would wipe out the parking lots. As Yordan declared: "More people, it seems clear, are again driving their cars into the city, a practice many had discontinued for lack of parking facilities. The result is likely to be more traffic congestion in the streets."[14]

"Gradually the parking lot is emerging from its ugly-duckling stage. In some communities, notably in California and Florida, it is putting on trimmings and calling itself an 'auto park'; it boasts a neon sign, a neatly painted fence, sections marked off with white lines for varying periods of parking, night illumination and a uniformed attendant," Yordan elaborated. Nor was the end in sight as Yordan speculated about the bright future of the lots: "Designers of communities for tomorrow have evolved plans that will lift the parking lot to the grandeur of a parking plaza or center, with landscaped borders, and with waiting rooms, reading rooms, lounges and refreshment stands. There will be telephone, mail and messenger services, and possibly a place where the children may be left while their parents go to the store or the theatre." Town planners would not hide away such facilities in back alleys, but put them where they were most needed. Some parking lots allowed the motorist to park his own vehicle, Yordan said, but if the place was crowded or small, the lot managers had learned from bitter experience to perform that task themselves. If they did not, then, too often fenders got smashed, auto bodies scratched, running boards bent, and headlights or taillights broken. Yordan did concede, "The depression, it is generally agreed, gave a great impetus to the parking field. The yards offered not only stopping places in crowded districts, but at rates generally below those which garages, with higher overhead could charge." Parking lots generally charged motorists from 25 cents to 50 cents, depending on the length of stay, compared to garages where the charge ranged from 50 cents to $1.[15]

From a survey made by the New York State Bureau of Municipal Information in 1938, it was revealed that 53 municipalities in New York State provided parking lots in their business districts, while 97 reported they offered no such facilities. Ithaca charged 15 cents per day, 75 cents per week and $3 a month, while at New Rochelle parking was free for 2.5 hours to those holding purchase slips from area merchants; others were charged 15 cents to 25 cents. Municipal parking was free in the other 51 municipalities. Capacity of the lots ranged from 25 cars in Hastings-on-Hudson (7,097 population) to 50 vehicles in Sherburne (1,077) to 500 in Lynbrook (11,993) to 775 in Garden City (19,000) and to 1,000 in Valley Stream (11,790). Nine of the communities provided attendants regularly at the lots, ten provided attendants as needed, such as on Saturday nights; and 33 provided no attendants. The report noted that the provision of off-street parking lots was a "new municipal activity" engaged in by cities in 16 states while a number of other cities were planning parking facilities to serve the business district. One of the largest municipal parking areas in America was in Grant Park, Chicago, on the lakefront adjoining the Loop district, accommodating 3,500 cars at 25 cents for 24 hours. Many cities provided such lots by utilizing land they had owned for years or acquired for purposes other than parking. Another method was the outright purchase or lease of privately owned land for the specific use as parking lots. For example, Winnetka, Illinois, provided space for 150 cars on two lots bought at a cost of $18,000; Flint, Michigan, accommodated nearly 350 vehicles on land bought for $110,000. Quincy, Massachusetts, paid $68,000 in 1931 for an area that held 150 autos and paid rent on an additional piece of land that parked 1,500 cars at no charge to motorists. Red Bank, New Jersey, leased six lots at a total rental of $3,500 a year; those lots held 500 cars that could be parked there for free.[16]

Yet, despite the boom in privately owned parking lots, *American City* was critical of them in a 1939 article for the fees those private lots charged and "moreover, the privately-owned lot may be considered a temporary use, since the land will be converted to more profitable uses if opportunity offers. Finally, the majority of parkers balk at paying the high parking fees charged at some private parking areas." If a motorist had to park at some considerable distance from where he was going the value of the parking privilege was correspondingly decreased. Thus, it could be said generally that the parking privilege was worth ten cents in some locations, 15 or 25 cents in other locations, independent of the length of time they parking space was used. Whatever the cost, it "is clear from the studies that have been made in some cities that the charges of garages and some parking lots are higher than the mass of motorists will pay." The article argued that most municipalities could not expect to provide free off-street parking space for all cars seeking it, but the officials of many cities, and traffic experts "believe that the provision of off-street parking is coming to the front as a municipal responsibility, not only because of universal car ownership but also because it is cheaper to provide off-street parking than to widen streets and, in many instances, cheaper than to provide curb parking." The article argued further, "Only city ownership can assure continued operation and relative permanence of location of parking lots in retail business districts. An improvement in business would undoubtedly bring a demand for land for the erection of new structures, which in turn would bring more cars to the business section." Properly placed, city-owned lots could be made to pay their way, it was argued, if they charged motorists a fee ranging from ten cents to 25 cents per day. A suggestion was made in Los Angeles that a uniform parking fee should be assessed against all registered motor vehicles in the Los Angeles area in an amount sufficient to cover the cost of acquiring land for municipal off-street parking lots, and to cover the operating costs of such facilities. However, this article stated that such funds should come from a city's general tax levy because "the provision of municipal off-street parking areas may involve considerable expense, but so also does the provision of wider streets, better pavements and express traffic ways. Furthermore, expenditure on these facilities is likely to be rendered ineffectual to a considerable degree without adequate and properly located terminal facilities."[17]

Data was gathered in 1939 on off-street parking in 34 municipalities by the Committee on Parking and Terminal Facilities of the American Automobile Association. Those communities provided 42 lots holding 3,660 vehicles and three buildings with a total of 546 spaces. Merchants provided 70 lots for 6,822 cars and 12 buildings with 2,360 spaces. Private operators provided 1,330 lots with a total of 115,000 spaces, plus 461 buildings with 78,000 spaces. Thus, there was available in those cities a total of 125,480 spaces in parking lots and 80,906 spaces in parking garages for a grand total of 206,386 spaces. Average fees for parking in lots were as follows: 20 cents per hour, 26 cents for two hours, 41 cents per business day, $1.21 per week. In garages, the average fees were 24.5 cents per hour, 31 cents for two hours, 55.5 cents for all day, and $3.01 for a week. Parking lot investment (private ones only) amounted to $34 million and totaled $60 million for privately owned garages. With the wages and operating costs being paid by private operators, it worked out to the private lots having a cost of $32 per lot space and $74 per garage space. If the cities were to take over all those facilities, the annual cost to the cities would be interest (at 3 percent) of $2.8 million and operating costs of $10 million, for the 206,386 spaces. Per space per year it was $62, with $48 of that being operating costs only. On a daily basis the cost of those spaces was 20 cents, with 16 cents of that amount being operating expenses. However, the article felt the general public was not ready for that kind of subsidizing by the municipalities.[18]

Rallying to a cry for united action, a group of Murray, Utah, businessmen agreed, in 1941, to motions to establish three free parking lots in Murray and to set a parking time limit along two of the city's central business thoroughfares, State Street and 48th Street South. That action climaxed months of effort on the part of Murray merchants who had long been aware of the need for more parking space. The threat of losing customers because of inadequate parking facilities had often been raised. Under the accepted motions, the plan was to grade and gravel four different lots. A committee of six businessmen was to begin the work of collecting the approximately $400 that was needed to cover the costs of grading and spreading gravel over the properties. Orlando Erickson, chairman of the parking lot committee, said it was the serious intention of all the interested businessmen to take a share in the actual labor of developing those lots, such as removing refuse and weeds, digging post holes, and spreading the gravel. The proposal to submit a petition to Murray city officials to impose a two-hour parking time limit on the two streets was said to have largely resulted from the practice of certain townspeople of parking their cars in the same place for eight to ten hours.[19]

Within a week, the Murray businessmen had raised the necessary $400 and about three months after that the three free parking lots with a total capacity of about 200 cars had opened and were available to the general public.[20]

Chapter 6

Other Facilities

As early as 1914, parking space for autos in the business section of Los Angeles was reported to have become a serious question. With the growing demands of merchants to prohibit cars from standing in front of their places of business in the CBD where it was not restricted, motorists were finding it increasingly difficult to leave their cars while on business. On Olive Street and on Eighth Street merchants had taken it upon themselves to erect signs warning drivers not to park in front of their places of business. In that way they were said to have assumed the legal right held by hotels and theaters to reserve space in front of their doors for their own cars. Where, wondered the article, was the motorist going to leave his car? Parking spaces open to the public for a nominal sum had been tried, the reporter explained, but such space had been available only in out-of-the-way locations while the "vital need" was in the very center of the city. Some of the merchants had suggested to the Automobile Club of Southern California that a municipal parking space be set aside to meet the 1915 demand, but after consideration, that plan had been set aside. However, the automobile club then came up with a plan, as outlined by club secretary S. L. Mitchell. He noted that, of the several office buildings then being built downtown, some had cellars, and all had large, flat roofs. So the club's plan suggested that a freight elevator be installed in those buildings and be used to lower or raise cars to the proper level, whether it be in the basement or on the roof. And, in buildings then in the planning stage, architects could make provisions for special parking floors, something that was said to have been "tried with success in many eastern cities." Of the plan, said a reporter, "Office owners in the building would have first call on the parking spaces, which could be reserved automatically with the lease of the office. Then the remaining spaces could be thrown open to the general public, thus removing from the street the cars which are often left standing the entire day, occupying space which should be given to the man who leaves his car for only ten or twenty minutes."[1]

In December 1925, Seaboard National Bank of Los Angeles opened a branch at 3152 Wilshire Boulevard with a service of car parking for its customers. Said bank president George L. Browning, "At the Wilshire-Vermont office you drive right into the bank's automobile entrance, which is alongside the main banking room. While you transact your business, our uniformed chauffeur cares for your car in our spotlessly clean garage." Once the customer had finished his business, "Your car appears at the door ready for you to drive away. With this service your car is no more trouble than your coat at the hotel check room. No congestion, no delay, and no charge. Your banking-traffic problem is solved."[2]

Clients of the Janss Investment Company were able to drive their cars into the company's offices in the new Subway Terminal building in downtown Los Angeles on June 1, 1926, when it opened its new, greatly expanded office. Praising the new facility for various features, company president Edwin Janss added, "An example is shown in the arrangement whereby the entire west wing of our floor which has a street level entrance on Olive Street has been converted into a private garage. Our clients in the future may drive directly into our offices without the delay or inconvenience of having to find a parking place for their cars."[3]

Part of the space on 22 of the 44 stories of a new (1926) Chicago skyscraper known as the Jeweler's Building was used for a garage, with a total capacity of 572 automobiles. Those parking spots were in the middle of each floor with offices on the outer parts of the floor. And, it was automatic. According to a news account, a feature of the installation was that, from the time a car entered the building until the owner retrieved it again, the auto was not touched by human hand. That was accomplished by an arrangement of tilting racks on each of the four elevators used and on the storage parts of the floors. After the driver steered his car onto a loading platform before one of the elevators an attendant determined, from a master control board, what space was empty on a particular floor. He then took a key bearing the designation of the stall assigned and gave it to the motorist as his claim check. Next, by pressing a button, the car rolled into the elevator as the loading platform was tilted. Then the elevator operator dialed an indicator with the car raised to the selected floor, where the doors opened automatically with the platform tilting and allowing the vehicle to roll off and into the storage rack. One advantage of the system was said to be the absence of gasoline fumes, as the engines of the cars being parked and retrieved were never running.[4]

Roofs of buildings continued to draw attention, as one of the more fanciful proposed solutions to the problem. In 1928, the Los Angeles Traffic Commission was reported to have viewed the use of roofs as parking lots for the storage of autos during business hours as a partial solution of the parking problem. Supposedly, there were a number of one- and two-story buildings close to the center of the CBD whose roofs could be reached by means of ramps from alleys — if, of course, such ramps were added to the structures. The average height of buildings in the Los Angeles CBD was only 3.2 stories and for taller buildings, it was pointed out, freight elevators could be used to lift cars to the roofs. Mostly, that type of solution was seen as being applied to the tenants of these buildings with their vehicles parked all day long.[5]

Leon R. Brown was safety engineer for the New York State Railways, based in Rochester, New York. He noted, in 1929, the recent development in traffic relief through the establishment of parking spaces near transit facilities in the outlying districts of cities — what would be described, many decades later, as park-and-ride facilities. A number of cities had established such a service, Brown wrote, notably Philadelphia, Akron, Poughkeepsie, and Baltimore. In all those cities, parking stations were provided at the end of streetcar or rapid transit lines of the street railway companies and a round-trip ticket to downtown was given to the motorist for 25 cents. For the year 1927 it was reported that 209,000 automobiles had been kept from the downtown streets of Philadelphia through the parking stations established at the outskirts of the Philadelphia Rapid Transit Company, and the company had thus gained 500,000 extra streetcar riders. Figures for the year 1928 showed a 15 percent increase in ridership over 1927. The greatest use at any one of three Philadelphia lots was over 800 cars in a day. In Boston, two car-parking areas on land owned by the street railway had been established adjacent to rapid transit terminals. They were leased out to be run by private operators.[6]

Arguing that the establishment of parking facilities at the end of streetcar lines had been so "successful," Brown said the question had come up as to whether the establishment of parking spaces on the outskirts of cities with a limited bus service to the downtown area would also be successful and provide relief for downtown congestion. However, as far as he knew, there were no instances of that plan being in use anywhere in America, although discussion of implementing such a service was said to be under way in St. Louis. A "deluxe" bus service in Rochester, New York served an exclusive residential section of the city, providing a service that took people directly to the business district. The bus picked them up and dropped them off, door to door. For some that saved the expense of owning two cars, as the family could have the use of the vehicle during the day. Brown also remarked that, while a provision for municipal parking was much discussed by traffic engineers in large U.S. cities, it had not been carried out to any great extent with Chicago being the only city that had any large municipal parking space. He saw the principal difficulties met in trying to provide municipal parking areas as being the lack of available space and the problem of financing those projects. "The method of financing and operating municipal parking has aroused considerable discussion and involves the question of municipal ownership and operation, which is contrary to American ideas," he explained. "The expenditure of large sums of money to provide free parking space which benefits comparatively few autoists is generally objected to by the public at large, which in most cases profits only indirectly if at all." Solving the parking problem in the CBD, argued Brown, meant that the establishment of privately owned lots and ramp garages had to be encouraged and "free municipal parking stations would discourage such practice." Therefore, any municipal lots that did exist should charge a fee. In conclusion, Brown observed, "Some traffic experts have even gone so far as to suggest that all autoists should be taxed or assessed for the privilege of storing their cars all day in any street," although he acknowledged he knew of nowhere that such an idea was imposed.[7]

Late in 1929, Miller McClintock, director of the Erskine Bureau for Street Traffic Research at Harvard University, in a report to the American Institute of Architects, argued that automobile parking space built in office buildings in large cities offered a solution to the traffic problem so logical as to appear inevitable. Such buildings, he said, were then more prevalent in America in Western cities than in Eastern cities because car ownership was more common in the former areas. One example he cited was the Subway Terminal Building in Los Angeles, wherein two entire floors were used for parking. Access to the garage was by means of doorways opening directly onto the street with the street being of such a grade that no internal ramps within the garage were required. McClintock was somewhat amazed by the convenience of such an arrangement and enthused, "That building affords this facility, as do other structures of this type that a tenant may drive into that garage, leave his car, get into the passenger elevator and go to his office without the necessity of getting out upon the street at any time."[8]

H. M. Gould remarked at the start of 1930 that there were miles and miles of streets in Detroit with pavement widths of 26 to 36 feet, but with curb parking allowed on both sides of those streets, many vehicles had been forced onto the comparatively few wide streets, increasing the congestion for moving vehicles on those thoroughfares. For Gould, a simple remedy lay in prohibiting parking on one side of every street whose pavement width was 36 feet or less. Several months earlier a test of staggered parking was made on one of Detroit's narrow but important thoroughfares, Vernor Highway from Van Dyke to Drexel. Parking was limited to one side of the street, but alternate sides were used, block by block. Cars driven away from their usual parking spaces because of this plan were said to have found space in back yards, garages, and other off-street places. As well, the plan had the effect of employees driving their cars off the street and into parking lots of manufacturers. Said Gould, "The latter will use the street for parking in preference to a parking lot even though the manufacturer has gone to great lengths to provide the off-street space." Gould also observed that at least one apartment house owner had recognized the necessity of providing off-street parking space for his tenants, and a garage had been incorporated into the building.[9]

At the end of 1930, reporter Al Parmenter wrote of a parking crisis in Los Angeles, and that as in other American cities, L.A. had too little curb space for the cars using the CBD area. The city was faced with a traffic problem that demanded a relief from congestion, provision for an easier flow of traffic, and easier parking. Parmenter noted, "Curb parking does not fit a metropolitan traffic scheme. The day is coming and not far distant when all parking will be prohibited at the curb.... The automobile driver cannot park at the curbing in the downtown traffic area much longer." Streets were for movement and when parking interfered with that purpose it became an "unabated nuisance." Opposition to the prohibition of curb parking came from merchants and property owners and was based on the belief, he argued, that from 25 percent to 50 percent of business was derived from curb parkers when, in fact, surveys indicated that less than 1.5 percent of business was derived from that source. For part of the solution Parmenter looked enthusiastically at an experiment in Detroit that was supposedly just about to get under way there. Plans were to establish an underground mechanized garage in downtown Detroit to be municipally owned and operated. Under consideration by the Detroit City Council was a plan for a 3,000-space parking lot to be built beneath city parks and streets as an initial step towards imposing a parking ban on all Detroit streets in the future. A nominal fee was to be imposed on motorists, just enough to meet the costs of the project. And it was even more fanciful, as the reporter explained, "A further proposal is to connect these underground spaces with the sidewalks by tunnels and even to provide a subterranean sidewalk that would provide a secondary and below street-level entrance to stores." He added, "Parking of cars would be accomplished by means of electrically operated mechanisms, obviating the use of gasoline-burning motors and the resultant need of extensive and costly ventilating systems." It had been calculated by surveys in Detroit that it was possible to park 3,753 automobiles at the curb on downtown streets, so the proposal would theoretically look after 80 percent of them. According to Parmenter, the Automobile Club of Southern California admitted it was highly skeptical of the Detroit plan. For one thing, it was said to be enormously difficult to get such a large number of cars smoothly back into the traffic flow in the afternoon rush hour without gridlock and/or chaos.[10]

Detroit's underground plan, which of course was never built, envisioned a subterranean lot that was four to six stories deep. From a street level entrance the motorist would proceed down a ramp to the first level, or reception floor, where he received a parking receipt and then depart. A conveyor carried the car to an elevator that, in turn, lowered the vehicle to a parking floor to be discharged mechanically to an electrically operated transfer truck running on rails. That transfer truck, with the car on it, would travel to a parking stall selected by an attendant by remote electric control, and the truck would be shifted sideways into the parking space whereupon it would deposit its load.[11]

As an idea, roof parking continued to surface off and on. As of 1937, the latest place for parking the shopper's car was on the roof of the very store in which he was making his purchases. Fred Meyer, Inc., a Portland, Oregon, department store with nine outlets was described as a pioneer in that attempt to dissipate traffic congestion and bring residential neighborhoods closer to shopping centers. The roof of its single-story, 22,750-square-foot Hollywood store was covered with a car park, free for the use of the store's patrons. Marshall Field Company in Chicago had its roof parking facilities next door while a new building was being erected adjacent to the company's Evanston, Illinois, department store, the interior of which was to be leased to Firestone but the roof would remain under the control of Marshall Field to provide parking space for the store's customers. By this time, more and more city traffic engineers were recommending to their municipalities that new business structures erected in congested areas should be required by law to contain off-street parking for all the new traffic they created.[12]

Another new development that occurred in the 1930s was described, in a 1937 article in *American City*, as the "park and shop" markets. Shannon and Luchs, realtors in Washington, D.C., told a reporter of their experiences with such projects: "In 1930, they build their first group of stores to bring special joy to the heart of the motor shopper. The plan provided that the stores be built as far back as possible on the rear of the lot, allowing no more back yard than necessary for an adequate delivery lane. The excess land, which usually lies idle and strewn with rubbish behind shops, is properly surfaced for the working of customers' cars at the front." The first project by Shannon and Luchs was the Connecticut Avenue Park and Shop, which faced onto Connecticut Avenue, the main highway to Chevy Chase and the center of the apartment district. A second project was the Colonial Village Parking Stores, built in 1935, located on Wilson Boulevard (the home-bound side), the main highway to Clarendon, Virginia. It also adjoined an apartment development. Project three was the Bethesda-Chevy Chase Shopping Center, completed early in 1937. It was located almost seven miles from the center of Washington and adjoined the suburbs of Bethesda and Chevy Chase. "The shopping in this territory of detached homes is almost all done by the use of automobiles and the parking area is not only a convenience but also a necessity" said a reporter. "This new idea in parking spaces has proved to be successful. The customers like it, and the merchants have been sufficiently taken by it to follow the new developments with additional stores." By late in 1937, Shannon and Luchs managed five groups of stores planned in that manner — that is, park and shop — with several more in the planning stages. No specific details were provided in the text as to size, number of stores and so on, but photographs and line drawings indicated perhaps ten to 15 stores at most, of the 1,000- to 2,000-square-foot variety, and parking for perhaps up to 35 or 40 cars, at most, in the front part of the lot. In other words, they were much like what today we know as strip malls.[13]

A news account in October 1939 proclaimed that the first large retail store in the U.S. to have a roof parking area incorporated in the original plan was the Sears store on Pico in Los Angeles. In laying the huge concrete slab that formed the main part of the roof it was necessary to make it almost ten inches thick — six inches thicker than usual — so it could withstand the extra load of 266 automobiles. Nearly 80,000 square feet of the roof area was devoted to parking space with the remainder taken up by equipment sheds that housed elevator shafts, and stairways leading to the store and escalators going from the roof to the basement. And, for the convenience of customers who parked on the roof, a desk where heavy packages could be picked up was located there.[14]

At the end of 1939, downtown St. Louis businessmen were hopefully watching Park-N-Shop, a new service designed to eliminate the expense and inconvenience of parking for shoppers. They hoped it would, as the promoters predicted, bring back customers who were then buying in outlying, neighborhood retail centers rather than driving into the congested CBD, where curb parking was a matter of luck and parking lots were crowded and inconveniently located. Some 70 retailers and one bank had entered into one-year contracts with Park-N-Shop to park the cars of their patrons and to provide a free bus service between the garage and the shopping district. Stores that subscribed to the plan paid a monthly fee of $2. Shoppers who parked at the garage and went on to purchase goods at a participating member retailer presented their parking check when making a purchase. Each endorsement stamped on the check by the retail establishment entitled the shopper to one hour's free parking. The stores paid Park-N-Shop ten cents for each endorsement. Park-N-Shop operated two 22-passenger buses throughout the day, traveling a 1.5-mile route through the downtown section. There was a bus every 7.5 minutes, with a total of 13 stops on the route. Space for advertising cards in the buses was rotated weekly among the subscribers. Originating that idea was the firm that owned a three-story parking garage. Park-N-Shop began operation on November 15, 1939, with 50 subscribing stores, but that total passed 70 within three weeks. A substantial expenditure was said to have been made by the garage for a waiting room. A $5,000 initial advertising campaign made use of both newspaper space and spot announcements on three radio stations. Three weeks after it started, Park-N-Shop was handling more than 100 cars a day with predictions that the service would grow to such an extent that it would tax the capacity of the garage, which could accommodate 1,000 cars, within a year. Three large department stores that operated their own garages were not participating in the scheme.[15]

Just 18 months later an update indicated the Park-N-Shop plan in St. Louis was thriving. By June 1941 more than just stores were involved, with 30 doctors, dentists, lawyers and other professional people subscribing to the service, Park-N-Shop buses, which formerly stopped running each day with the closing of downtown stores, ran until midnight for the convenience of patrons of two of the larger theaters and a number of cocktail bars. Retailers who subscribed to the plan still paid a monthly fee of $2 and ten cents for each parking endorsement they stamped on patrons' checks. Park-N-shop had also added a stamp plan for clients not using the endorsement method. Under that aspect of the plan, books of 100 stamps were sold for $15 (15 cents each) and redeemed for parking at a value of ten cents. A special stamp for the theaters entitled the patron to parking privileges for the duration of one complete performance, upon presentation of the stamp and ten cents. The number of retail stores participating in the plan had increased to 130, making it necessary for Park-N-Shop to acquire a third bus. Bernard Von Hoffman, president of Von Hoffman Realty & Investment Company (owner/operator of the garage and the Park-N-Shop system), said the service carried 30,000 passengers each month.[16]

As of 1940 it was reported that five cities and two counties had passed ordinances requiring that, in the case of new homes and multiple dwellings, parking facilities adequate for their occupants had to be provided. One of the five cities was Los Angeles, and its ordinance read, "In connection with each and every duplex, double dwelling, multiple dwelling, apartment house, bungalow court or multiple-family use of a lot there shall be provided on such lot garage space in a building for at least one automobile for each family unit or apartment contained on such lot." Theaters were required to provide off-street parking space in Evanston, Illinois, with one parking space having to be provided for every ten theater seats. Also, Evanston joined the group of cities requiring apartment buildings to provide their own parking spaces — in that case, one space for every two dwelling units.[17]

C. T. MacGavin, with the Bureau for Street Traffic Research at Yale University, remarked in 1940 about what certain retail stores had done in an effort to solve the parking problem. Some "have created parking space in the rear of their buildings, served by modernized rear entrances which rival their front marquees and display windows. Some of these stores have uniformed attendants to park customers' cars. There have been reports that more people now come through the back door than through the front."[18]

Chapter 7

Parking Meters, the First Two Years

Over the course of a few weeks in July and August 1935, a great many American municipalities were watching the efforts underway in Oklahoma City, Oklahoma, to solve the overtime parking problem through the use of a new device, a meter conceived and manufactured locally in Oklahoma City. First of all, the curbs in the parking blocks of the downtown area were marked off in 20-foot lengths, with a meter mounted four feet high, one for each of those intervals. A total of 200 meters were installed at the start, with the possibility of moving to 1,000 later if the experiment was deemed successful. A motorist deposited a nickel in the meter, whereupon a green indicator rose and remained thus in view for a period of 60 minutes, after which it fell back into place. Prior to the parking meter there was no easy, efficient way to determine when a parked auto was over the time limit. A police officer had to jot down lists of license numbers and times, or mark the vehicle in some fashion — chalk marks on the tire has been the traditional method from the beginning — and remember times. But with this new device, one motorcycle patrolman, with an eye to the meter indicators, could cover the entire area.[1]

Reportedly, the attitude of the public was favorable to the meters because on that first day the devices were well used. The average take on that first day was 50 cents per meter, despite the fact that only 20 percent of the CBD was equipped with meters, and all the rest of the CBD curb space featured free parking as usual. The legality of the city's parking-meter ordinance was sustained in District Court on July 24, although the case could still be carried to a higher court. The Dual Parking Meter Company of Oklahoma City was reported to have installed those meters at no cost to the city and would take all the receipts until the devices were paid for. After that point was reached the meters became the property of the city, free and clear. Oklahoma City Police Chief John Watt stated on July 18, "These meters have been installed for only two days and we cannot give you any particular comments as to the reaction of the citizens at this time; however, we believe that they are going over in a big way. They are placing the checking of on-time parking on a mechanical basis instead of on the officers." He felt they would make it easier for the average man to find a parking place, easier for him to park and get out of his space.[2]

When *Business Week* devoted a small piece to the new device, it described how they worked as follows: "Its simple plan of operation upsets the time-honored freedom of the streets by converting them into nickel parking lots. The meters collect fees in advance, compute and record time and, if necessary, call a cop. They cannot argue nor show favoritism." Those meters could be set for varying time limits, from 15 minutes to two hours, and the motorist could plainly see how much time remained. "The ease of checking up parking violations allows one motorcycle officer to cover at least 4 times the usual area," was also mentioned as a feature.[3]

O. M. Mosier, City Manager of Oklahoma City, explained the workings of the first few months of the city's experiment with meters. First, though, he noted as background that the downtown parking problem in Oklahoma City was becoming more acute. In spite of ordinances limiting parking, there were so many abuses of parking privileges that it was almost impossible for shoppers to find parking space, even after considerable cruising, because all space had been occupied by cars owned by businessmen and their employees. Numerous cars received dented fenders from impacts due to parking too close together. Policing was unsatisfactory, depending upon the marking of tires with chalk, and that might not be done for a considerable time after cars had been parked. Numerous disputes arose. Then, in the summer of 1935, Oklahoma City turned to parking meters as a remedy for those ills and 200 meters were installed as an experiment. Some of the devices were set for 60 minute intervals, and some were set for 30 minutes. For that experimental installation meters were placed along only one side of several streets in the heart of the congested downtown district. "The legal principle of the parking ordinance is not taxation for the use of the streets, but a fee for the cost of regulating, parking and keeping traffic moving," Mosier explained. "Such regulation not being needed at night, meters are not required to be used after 6 P.M. Nor are they in effect on Sundays or holidays." The public was prepared for the devices by advertisements in print media and by radio spots that pointed out the "abuses and evils" of the old system and enumerated the prospective benefits of the new method. Reportedly, that advertising and "propaganda" served its purpose in making the public open-minded for a trial run. However, Mosier admitted that many people, including public officials and police officers, were skeptical as to the practicality of regulation in that form. Parking meters went into operation in Oklahoma City on July 17, 1935, and by 1:00 P.M. the system was declared a success by city officials — due entirely and solely to the fact the public was using the meters.[4]

After just two days of use, operation of the meters was temporarily enjoined by the District Court with the plaintiffs alleging the coin-operated devices impaired their right to the free use of the streets as provided by statue. However, a few days later the court dissolved the injunction holding that "use" of the streets meant "travel" and that parking, which could be prohibited altogether, could be regulated and a fee charged. Thus, the meters were returned to operation and remained so, through to the time that Mosier was writing. And for the ensuing four months the two sides of the city's downtown streets had provided comparisons that were obvious to the city manager: "On the unmetered side is confusion, cars jammed together, fenders being bent, cars being pushed in front of fire hydrants, and traffic being impeded by those who are trying to back into the cramped parking spaces, while shoppers can hardly find parking spaces open." But, explained the city official, "On the metered side is order, sufficient room for every car to be parked and driven out quickly and easily, and there are usually parking spaces open so that shoppers can park within a block of any store or bank." Women, in particular, were said to have praised the metered system for the speed with which parking spaces could be found and for the ease of getting in and out of spaces. Police had found the machine indicators to be much more reliable in regulating parking time limits than any system they had formerly used.[5]

Because Oklahoma City was so pleased with the first few months of the operation of the devices it placed an order for 300 more parking meters with an estimate that the city would require in total about 1,808 meters to cover all of the CBD. With property tax revenues for cities often being sharply curtailed in the Depression years, Mosier admitted the meters were looked to as a welcome source of city revenue: "In searching for revenue substitutes, the Council has looked first to those who have made city regulations necessary, and to those who receive the benefits of city services. In these respects the parking fees met the requirements of being fair contributions to the cost of city governments." Collection for the first four months of parking meter operations in Oklahoma City were as follows: August, 27 days of operation, $1,979.91 (receipts from 174 meters); $73.33

(average receipts per day); 42 cents (average receipts per day per meter); September, 24, $2,088.97, $87.04, 50 cents; October, 27, $2,331.51, $86.35, 50 cents; November, 25, $1,977.99, $79.12, 45 cents. The drop in November receipts was explained as due to extending the parking time in several zones, from 30 to 60 minutes. To that date, said Mosier, revenues from month to month had been "remarkably consistent, a feature much to be desired of the revenues anticipated in the annual budget." Mosier concluded, "While there are some opposed to the meter system, the public and the downtown merchants have accepted the meters favorably. Merchants on the unmetered sides of streets have requested the complete installation of meters. Taxpayers have accepted favorably the idea of better traffic control on a self-supporting basis."[6]

And other cities began to follow suit. In late 1935, C. G. Beckenbach, an engineer in the traffic division of the Dallas, Texas, Police Department, explained that for some time the parking of cars had grown increasingly vexing to city officials. In Dallas, as elsewhere, attempts had been made to deal with the situation by establishing loading zones, extra safety zones, time limits, and so on. "Because of the high cost of adequate personnel to administer parking regulations and because they were so easily evaded by the simple expedient of erasing chalk marks or moving the vehicle a few feet periodically, it was found impracticable, if not impossible, to secure enforcement. A considerable amount of the downtown traffic officer's time was spent in assisting motorists, particularly ladies in extricating their cars from tight places." Also, because of the limited parking space available, it was a frequent occurrence for an exasperated motorist to double-park his vehicle, leading to even more congestion. Added to those troubles was an urgent need in Dallas for more traffic officers and for a modernization of the traffic signal system, together with an extension of the system to new areas. But there was no apparent source of funds for any of those purposes. Then, in July 1935, there came to the attention of the Dallas city officials a device known as the parking meter. "Rather extravagant claims were made for this device and for some time there was hesitation about even investigating it," Beckenbach admitted. However, they watched the Oklahoma City trial closely and were convinced.[7]

Installation of 1,000 parking meters was made in Dallas between November 1 and November 30, 1935, and, declared Beckenbach, the following results were obtained: (1) all-day "parking hogs" were removed from the streets; (2) one or more parking spaces were available at all times for those having legitimate business; (3) spacing of meters at 20-foot intervals gave each parked vehicle adequate room to enter and leave its parking space; (4) bumpers and fenders were rarely, if ever, damaged when entering the 20-foot space; (5) there was little or no wait for cars to go into or out of parking spaces; (6) double parking was eliminated; (7) the quick finding of parking space reduced the amount of moving traffic, making possible a more rapid traffic flow; (8) there was a net revenue of about 40 cents per meter per day, an amount that was ample for all traffic improvement needs; (9) motorists and merchants were "immensely pleased" with the new conditions;) and (10) there had been a reduction in traffic accidents in Dallas. At least part of that accident reduction was due, argued Beckenbach, to the fact that the nerves of motorists were not frayed and irritated as had been, although he admitted his belief was hard to prove. Three time limits were used in Dallas meters; a 20-minute time in front of banks, a 40-minute limit close to stores doing a quick turnover business, and a 60-minute limit for meters near department stores. All operated on a five-cent charge. Dallas City Manager Hal Moseley declared, "We have a voluminous file containing letters from all classes of professional men as well as laymen commenting very favorably on results obtained." He added, "The letters have been received not only from local citizens but also from visitors from other parts of the country. Moreover, up to the present we have received no letters protesting against this manner of regulating parking."[8]

Nevertheless, there was opposition to the devices. An indignant editorial about the meters appeared in the *Los Angeles Times* on May 12, 1936. At the time, the devices had not appeared in any California communities but had been proposed for Los Angeles, San Francisco, and other cities. "The scheme is being fought vigorously by the California State Automobile Association and it is to be hoped that motorists of Los Angeles will join them in opposition," the editor wrote. In his mind, the legality of such a scheme was questionable: "To make the motorist pay for the use of public thoroughfares for whose building and maintenance he has already paid is certainly double taxation and probably as contrary to law as to equity. Even if constitutionally possible, such a system would do nothing to solve our traffic problems, alleged to be one of the chief objects of this innovation." Also, he said, the unfairness of the scheme was seen in the lack of discrimination employed in imposing the parking meter device: "Under its provisions the autoist using the space for only a few minutes would have to pay as much as he who uses it for the full period permitted. Another objection is the generally accepted legal principle that fees collected under the police powers of a city may not exceed the cost of operation, as they certainly would in this case. It would be just as sensible to tax pedestrians so much a block for using the sidewalks."[9]

On the other hand, a pro-meter editorial appeared at around the same time in *The New Republic:* "We hereby predict that the next great American gadget will be the parking meter," exclaimed the editor "This device, which first appeared a few months ago in Oklahoma has already spread to Texas, Florida and Michigan and seems likely to sweep the country. The revenue from these meters is said to be amazingly large; they pay for themselves in a few months, and thereafter they pour money into the city treasury." According to the piece, the device did away with the all-day parking hog, traffic congestion had been enormously lightened, stores were more accessible to potential customers, and the revenue from the machines helped curtail taxation. And, he added, "Very few motorists complain of the scheme and many, it is said, warmly approve it."[10]

Almost a year after the first meters began to operate, *Business Week* remarked that the devices had been installed in many cities and that automobile clubs across America were getting all worked up over the parking meters. Dallas then had 1,400 meters in operation; Houston, 1,000; El Paso, 500; Oklahoma City, 775; Kansas City, 2,000; Miami, 400; St. Petersburg (Florida), 150; and Fort Worth and Salt Lake City were each using some in a trial situation. Other cities were seriously toying with the idea — including New Haven, Syracuse, Baltimore, Washington, Toledo, and San Francisco. Topeka merchants had recently visited Oklahoma City to see for themselves how the devices worked and were so convinced that they petitioned their city commissioner to have them installed. But the American Automobile Association had just passed resolutions condemning the scheme in all its forms. Local automobile clubs in Parkersburg (West Virginia), Tulsa, Davenport, Chicago, Denver, and Spokane had fought them, successfully in several cases. However, the local automobile club in St. Petersburg, Florida, declared itself in favor of meters, as did the El Paso club. Principle objections raised against the devices were that it was one more tax on the "harassed" car owner; it made him pay for a device to help apprehend him for parking violations; it would not relieve traffic congestion; it enriched a private company, the Dual Parking Meter Company of Oklahoma City, by municipal ordinance; and it sold to a few citizens the use of the streets that belonged to all. According to this business publication article, how great a burden to car owners that "tax" could become was indicated by the fact that Toledo was then planning a trial of 1,000 meters as a means of raising $45,000 of additional revenue for the city. And the meter manufacturer estimated that 100,000 devices could be used in New York City and would produce revenue of $12 million, of which all but $2 million would be net. Dallas then averaged an income of 40 cents a day per meter, or around $10,000 a month. As the reporter explained: "The parker pays five cents for a specified parking time (usually an hour), two-thirds of which goes to the meter company until the installation is paid for. The meters cost $58 each."[11]

Proposals to install parking meters met with a cold reception in Canada in 1936, according to Dr. Styles W. Wherry, president of the Utah Motorist Association. Reports were that metered parking propositions had been considered and rejected by four Canadian cities — Toronto, Montreal, Hamilton, and Kitchener — while the Chamber of Commerce of London, Ontario, was making an aggressive fight against the installation of the devices. In Toronto, explained Wherry, "The slot machine plan of parking" was turned down by the municipal authorities following a study of the subject from November 1935 to June 1936. The members of the board of directors of the Ontario Motor League took the position that the meter plan did not solve the parking problem and recommended strict enforcement of existing regulations rather than using the mechanical devices. City authorities in Montreal were approached by one of the parking meter companies but did not give the plan serious consideration. "Not one single request for installation has been received from the public," Wherry added. In Hamilton, Ontario, the meter proposal was rejected when 170 merchants signed a petition against that scheme for parking. Hamilton's board of control, after a long discussion on the topic, referred the matter to the chamber of commerce, the Hamilton Automobile Club, and the merchants. Each group reported unfavorably on the idea, whereupon the matter was dropped by the city.[12]

When Salt Lake City was installing meters in the summer of 1936 "to grab nickels," the editor of the *Murray Eagle* [Utah] newspaper was moved to grumble that whenever the automobile was mentioned around a state house, a new tax was placed on the owner. "The grand finale seems to be here, now when nickel consuming machines leer at you from every parking place," he added. "Business men of Salt Lake County outside of the nickel trap area should feature free parking and secure additional trade from the hounded man with automobile parking fees to pay. Merchants should profit by this mechanized gypry on the part of the tax-frantic Salt Lakers."[13]

St. Petersburg, Florida, City Manager A. F. Thomasson oversaw the installation of 150 parking meters in his city on January 6, 1936, at a cost of $58 each to be paid for from the receipts of the meters, with an allowance of $1.25 per meter because the city did its own installation, rather than leaving that chore to the meter manufacturer. Five months' receipts totaled

$5,420.40, an average of $36 per meter for the five months, or around $7 per meter per month. The largest amount received from one meter was $71.30 for the five months. A total of 68 of the meters in the "less active" locations were discontinued on May 1, at the end of the busy winter tourist season, leaving 82 meters remaining in operation — the most active ones. Thomasson estimated, from that experience, that the meters would be entirely paid for by January 1, 1937, or a little less than a year after they went into operation. Maintenance costs totaled roughly $100 annually (for all the meters combined). With ordinary care, the meters were expected to have a life expectancy of many years. The use of slugs in the devices was prohibited, with a fine for violators, but Thomasson said that practically no trouble had occurred from that source. Collection of the coins from the meters, during the height of the tourist season, required the labor of two men for four hours every three days. Accounting for the coins involved about 2.5 hours per day as the receipts were posted to the credit of each meter. With respect to legal objections, Thomasson said lawsuits seemed to have stopped by the time he was writing. All suits that got as far as a decision point were decided in favor of the city; all plaintiffs had argued pre-emption of the streets for private use and rental of street space by the city. With only a couple of exceptions, merchants accepted the devices and applications were soon received from other merchants requesting additional meters installed around their property. Thomasson concluded, without details, "Installation called for alternate meters in congested districts, and it would probably be a mistaken policy to install meters solidly in any district, but this has been done in some communities."[14]

An editorial in *American City* in August 1936 noted that practically every city in America with a population of 20,000 or more had a parking problem. After mentioning the various measures that had been tried to relieve the problem (prohibitions, time limits, and so on) he said, "Where these regulations are enforced, they cause ill feeling, because of necessity they are usually unequally enforced. Where they are not enforced, they are useless except as they are vicious like any other law that is permitted to lie dormant on the books." Then he moved on to the main topic, his favorable assessment of parking meters. One month after the Oklahoma City meters went into use, Police Chief John Watt said, "The parking meters are going over in good shape. The public has accepted them and I have yet to find any one who has used them and is not for them." After the first installation of 174 meters in July, Oklahoma City increased its total to 575 in December 1935. By the time the *American City* editor wrote his article, those meters had all been paid for out of their earnings. According to the editor,

"In the cities where the meters are used, their efficiency appears to be undisputed. In fact they have worked out so satisfactorily that they are in the class of hot cakes and are being considered in cities of all sizes throughout the country."[15]

The editor also argued that the principal current objection to the devices came from the American Automobile Association and its local motor clubs. On June 6, 1936, the AAA objections were outlined as follows by organization president Thomas P. Henry of Detroit: (1) one more tax and one more harassment on car owners already suffering from too many of both those veils; (2) because of their popularity with the merchants, there inevitably would be continued demands for extension of the system throughout the entire business districts of the cities once it had been started; (3) in effect the system made a motorist pay a tax for a device the primary purpose of which was to make it easier to apprehend and fine him for parking violations; (4) the scheme would not relieve traffic congestion because whether the motorist pays or not, the curb area was still in use as a parking zone and was not available as a traffic lane; (5) adoption of a parking meter system meant the enrichment of a private company at the expense of the motorist through municipal ordinance; (6) while the five cent charge was claimed to be nominal, nevertheless, the aggregate charge against motorists eventually would be tremendous, particularly if merchants were successful in having the system extended throughout the business districts; (7) although an Oklahoma court upheld the parking meter ordinance of Oklahoma City that court noted the revenue raised by the city, from its police power in general, should not exceed the cost of regulating the behavior. The largest installation of meters to that date was reportedly at Kansas City where 3,000 had been ordered at $58 each, the manufacturer to receive 85 percent of the revenue until the machines were paid for; but after eight months they became the property of the city, whether paid for or not. Another clause of the agreement allowed the city the right to cancel the deal after four months, in which case the manufacturer had to remove the meters within two weeks.[16]

And it all began in the mind of newspaperman Carlton Cole Magee, who was 63 years old in 1936. The by-then former Scripps-Howard newspaper editor stood poised to become rich from the sale of his invention — the parking meter. First-year sales of the device had reached close to $500,000. In the words of a reporter in *Literary Digest*, "Last week in eleven cities, motorists slipped nickels into 8,702 Original Magee Park-O-Meters for the privilege of parking on their own streets. In a score of other communities, city fathers poised pens above contracts, waiting only for legal questions to be straightened out. The invasion of shoulder-high hitching-posts, surmounted by nickel-devouring meters threatened to spread to every congested community in the nation." On those meters a white arrow moved slowly across the dial, indicating time remaining. Just two years earlier, in 1934, Magee, then editor of the *Oklahoma City News,* received an assignment from the Oklahoma City Chamber of Commerce: "Solve the local traffic problem."[17]

Because public-spirited citizen Magee had tinkered with machines and had produced a homemade self-starter for automobiles long before they appeared commercially, his thoughts ran to a solution by mechanical means. In four months time he had figured out what he wanted, but lacked the time and skill to produce it. Therefore, he offered $3,000 to postgraduate students at the Oklahoma Agricultural and Mechanical College to devise a slot-machine meter that would sell parking-time to motorists, and then alert traffic officers when that paid-for time had elapsed. From the plans produced, the Macknick Company of Tulsa, precision machine manufacturers, developed the Dual Park-O-Meter, dual because it served two purposes — it controlled parking and it provided revenue. Magee capitalized his Dual Parking Meter Company at $50,000, quit the newspaper business, and became a manufacturer. While 27 employees in the Dual plant worked to keep up with the orders, 300 field salesmen drove home a simple, convincing sales talk: the meters earned their way: they helped fill impoverished municipal coffers. For each $58 Dual parking meter, a city paid no cash down. It did not even have to pay the extra $1 per machine if the community had the Dual workers install the devices, at the time the work was done. It all came out of meter revenues, with 85 percent of the take going to Dual, usually for around six months or so. Cities kept 15 percent initially so they had enough income to pay their collection, accounting and repair costs. The *Literary Digest* admitted that, while city officials and merchants applauded the devices, "Motorists failed to take them to their bosoms." In Kansas City, motorists named the devices "nickel nabbers" and "one-armed bandits." In San Antonio, drivers dubbed them "gypometers." One tactic used that "exasperated police" involved motorists driving around from one meter to another, looking for one with time left, or the one with the most time left. The biggest critic of the parking meter remained the American Automobile Association, which advised its 750 affiliated clubs to fight the devices.[18]

Years earlier, Magee had abandoned the job of supervising schools in Carroll, Iowa, and later abandoned the practice of law in Tulsa, Oklahoma. In 1922 and 1923, as editor of the Albuquerque (New Mexico) *Journal* and later the New Mexico *State Tribune*, he had locked horns with U.S. Senator Albert B. Fall. Magee's disclosures in print precipitated the still-infamous Teapot Dome Oil investigation that sent Fall to jail. That being done, Magee accused District Court Judge D. J. Leahy of New Mexico of corruption. Leahy charged Magee with libel and contempt, heard the cases himself and, not surprisingly, found him guilty and sentenced the crusading editor to jail. New Mexico's governor intervened and pardoned the newspaperman. In 1925 Magee stumbled upon Leahy in an East Las Vegas hotel, whereupon the enraged jurist knocked Magee down and kicked him. Suddenly producing a gun, Magee shot at Leahy but missed, killing a spectator. After being acquitted in court of manslaughter, he left for Oklahoma City.[19]

The Promised Land for the fledgling meter manufacturer was, of course, New York City, which offered the biggest potential market of them all. Dual had one of its best salesmen, J. N. Jordy, waging a one-man drive to sell meters to New York City. "As persistent as he was eleven months ago [September 1935] when he started his campaign, Mr. Jordy continued to scurry about the five sprawling boroughs of the metropolis, mapping likely spots for parking meters. He button-holed traffic inspectors, aldermen, Borough Presidents, city attorneys, even the State's Attorney General.... For his cause he had mobilized impressive boards of trade, and chambers of commerce. With their help he hoped to get an NYC contract that could ultimately call for 200,000 meters costing $11,600,000. After that Jordy's somewhat grandiose plans involved going to Paris and London to sell the parking meters."[20]

Parking meters finally made inroads into the California market as both Huntington Park and Long Beach installed the machines for a trial, in the summer and fall of 1936.[21]

When the American Automobile Association held its convention in Detroit in November 1936, among the resolutions adopted by the convention was one condemning parking meters as an "illegal and burdensome" means of raising revenue.[22]

For Long Beach, California, November 28, 1936, was the first day the meters in the business district went into operation. Despite the fact that the Christmas shopping season was underway, the metered spaces were said to have been only lightly used. According to a reporter, that condition was the experience of other cities — light use of meters for a few days until motorists accepted the five cents per hour "toll machines." Other cities reported that thereafter the spaces were filled. In using the first metered parking in Southern California, motorists told the reporter that they appreciated the ample parking spaces and the absence of vehicle ramming. A group of uniformed policemen were on hand that first day in the Long Beach CBD to explain the machines. For a limited time, motorists were to be allowed ten minutes grace over the one-hour meter limit before being ticketed for a $1 fine.[23]

At the start of 1937, the American Automobile Association reiterated its stand against the parking meter. Resolutions were adopted at the group's annual convention condemning the devices as "an illegal and burdensome means of collecting more revenue from the already overburdened motorist."[24]

In the first week of 1937, climaxing months of surveys, discussion, and controversy, the Salt Lake City commissioners decided that the five-cent parking meters were a good thing and declared they would keep them. By a unanimous vote, the commission decided to retain the 200 meters then in operation on downtown streets and to purchase about 800 more of the machines to cover the entire downtown district. During the previous two weeks, when it became incumbent on them under terms of an agreement with the meter manufacturer to make a decision, commissioners were flooded with petitions. Some demanded the immediate discontinuance of the machines; some praised the devices. Newspaper polls indicated a fairly even split of public opinion with respect to the meters. Commissioners, fortified by Florida court decisions upholding the legality of the machines, and by contracts allowing cancellation in the event of an adverse court ruling, decided in favor of meters.[25]

By early in 1937, meters were threatening to arrive in Los Angeles. The use of the machines on downtown streets had been suggested in a resolution introduced to the city council. That body was then waiting for City Attorney Chesebro to give an opinion on the legality of the proposal. An unnamed traffic cop, in favor of the meters but tired of trying to convince motorists they had overstayed their time under the old human-led systems remarked, "You can't argue with a meter." The reporter observed that motorists drove around searching for a spot vacated by a driver who had used up only a small part of his allotted hour. Those searchers parked and often returned to their machine before the free time expired. He regarded that as evidence of motorists having found a way to beat the system. After a two months' trial period Long Beach, where 400 meters had been installed, was sold on the device. Businessmen in the city were said to have felt it had done them much good and even parking lot operators had benefited. Long Beach motorists declared they had an easier time finding a parking place than before the devices were installed because so many cars had previously been parked overtime. Not every city in California, however was convinced. Hermosa Beach had earlier been on the point of installing the machines but suddenly balked at the idea and declined to use them. At least one victory for the opposition forces had been won in court. In Alabama, the State Supreme Court outlawed the machines in Birmingham as "an unauthorized exercise of the taxing power of the city."[26]

Meanwhile, on the other side of America, in Albany, New York, groups of motorists and advocates of parking meters, particularly for New York City, clashed on February 25, 1937, at a public hearing on proposed meter legislation. Spokesmen for motorists declared meters were unsound and impractical as well as unconstitutional and were merely another instrument "for socking the motorists." J. Jordy of the Dual Parking Meter Company insisted the devices worked successfully in many cities and asserted that, with 200,000 machines installed in New York City, there would be an income to the city of $80,000 a day. William Gottlieb, of the Automobile Club of New York, opposed the bill which would have permitted cities and towns to install the meters, saying, "This is just a combination of an alarm clock and a slot machine which is to be used for further socking the motorist, who is already paying enough in taxes. This is merely an attempt to legislate for the sale of a device for which the motorist would pay. I hope this will never come up here again. There would be no need to stand here and discuss this proposition except for the activity of the manufacturers of these devices." Jordy admitted frankly that he was at the hearing as a lobbyist and, again pointing out the potential revenue of $80,000 a day to New York City, declared, "Think how that money could be used for safety campaigns or for police personnel."[27]

A week later the Merchants Association of New York disclosed that it had asked state legislative leaders to support measures enabling New York City to make a practical test of the parking meter. In its message to both branches of the Legislature, the association declared that parking in New York City was a problem that could not be satisfactorily handled by the police department with its present personnel, even with an enlarged staff. Moreover, it continued, strict enforcement of existing regulations would have flooded the courts and been interpreted by many people as a "form of persecution." Said the group, "There is ample ground for believing that many people abuse the privilege of parking on the streets, which are, of course, primarily for the purpose of accommodating moving traffic rather than for the storage of automobiles."[28]

Bakersfield, California, joined the ranks of cites in that state with parking meters when it installed 200 machines that went into operation on its downtown streets on March 12, 1937. As with most meters across the land, motorists got 60 minutes of parking for five cents. City officials hoped the machines would solve their parking problem, which they described as having grown acute in recent months.[29]

One of the other companies that moved in quickly to manufacture parking meters, in competition with Dual, was the Mark-Time meter, manufactured by M. H. Rhodes Inc. of New York. In 1937 it requested the engineering laboratory of an unnamed university to make tests of the accuracy of the meter's timing mechanism and the range of temperatures under which the Mark-Time model could operate. It was reported that the meter would operate satisfactorily in air temperatures ranging from 150 degrees above zero degrees Fahrenheit to approximately 70 degrees below zero, and that the maximum timing error would be no more than two minutes per hour — and that only at temperature extremes. Also, when the timing mechanism was off it always ran slow — that is, it always favored the motorist. Coin boxes for the machine were described as theft-proof and the Rhodes firm boasted that there had never been a theft from a single Mark-Time meter in operation.[30]

As of July 1937, parking meters had been around for two years, and that prompted a number of round-up style articles and reviews. Since the day they began in Oklahoma City, some 40 cities had installed them and more were considering their installation. Most recently, on June 22, 1937, Montclair, New Jersey, installed 65 meters on its main street with 200 more to be added on another main business street. Motorists who parked beyond the one-hour limit received a summons to appear at police headquarters within 24 hours and pay a $1 fine. Should the violator fail to appear, he was subject to a $50 fine or 30 days in jail. Public Safety Director Michael P. Duffy of Newark, New Jersey, had decided to install meters on a trial basis in all downtown streets; at least 2,000 meters would be needed. Duffy had secured the approval of both the Broad Street Association and the Market Street Association, which together had as members most of the establishments in the business district. When cities considering the installation of meters asked his advice, statistician H. H. Whitehead of Oklahoma City replied as follows: "1. Start gradually with a few blocks in the most congested areas. Then let merchants petition extensions. 2. Sell the people through radio and advertising before installation." With respect to the Oklahoma City devices, Whitehead said the merchants were favorable to meters, some were then petitioning for more; the general parking public was also favorable and meters were not an issue at the previous civic election. There had been no vandalism and the metered areas were patrolled by the police day and night. As to the durability of those machines, Whitehead declared, "Our meters were the first installation made. Naturally they lacked features of mechanical perfection. They have given good service for nearly two years, and are now being replaced by meters which will overcome the defects of the earlier machines." As part of its two-year anniversary article, *American City* looked at parking meter data supplied by 11 cities. The total of 6,842 machines in those cities had been in service an average of 9.7 months and had combined to earn about $53,700 per month, or $7.85 per meter per month. Revenue had totaled $536,657 with all costs of collecting the money and repairing the machines having totaled $55,124.[31]

J. Fred Thomas, mayor of Sharon, Pennsylvania, remarked that his city had installed 84 parking meters and "our collection will average better than $100 a week. These meters were not installed as a source of revenue for the city, but rather to have our streets take more cars than they had done previously." Captain of traffic, B. B. Smith of Dallas, said his city had experienced no legal obstacles or test cases and that he knew of no opposition to the meters on the part of the public, merchants, or any agency or organization: "The merchants are strongly in favor of meters; the automobile club sponsored their installation; the general parking public finds them very satisfactory. Meters are most serviceable and most satisfactory when there is fair and impartial enforcement. Any ticket-fixing with reference to metered parking would spoil the effects and materially lessen the benefits accruing from such a system. Meters have proved to be beneficial to Dallas in providing for additional traffic-control equipment, benefiting traffic conditions in general." T. R. Burnett, captain of traffic in El Paso, said the local automobile club and the AAA approved the January 1936 installation of meters in his city, as did 80 percent of the merchants and general public. In St. Petersburg, Florida, merchants and the public were favorable to the devices, according to Police Chief R. H. Noel, while automobile club members were divided in opinion. San Antonio's meters had made more money available for traffic control generally and the attitude of merchants, the automobile club, and the general public toward them was described as "very good" by Police Chief Owen W. Kilday. "The parking meter has solved the traffic situation with us in a very pleasing manner. Traffic flows easily, parking spaces are always available, double parking entirely eliminated," he enthused.[32]

A trade publication, *Transit Journal*, studied the parking meter from a variety of angles on the occasion of its second anniversary. Among the conclusions it drew, as published in *Business Week*, were that "the meters may be opposed, but they do help the flow of traffic by eliminating double parking; they offer a compromise and may turn out to be a transitional step toward a more intelligent attitude on the use of streets for movement rather than for storage; they emphasize that parking is a privilege rather than a right and that an individual who impedes traffic while saving time for himself robs many others of theirs."[33]

Another who evaluated the devices after their first couple of years was Leon R. Brown, safety engineer for the New York State Railways (Rochester) and chairman of the traffic committee of the Rochester Engineering Society. During the spring of 1937 he visited many of the cities where meters were used, to evaluate them. On his journey he saw the machines in operation, and talked to various city police personnel, automobile club executives, chamber of commerce officers, merchants, shoppers, and so on, and prepared a report that he presented as a paper at the New York State Conference of Mayors and other municipal officers, on June 29, 1937. He said there were about 20,000 meters in use in 35 U.S. cities and that "one of the important benefits of metered parking is the spacing of parked cars 20 or 22 feet apart. This permits ease of access and egress, thus saving time and avoiding congestion. It is said the motorist's saving on prevention of bent fenders and bumpers more than offsets the small charge." Because of the spacing, he pointed out, there was room for around 20 percent fewer cars than before, but it was found that about three times as many cars parked in them. Also, the meters had worked to completely eliminate double parking: "This facet and the time saved in getting into and out of parking spaces have caused traffic to be speeded up as much as 15 per cent." Brown exclaimed that it was his belief from personal contact in the cities with meters that at least 90 percent of people in the various groups involved liked them. When only one side of a street had meters, merchants on the other side demanded them. When one town had them, the merchants of nearby towns demanded them, showing that "they drew out-of-town shoppers rather than driving them away."[34]

Brown also emphasized how easily and efficiently police officers could monitor the meters. In all the metered towns he visited he said he could find no cars parked past the time limit unless they had already been tagged by the police. On the other hand, in the 11 annual parking surveys his group had made in Rochester (a city with no meters) it was found that over 50 percent of all cars had overstayed the limit, a condition due to the fact that cities without metered limits could never adequately enforce parking time limits. Every meter produced on average about 40 cents a day, which meant the yearly collection at that rate from 1,000 meters would run to $120,000; money that could be used by a city for more traffic police, and more police traffic equipment. Acknowledging that opposition to meters came principally from the automobile associations, Brown declared he found that where meters were used, the automobile clubs had withdrawn their objections. He concluded, "I believe the solution of the parking problem is nearer than every before"— meaning, of course, the utilization by cities of parking meters.[35]

Time magazine also published a small piece marking the second anniversary of the machines. After noting some 20,000 of the $58 meters were in use in the streets of 40-odd American cities, it added that Denver's city council had just voted to install them and Baltimore was considering doing so as well. Reportedly, many cities were enthusiastic about their meters. Dallas, for example, got about $140,000 yearly from its 1,500 devices and felt they had solved the city's traffic problem. But not all cities were sold on the idea. Topeka, Mobile, Salt Lake City, and six other cities were said to have installed them, and then removed them. A week earlier, City Manager H. F. McElroy of Kansas City, Missouri (1,400 meters in use), complained, without detail, "The meters solve none of the parking problems." Also mentioned was the Birmingham, Alabama, situation wherein after the city had installed 500 meters in September 1936 the state Supreme Court — after a test case was brought by motorists — barred them from the city.[36]

Chapter 8

Parking Meters, Part 2

C. G. Beckenbach, Dallas traffic engineer, discussed his city's installation of meters at length in the fall of 1937. When Dallas installed its first 1,000 meters in November 1935, it was decided then to under-meter rather than to over-meter. That procedure left the fringe districts without the advantage of meters, and within 30 days it brought a deluge of demands for more meters for the city. As a result, nearly 500 additional meters were added, although even as Beckenbach was writing, there were still said to be petitions on file in Dallas for more meters. These were being held in abeyance pending "complete proof" that additional meters would answer an actual public need. "We have never had to remove any meters once installed," boasted the city official. He added, "The carefully planned publicity and demand campaigns that were carried on just prior to and during the original installation served their purpose of allaying complaints until the advantages of the meters were proved to be real." Before the first installation, a random phone survey of 1,000 Dallas citizens and merchants was carried out; it found only 4 percent opposed to the use of parking meters.[1]

Dallas's original 1,000 meters were all "manually" operated (that is, a coin was inserted and then a handle was turned by hand to start the timer and raise the flag). "They are still in use, but are not giving the service and showing the durability which we are getting from the 500 meters of the second type, in which the coin trips a lever which raises the flag and starts the clockwork," he explained. "There was some difficulty in making the clocks of the manual meters start, and it was also possible to cause them to lock so that the flag would not fall. None of this trouble exists with the automatic machines." Dallas was then making 5.13 repairs per meter per month on the manual type, and 1.43 repairs per meter per month on the automatic models. Meter collection per month consistently brought in from $12,500 to $13,750, with the odd exception for cold or short months; for example, January and February collections were, respectively, $10,200 and $11,300. On a per-meter basis, receipts were 40 cents per day in the congested area and 20 cents a day in the fringe area. From a Dallas use analysis of the meters it was discovered that paid users averaged 37.5 minutes, with 42 percent stopping for 45 minutes or more. By contrast "free time" parkers averaged a stop of 21 minutes each. A specific check was conducted on one block in a retail-shopping district (small dress and hat shops prevailed). The block contained 18 one-hour meters which were in use from 7:00 A.M. to 6:30 P.M., meaning there were 207 parking hours available at the meters in that one block during the business day. Parked vehicles totaled 134, making the effective use of available space to be 64 percent. Vehicles paying a nickel to park and not overstaying the one-hour limit numbered 92 (68 percent); vehicles paying to park and overstaying the limit totaled nine (6 percent); vehicles not paying but parked on somebody else's un-expired time were eight (6 percent); vehicles parking on un-expired time and overstaying what remained of the 60 minutes numbered three (2 percent); and vehicles parking in violation, by not paying to park at a meter with no time on it totaled 22 (16 percent).[2]

A brief review of legal decisions, in November 1937, with respect to parking meters revealed that cases in Oklahoma, Texas, and Florida involving claims by the motorist that parking meters created an illegal obstruction to traffic were rejected. In Alabama, the owner of land abutting on such a parking space brought suit on the ground that the right of access to his property from the street was obstructed, and the ordinance was held void. The case in which the Alabama Supreme Court outlawed meters on the ground they constituted "an unauthorized use of the taxing power" was also cited. A thorough study by the justices of the Massachusetts Supreme Court, however, had resulted in the opinion that a properly worded parking meter statute would be valid, and valid ordinances might well be passed under it. It was an opinion expected to be of influence in other states. A reporter concluded, "To date legal opinion indicates that parking meter ordinances are reasonable if properly drawn: the spaces allotted must be suited to the streets, the traffic, and the needs of the abutter, and the charge must be no more than sufficient for the purpose of regulation; it cannot be imposed as a source of general revenue."[3]

Another who weighed in on the debate between the manual and the automatic meter was Lewis R. Greene, chairman of the police commission, Westerly, Rhode Island. He made the case for the simple, manual meter in 1937—you inserted a nickel and spun a handle that automatically wound a clock. Meters were then in a state of rapid development. Where there was just one manufacturer a little over two years earlier, by late 1937 there were said to be a dozen makers, with each one striving to produce a better machine. Automatic meters were something like an eight-day grandfather clock, but the time did come when they had to be wound manually — that is, a city employee had to go around with a key and rewind all the automatic meters. Since the running down of the automatic meters was a function of use, it was not easy to determine when one needed rewinding. When Greene was deciding which type to buy for his city he took into account all the actual costs, such as a city worker going around to rewind all the devices. Also, there were a great many more parts in the automatic meters and that was said to have increased the incidence of problems and repairs, compared to the manual meters.[4]

Forth Worth, Texas, police chief A. E. Dowell remarked at the start of 1938, "Since the parking meter found its place in Fort Worth, vehicle and pedestrian accidents in the metered area, which covers 30 per cent of the business district, have fallen off to almost zero. Safety is our chief argument for parking meters, though the disappearance of the all-day parker is another boon." During the summer of 1936 the city of Fort Worth installed 619 meters and 374 more in the fall, a total of 993 Dual automatic models. For the seven months from January 1 to July 31, 1937, those meters had a total income of $52,820, or $7.53 per month per meter. Monthly costs included: servicing (including replacing, repairing, purchasing parts, a repairman's salary of $125 a month); overhead, one collector at $125; one clerk, $80; four police officers, $520; one three-wheel motorcycle, maintenance of, $50; for a total monthly cost of $775. Thus, the cost to service, administer the meters, and to tag violators, amounted to 12 percent of the income. Surplus funds were credited to the city's general fund. When city officials wrote to Fort Worth asking their advice about the devices, Dowell wrote to them, in part, "The approval of the installation of parking meters is a matter of education of the people involved, including the public, the city officials, the police officials, and the merchants. Upon installation, the meters gradually sell themselves on merit; to the motoring public, because of improved parking facilities and the quicker flow of traffic; to the city officials, because of the revenue received and the satisfaction expressed by the public; to the police officials, because of the improvement of traffic conditions; and to the merchants because of the added parking facilities provided for their customers."[5]

Dowell also wrote to Boston Mayor Frederick Mansfield, who had requested information. First he told him of his high regard for the devices and then he said he felt some part of the meter receipts should definitely be set aside for traffic betterment, rather than going into the general fund. By doing that, Dowell felt an ordinance would be better positioned to withstand any court challenges that might arise. With respect to introducing meters, he told Mansfield, "First select your most congested districts, and do not undertake to meter beyond the limits of the present congestion. This will permit those who fight the meter to park just outside the metered area. You will most likely find that those who opposed the meter soon learn the purpose of the meter." Dowell concluded, generally, "I think that the parking meter is one of the most forward steps in traffic engineering since the installation of traffic-signal lights. There is no question but that the parking meter is not only a money-maker but a distinct help in handling traffic."[6]

Toledo, Ohio, Traffic Engineer Paul Robinette explained, in March 1938, that in the beginning and up to November 1936 (before the city installed meters in the CBD) Toledo, like most cities in that class, had a parking problem. There was a concentration of business in the limited CBD, which was about four blocks square, and narrow streets in short blocks on which the incompatible demands of curb parking requirements and the need for a more expeditious movement of traffic battled it out. As in most cities, Toledo responded with a variety of regulations but nothing was successful — all ended in "utter confusion," he explained. Had sufficient resources been available to enforce all those regulations, the system might have worked — but they weren't. To enforce parking time limits meant cars had to be checked soon after parking and get tagged soon after overstaying. The old system of chalking the tires meant two rounds for the police officer, and the legal hour's stay often actually became three hours or more. "The public are very observant and soon learned to note the rounds of the arm of the law, and even jumping the schedule didn't fool them very often," said Robinette. "They often learned, quite rapidly in fact, that simply rolling a car a few inches after the chalk mark was applied was just as effective as driving around several blocks looking for a new hole to get into. This perpetual chase had no other than nuisance value. We know that a car occupies just as much space in one block as it does in another, and chasing the long-time parker from one point to another was futile in bettering conditions." With curbs usually parked full on both sides, Toledo found the need for making short-time vehicle stops led to more double parking and even more congestion. To overcome that, in a move Robinette described as "ridiculous," the city banned parking entirely on one side of those CBD streets for the sole purpose of giving those people who had formerly illegally double parked an opportunity to park at the curb (illegally) and thus interfere less with moving traffic.[7]

Robinette conceded that, with the conditions that then prevailed, amounting to "a form of municipal government in which ability to have tickets fixed was a matter of political patronage — a full regiment of the United States Marines would have had difficulty in giving adequate enforcement. Tickets meant little or nothing, and because of this the early birds took possession of the curb space" and, after that, shoppers and others coming into the CBD parked outside the area and walked in. Others confined their shopping to the outlying community shopping areas and avoided the CBD entirely. Dissatisfaction with the conditions was heard from all sides. Merchants found their establishments almost inaccessible; the movement of goods in and out of the district was extremely difficult and people seeking parking spots often cruised round and round the CBD, adding to the confusion. Then Toledo got rid of the old-style political machine control form of city government and adopted the more modern, and efficient, city manager style of governance.[8]

One of the first problems tackled in Toledo by the new city manager was to clean up the traffic problem in the congested area. Ticket fixing was immediately stopped and enforcement of existing regulations was tightened. But it was also in the depths of the Depression and Toledo had a "magnificent deficit." Therefore, it was impossible to place a sufficient number of policemen in the CBD to provide an adequate enforcement of the parking regulations. Even though enforcement was tightened and tag fixing was stopped, the lack of personnel prevented any definite improvement. So the issue came down to finding some means by which that limited number of men could make their service more effective. And the answer to that issue, explained Robinette, was parking meters. It meant some cops could be removed from the traffic department and assigned to other duties because an officer could work so efficiently with meters. Therefore the city enacted enabling legislation and 1,000 meters were purchased. Because of a certain amount of reconfiguring of parking spots — changing loading zones, for example — and because metered spots were larger than spaces without meters, the 1,000 machines extended over an area that formerly accommodated 1,600 cars. All the devices provided 60 minutes of parking for five cents, except for 60 meters in one street through the heart of the financial district, which were timed to give 30 minutes.[9]

Results of the Toledo experiment were dramatic. According to Robinette, "One had to see it to believe how completely the parking meters took command of the situation. One day it was bumper-to-bumper, and ill-tempered confusion; very soon it was timely movement in and out of the stalls all day long. The long-time parker removed his car to a lot or garage or out of the district. The motorists now using the street facilities had business to transact there and usually did it quickly." Where formerly 1,600 cars had been parked, with an average daily turnover of four, making a total of about 6,400 cars parked daily in the CBD, the metered plan with just 1,000 spaces was daily accommodating at least 7,000 motorists who paid the fee, plus from 4,000 to 7,000 more who did not pay but parked in vacant spots where time still remained on the meters. Actual checks, declared Robinette, showed that each parking period served from 1.5 to 2.5 cars per meter. Seldom was the stall occupied to the full limit of the time by the original occupant. Bus traffic served as a marker for traffic-flow velocity. By request, exact running times of all bus schedules were compiled for the four weeks just prior to the meter installation as well as for the four weeks after the meters were installed. With meters in operation, the running times of the buses were reduced (improved) by an average of 9 percent.[10]

Merchants in Toledo also liked the new meters, declared the engineer. George C. Morrison, secretary of the Retail Merchants' Board said, in part, in a letter to Robinette, "Customer reaction, merchants' opinion and the opinion of the average motorist, are all very favorable. These men have reported that they do not receive any complaints from their customers, and they have stated on numerous occasions that the flow of traffic in the downtown section has been speeded up noticeably since meters were installed. The average motorist usually finds a parking space in the vicinity of the store at which he desires to transact business and does not voice any objections to paying his nickel for ample space in which to park his car." Originally, the Toledo Automobile Club opposed the system as a "matter of principle," but were said to have quickly changed their mind. In a letter to Robinette, D. D. Hatcher, secretary-manager of the Toledo Automobile Club, said at first the group was against meters because it looked like they were just "another grab on the motorist," and it was some time before the group became convinced the machines were of any benefit to traffic. "Our members, most of them, have complimented the meters, owing to the fact that when they come downtown now it is easier for them to park," he wrote. "Not only that, but it eliminates a lot of double-parking and in general, in my opinion, speeds up traffic. This might be hard for one who fought the parking meters like I did; but I am really pleased with the success of them." [11]

Later in 1938, the New York State Bureau of Municipal Information gathered data from 37 cities on their use of parking meters. The data was gathered from a series of questions directed to the municipalities. In response to the question, "Do meters reduce cruising of cars?" all 37 cities said yes, and in 23 instances voluntarily elaborated by giving figures ranging from a 25 percent to a 90 percent reduction in cruising around to find a parking space. When asked, "Do meters speed up traffic?" the answer was yes from 36 cities with the only negative response coming from Pona City, Oklahoma. In response to the query, "Has the city been held liable for dangers to parked autos?" all cities said no. When asked, "What per cent of the merchants are pleased?" a total of 27 cities replied. One reported 65 percent, two at 80 percent, one 85 percent, six 90 percent, one 92 percent, four 95 percent, one 98 percent, two 99 percent, and nine at 100 percent. In response to the query, "What per cent of the parkers are pleased?" there was again a reply from 27 cities. One reported 50 percent, one 65 percent, two 75 percent, three 80 percent, two 85 percent, six 90 percent, four 95 percent, one 96 percent, and seven at 100 percent. When asked, "What per cent of the city officials are pleased?" a total of 31 cities responded. A total of 27 of them reported 100 percent, with the other four cities giving the following percentages: 20, 83, 90, and 90. As a final query the cities were asked, "Is your meter system an unqualified success?" A full 15 cities did not reply; a "no" response came from Pocatello, Idaho, St. Petersburg, Florida, and Wichita Falls, Texas; "not exactly" was the reply from Austin, Texas. But the following 18 cities answered "yes": Atlantic City, New Jersey (60,000 population); Bakersfield, California (35,000); Clarksburg, West Virginia (30,000); Clearwater, Florida (20,000); Cumberland, Maryland (40,000); Dallas, Texas (209,000); El Paso, Texas, (102,000); Hagerstown, Maryland (33,000); Houston, Texas (400,000); Long Beach, California (170,000); Norfolk, Virginia (129,710); Oil City, Pennsylvania (22,000) Oklahoma City, Oklahoma (215,000); Omaha, Nebraska (220,000); Pittston, Pennsylvania (19,000); Toledo, Ohio (293,000); Uniontown, Pennsylvania (20,000); Wilmington, Delaware (115,000).[12]

Mayor Benjamin F. Turner of Passaic, New Jersey, remarked in May 1938 that his city (population 63,000) was the first in the East to experiment with the "modern" method of parking control and installed 140 parking meters in the CBD in January 1937 and added 386 more the following September: "The first installation was made with the consent of the merchants in the metered district. The second installation was made on the petition of other merchants who had observed the larger turnover of cars, the disappearance of the critical parking problem, and the general satisfaction shown." Passaic was the hub of a wheel made up of numerous communities and those out-of-town shoppers were described as the "cream" of the parkers in the CBD. However, they found the competition for space increasingly keen with their worst competition coming from the merchants and clerks who parked all day in front of their own or other places of business. Congestion in the four-block square CBD was getting worse. Public opinion, including that of the merchants, at last caught up with the facts and a deputation called on the Passaic Commissioner of Public Safety, John J. Roegner, demanding that one-hour parking be enforced. "The Commissioner inquired whether they knew what that entailed," said Turner "Parking was of all shapes and volumes — side, angle, nose, double, sometimes triple, and all-day. Our own townspeople, whom we all knew, were regular offenders. Endless, unpleasant and unprofitable arguments were foreseen, as well as an unpopular police force." Ten additional officers were estimated to be required to enforce the existing one-hour limit on the CBD's un-metered streets, and that alone would have added $25,000 to a city budget in trouble, as in most cities, because of the effects of the Depression. Three choices existed for the city of Passaic: prohibit parking entirely; compel the police to enforce the regulations; or install parking meters. Because Passaic did not want to prohibit parking and since they could not afford to enforce the regulations, the city turned to meters.[13]

Before the machines were installed, explained Turner, city officials talked to the merchants and got them to agree to a trial of the meters. The job of selecting a meter was given to City Engineer John J. Schneider, who invited manufacturers to send representatives to see him, with samples. Each man was given 15 minutes for a sales talk, and requested to leave his meter for 48 hours. A list of desirable features had been drawn up beforehand and the meters were examined, tested, and rated as to how they fared against the list. In the end the Mark-Time meter manufactured by M. R. Rhodes, Inc., of Hartford, Connecticut, was selected. Turner said the regulations, with the meters in operation, were enforced, but not harshly. For example, a car might stop at a curb while the driver bought a newspaper or a pack of cigarettes without his having to feed the meter. In the case of a car parked over the limit, a grace period of five to ten minutes was allowed. Concluded Turner, "Everyone in Passaic seems to like parking meters" and that repair work and servicing had been "negligible." Usually a police officer on patrol did whatever fixing or adjusting was necessary, whenever possible. On average, two meters a week had to have the unit removed from the post for repairs and when four of those had accumulated they were mailed as a group to Hartford in a special mailing case provided by the manufacturer, and requiring 18 cents postage. Sealed coin boxes from the meters were collected from the streets of Passaic in three half-days each week. With the success of the first installation of 140 meters with merchants and "everybody," businessmen on un-metered blocks requested that meters be installed on their blocks. Passaic officials said they would do so only on receipt of a petition. So a petition was drafted, circulated, and signed and led to full metering. Turner said that once the machines were all paid for it was hoped the accumulated surplus would accrue to the credit of the Department of Public Safety and would then be used for items long wanted, such as a new traffic-signal system.[14]

Revenues for the Passaic meters were as follows: from January 5, 1937, to April 30, 1937, (140 meters) $2,322.60; May $581.55; June $505.10; July $530.45; August $456.40; for an eight-month total of $4,396.10. Revenue for September (526 meters) was $1,643.40; October, $1,634.45; November, $1,475.35; December $1,927.45; January 1938, $1,053.30; February, $1,157.95; March, $1,326.10; for a seven-month total of $10,218.00. Total receipts from January 5, 1937, to March 31, 1938, were $14,614.10. In his general conclusion on the effect of the meters, Turner said that immediately after the first 140 devices were installed the all-day parkers disappeared as the merchants and clerks made way for shoppers. Double parking was reduced by 95 percent and the two-minute grace limit was "reasonably" observed. "The meter became a mechanical policeman. It commanded respect. Furthermore, it stopped most arguments between traffic officers and motorists, because the meter told the story, proved at once whether the motorist or the officer was right," Turner added. He found that only one in three or four parkers actually paid for the privilege, because so few people stopped for the full 60 minutes, "It is common to find four and five cars using space on the same nickel, and the observed record was 11 cars parked legally on one nickel."[15]

On February 25, 1937, Norfolk, Virginia, put into operation 246 Dual parking meters on representative streets of the CBD. Total curb length in that shopping area was 81,670 feet, but certain physical and legal prohibitions such as bus stops, loading zones, taxi stands, driveways, fire hydrants, and so on, decreased the curb space available for parking down to 57,606 feet. That distance was divided as follows: no parking, 20,968 feet; no parking 7:00 A.M. to 7:00 P.M., 2,518 feet; restricted time parking, 20,799 feet; unrestricted parking, 19,321 feet. Of the restricted time parking, 4,920 feet (24 percent) was given over to the meters, 246 machines times 20 feet each. L. W. Tazewell, director of traffic survey for the city, revealed that vehicle turnover on certain CBD streets was as follows: before meters, 6.2 cars per day per space; with meters, 9.7 (an increase of 57 percent); on another group of streets, before meters, 5.8 cars per space per day; with meters, 9.0 (55 percent increase). Before meters were installed, a parking space was anywhere from 14 to 20 feet of curb space. "Of all cars parked in the metered area, 37 per cent of them parked legally on unexpired time of preceding motorists. The free parking in the various blocks varies from 30 to 56 per cent and averaged 37 per cent," said Tazewell.[16]

Metered parking space in Norfolk was patrolled by one traffic cop on a motorcycle that made a complete circuit of the area in 20 minutes, tagging all the overtime vehicles, explained Tazewell. In the non-metered area, the method was to make one round, chalk-marking the tires of parked vehicles and then to make a second round, tagging cars that were chalk-marked. In a field check of one of the non-metered areas it was found the total number of cars parked was 950; five were tagged, 347 were overtime, 201 were chalk-marked, 749 were not chalked. Thus, only five tickets were given during the day of the check although 347 vehicles parked overtime and those cars accounted for 67.9 percent of the total vehicle hours. Two cars each parked between 8.0 and 8.5 hours without receiving a ticket. Of the 201 cars that were chalked, 55.6 percent were parked over one hour before being marked. Those 749 vehicles (79 percent of the 950 total) that were never chalked where parked an aggregate of 757 hours. Field checkers reported that cars were repeatedly moved to nearby positions when the owners noticed chalk marks and that in several cases the chalk marks were rubbed out by the motorists. From February 25 to March 24, 1937, a total of 1,067 tickets were made out for overtime parking on Norfolk's CBD streets: 471 (44 percent) were issued in the metered area (4,920 curb feet) and 596 (56 percent) were issued in the non-metered area (15,879 curb feet). "On a curb-foot basis almost three times as many overtime parking tickets are given in the metered area as in the non-metered area," observed Tazewell.[17]

Meters in Salt Lake City did not last too long and were soon removed from the streets of the business district sometime later in 1937 or in early 1938, due to the insistent lobbying against the devices by the business people. However, the question of whether or not to have meters was under vigorous discussion again, in November 1938, at least by the federated women's clubs of that city. As far as an editor with the *San Juan Record* (Utah) newspaper was concerned, the question was whether Salt lake City would continue to grant the free use of its curbs in the downtown district to the shopkeepers and their employees, or would it elect to reserve space at the curb, on payment of a nominal fee, to those people from the residential sections and out-of-town customers, so that they could reach the business establishments without undue effort and inconvenience. He added, "It is a serious reflection on the business acumen of Salt Lake merchants that they appear to prefer to use the curbing for their own cars free, to the exclusion of motorists anxious to spend money with them."[18]

By late 1938 it was reported by *American City* that 85 cities, large and small, in 26 states, had installed a total of 24,610 parking meters. And those communities were practically unanimous in praising the machines and what they had done in solving their cities parking problems; all were said to be "enthusiastic" about meters. Houston had the most meters in use, with 2,075; Dallas with 1,500; and San Antonio had 1,500. A total of eight cities had 1,000 or more of the devices in operation. At the other end of the scale was Bradenton, Florida, with 12 meters in use, and Clearwater, Florida, with 25. Ten cities each had less than 100 machines in use.[19]

At about the same time, *Fortune* magazine ran an article about parking meters and declared an annual $3 million, at least, in nickels was being dropped into some 30,000 of the devices in 77 American cities. There were reported to be over a dozen parking meters then on the market. Dual's biggest competition was M. H. Rhodes, Inc., whose meters were set in operation by flipping a crank. The original Dual meters also had to be cranked, but Dual stopped making them when it developed the automatics: too many people forgot the cranks. Rhodes was said to have sold 3,138 of its Mark-Time Meters from January 1, 1938, to October of that year. Then, there was the multiple-coin Miller Meter offering ten minutes parking for a penny, or an hour's worth for a nickel; the Jennings Meter with a rotating time disk and fixed pointer; the Red Ball Meter with a glass globe on top wherein appeared a red ball when the time was up; and the Park-O-Graph, Park-O-Matic, Parkrite, and Karpark meters—but Dual remained the manufacturer with the most meters on the most streets. Out of the estimated 30,000 on American streets, Dual accounted for about 60 percent of them. Since January 1938 alone, the firm had made installations in eight new cities and had signed additional contracts in nine communities it had previously metered. Standard price for the Dual automatic remained $58; prices on other Dual models and from other manufacturers ranged from $30 to $65.[20]

Cities still bought meters with no money down with the general procedure after installation, according to *Fortune*, being to split the take three to one between manufacturer and city until the machines were paid for. As each meter took in an average of 30 cents a day (six days) it usually paid for itself in nine months. Main benefits were said to be the elimination of the all-day parker and the virtual elimination of double parking. Numerous city mayors and chambers of commerce heartily approved of the devices and in 1938 the U.S. Congress gave the District of Columbia Commissioners the authority to install meters in Washington for a trial period. "But a good many people still hold Mr. Magee's idea in very bad odor," explained the article. The citizenry of Mobile, Alabama, abandoned meters after a short test; Milwaukee, Wisconsin, refused even a test four times; and the city fathers of Topeka, Kansas, felt they were basking in such reflected disfavor that they yanked their meters out until after an election. Local automobile clubs are divided, but the American Automobile Association lined up its 750 member clubs against meters from the start."[21]

To find out about parking meters, the National Association of Building Owners and Managers queried, late in 1938, contacts in 21 cities that used meters. Results indicated the cities were in substantial agreement that the devices were definitely helping to solve parking and traffic problems; that traffic moved more rapidly and more parking space was available; and whatever initial opposition existed was soon overcome with almost everyone quickly coming to regard the meters with favor. And, added a reporter, "It appears, too, that parking meters offer a welcome — though incidental — source of revenue." From the survey it was found that nine cities each had 500 or fewer meters; six had between 501 and 1,000; five had between 1,001 and 1,500; one city had between 2,0001 and 2,500 machines. Cities with populations ranging from 25,000 to 100,000 averaged 357 machines each; from 100,001 to 200,000 averaged 625 meters; from 200,001 to 300,000 average 1,003 meters; and from 300,001 to 400,000 averaged 1,486 meters in use. In seven of the cities (33 percent) legal objections had been raised at the time of installation, but in court all those cases were rendered in favor of the devices.[22]

Under legislation passed in Albany in 1937 parking meters could be used anywhere in New York State, except in New York City, with any income accruing from the devices having to be earmarked for traffic control measures; that is, not to be treated as general revenue by a city. Many communities in the state quickly moved to install the meters. White Plains completed a six-month trial of the devices on December 1, 1938, and decided to keep them permanently. Watertown, Glens Falls, Oneonta, and Auburn had each had them in operation for several months, while Newburgh, Geneva and Buffalo had each contracted for an installation. Buffalo looked at all the models manufactured by seven different firms before deciding on one. At Auburn the meters received pennies instead of nickels. Any number up to five could be inserted at a time; each entitled the motorist to park for 12 minutes. Auburn collected 80,000 coins a day and the only major complaint in that city was that slugs sometimes appeared among the coins. White Plains expected to derive a profit of $18,000 a year. When a White Plains department store queried its customers, it found two-thirds of them favored the meters. The Civic and Business Federation of White Plains sent out 300 questionnaires to shoppers; 75 percent reported themselves to be in favor of the devices. Merchants, who had been 60 percent opposed, reported an increase in trade. Police, unable previously to enforce a 60-minute parking limit, found the average time of parking at a meter to be less than 30 minutes. John R. Crossley, vice-president of the Automobile Club of New York, remained strongly opposed to meters: "Parking laws can be enforced without using meters. There is nothing that can be done with meters that cannot be done without them, except collect nickels. I believe that cities will take the meters out after the experiments have been made."[23]

Salt Lake City reapproved parking meters and reintroduced the devices in early 1939. As they were being installed, the city commission discovered several parking lots had been created where owners were starting to charge a dime for the parking of automobiles. Apparently worried that those lots would perhaps cut down revenue from parking meters, the commission promptly changed the regulations and charged parking lots a high license fee to do business.[24]

As Salt Lake City reintroduced meters, the city of Ogden, Utah, in its tourism advertisements, pointed out that it had no parking meters — but did have city-operated free parking lots — and added, jokingly, it would appreciate a visit from people "unfortunate" enough to possess an automobile. A reporter added, sarcastically, "Salt Lake City officials plan to help the motorists get on their feet and walk, by laying on the parking charge and trying in other ways to put the car owner in his place."[25]

More grumbling over the Salt Lake City, Utah, meters was heard in 1940 when a newspaper editor noted that all of the profits from the meters were to go into a traffic safety fund to enlarge the police force and buy equipment for solving the city's traffic problem. But, said the editor, of the $75,000 that should have gone into that effort, $70,000 was used in other city departments.[26]

As of January 1, 1939, parking meters were in use in about 90 American cities, according to a survey by the American Society of Planning Officials and the International City Managers' Association. All those experiences were reported as having been successful. Toledo's 1,000 machines produced about 35 cents per meter per day, with total revenue of $109,140 in 1937. Dallas had 1,500 in use with gross receipts of $147,582 in 1937 and cost of just $12,000 to repair and maintain them, and collect the coins.[27]

Los Angeles remained meter free but the proponents kept trying. In 1939, a proposal to install the machines in the CBD was presented to the city of Los Angeles and ordered filed by the police commission on the motion of Commissioner Van M. Griffith. LAPD Chief Arthur C. Hohmann said that, after he had conferred with representatives of the City Attorney's office, it was a question in his mind whether public streets of the city could legally be used for the purpose of obtaining revenue.[28]

Pittsburgh, Pennsylvania, installed 437 meters in selected portions of four business districts in 1939 and then conducted surveys. Overall, they found slight increases in both traffic speed and volume when the pre-meter period was compared to the period with meters in use; average traffic speed increased 9.9 percent and traffic volume increased 5.71 percent when the meters were in operation. A survey of public opinion was made of motorists who were actually parked at a meter. When asked, "Do you favor the retention of parking meters?" 2,007 (95.3 percent) said yes, and 98 (4.7 percent) said no. The question, "Were you opposed to the installation of meters?" brought a yes response from 159 (7.5 percent) of the motorists, and a no from 1,946 (92.5 percent). Merchants in the affected areas were asked, "Do you favor the retention of parking meters?" with 168 (86.6 percent) replying yes, 20 (10.3 percent) saying no, and six (3.1 percent) expressing disinterest. When asked "Were you originally opposed to parking meters?" 64 (33.0 percent) said yes, 114 (58.8 percent) said no, and 16 (8.2 percent) expressed disinterest.[29]

Vandalism sometimes became an issue. Huntington, West Virginia, had 1,200 meters in operation in March 1940, and one night that month somebody expressed his disapproval. Police Detective Roy B. Hagely said that about 100 meters in the downtown district had been smashed by some type of heavy instrument and put out of commission. However, no coins were removed from any of the machines.[30]

After being in use for about two years in Bakersfield, California, CBD streets, meters were still a bone of contention, at least in some quarters. As part of a traffic survey report submitted in April 1940 to the city council by City Engineer Holfelder, was a defense of the devices. Said Holfelder in the report, "Certainly parking meter installation has been a material aid to the enforcing of parking regulations and has reduced the number of offenses needed to obtain the same degree of observance."[31]

Parking meters resurfaced as an issue in Los Angeles in the spring of 1940 with another movement to have them installed on city streets. In an editorial in the *Los Angeles Times,* the editor opposed the idea arguing that the objections cited by the Automobile Club of Southern California against meters did not adequately emphasize one of the most fundamental objections to the machines, that "parking meters are an effort to rent out public property meant for the general use of all and paid for by taxation, to private uses. Might as well put a toll charge on the use of the streets; the principle is much the same." With respect to the existing regulations and fining of motorists for over-parking, he argued they were designed to foster the free use of the streets by preventing their being taken over by parking hogs with the collection of revenue being incidental and punitive. Individuals were not given a "lease" on a particular public area. He declared that parking meters and parking fines did not amount to the same thing; their intent was opposite: "The parking meter makes street parking chronic, establishes it as a right, whereas the tendency of regulation is to do away with street parking altogether, which will probably be necessary in the not distant future. It will be necessary if traffic continues to grow in volume." As the Automobile Club pointed out, the *Los Angeles Times* editor continued, curb meters did not aid the enforcement of parking regulations nor did they eliminate the need for it, though they did add to its cost. They reduced the total parking space available because the spaces marked off each had to be big enough for cars of the longest wheelbase. "Much emphasis is laid upon the public revenue accruing from the use of the devices, but very little upon the fact that it comes entirely from motorists, already the highest taxed of any group, for the use of public property paid for and maintained by levies on gasoline," grumbled the editor. How much those "unjustified" charges came to was estimated by the California State Automobile Association when meters were under consideration by San Francisco. According to its figures, the annual cost to motorists of each 1,000 meters, operating ten hours a day for 300 days a year was $120,000, or 40 cents per meter per day. Acknowledging that the meters were then in use in some 100 American towns and cities, the editor stated the machines were in none of the cities of the "metropolitan class" where traffic congestion reached major dimensions. On the other hand, he noted, the devices had been considered and disapproved of by Detroit, Chicago, New York, Philadelphia, San Francisco, and other large cities, according to a report presented in December 1939 by the Traffic Advisory Board to the Los Angeles Police Commission. Los Angeles Mayor Bowron, who was interested in a new source of revenue, had recently suggested the devices be given a trial, notwithstanding that the city attorney had held that meters could be installed only under municipal police powers and not as revenue producers.[32]

A mere suggestion that meters be tried brought out the opponents as protests were filed with the Los Angeles City Council against the installation of parking meters. One came from the Downtown Businessmen's Association, which urged city officials to oppose the installation of the machines in the downtown district.[33]

In May 1940, the Automobile Club of Southern California submitted a nine-point protest to the Los Angeles City Council against parking meters that included the idea that even greater traffic congestion than presently existed would result from meters placed on the city's CBD streets. According to the club, meters would block the solution of the traffic problem and would tend to turn motorists away from the metered business district. A reporter declared, "Definite opposition of the club's directors to the meter scheme is based on extensive investigation of experiences in other cities where it has been tried." Stated the report: "Trial installation of the nickel-grabbing meters would entrench curb parking and make it virtually impossible to eliminate storage of vehicles along certain streets. Such storage should be eliminated in order to move traffic more speedily," and that "more off-street parking facilities must be provided, but parking meters that would perpetuate curb parking would serve no beneficial purpose." As far as the auto club was concerned, "Congestion will be increased by autoists roving around blocks looking for free time left by the persons who only parked for five or ten minutes," and "there would be less parking space than at present, because meters would necessitate making space for cars of greatest wheelbase." As a last shot, the report concluded, "Parking meters have the sole advantage of producing revenue for the city by forcing motorists to pay a rental charge for parking space on the city streets. Sale of high-priced meters to the city also would enrich the manufacturers, with motorists paying the bill. All other benefits claimed for this device can as well be obtained by adequate enforcement of present regulations."[34]

The Los Angeles City Council was considering the trial installation of 5,000 meters as a possible source of $500,000 in yearly revenue, said the Automobile Club of Southern California as it continued its onslaught of protest against meters in May 1940: "Parking meter interests derive a huge profit margin. The machines cost from $6 to $8 to manufacture but are priced from $25 to $65 installed. Promoters make it easy for cities by taking the payment from meter revenue but motorists pay the entire bill." The club insisted: "When cities experiment with meters the devices are removed as soon as paid for. The promoters never lose. When the meters are removed by public demand, the promoters pocket the money derived, take back their machines and move elsewhere." (Most of those statements were false. A very few cities had removed the meters after installation, but the vast majority kept them, to the agreement of most people.) One argument that did make sense was that the use of meters did not free up streets: "Los Angeles needs traffic remedies, not barriers. It has outgrown its streets and must open up major routes for the free flow of traffic. Every effort should be made toward restricting parking on congested streets rather than licensing the practice." Businessmen and organizations opposed to meters being located in their districts were urged by the auto club to express their views in writing to the city council. Downtown merchants on Broadway had just voted 74 percent against meters, according to a survey.[35]

Reportedly, "scores" of organizations opposed to meters in Los Angeles told council representatives they were "a tax threat against motorists and a menace to business." Motorists forced to pay a fee for curb parking would simply turn away to become customers at shopping areas offering free curb parking, businessmen thundered. And meters, they predicted, would retard the development of off-street parking areas. Besides the auto club, groups opposing the proposed meter trial in Los Angeles included: Los Angeles Traffic Association the, Los Angeles Junior Chamber of Commerce, the Central Business District Association, the Downtown Businessmen's Association, the Restaurant Association of Southern California, numerous district business and improvement associations and "scores of labor organizations."[36]

According to the Automobile Association of Southern California, there was an ever-increasing opposition to the meter proposal and organizations on record as of early June 1940 as opposed, the club announced, included: the Hollywood Chamber of Commerce, the San Pedro Business Men's Association, the San Pedro Chamber of Commerce, the Miracle Mile Association, the Wilshire Chamber of Commerce, the Eagle Rock Business Men's Association, the Los Angeles Central Labor Council, the Los Angeles Traffic Advisory Board, and the groups listed above.[37]

Attorney Frank P. Doherty announced in August 1940 that even more opposition was surfacing against meters and that it was coming from civic-minded citizens and organizations in all districts of the city. He said there were already more than 50 organizations on record as opposed while not a single citizen, merchant or business group had appeared before the city council or the police commission to speak in favor. "If it were not for the parking meter salesmen and lobbyists with their self-seeking profit motives we would hear nothing more on the issue," said Doherty. "The purchase of such meters by the city constitutes the creation of a private monopoly invading the use of public thoroughfares. Motorists would be compelled by law to pay tribute to a private corporation for the privilege of parking on public streets."[38]

Doing its part in the lobby effort against the meters was the *Los Angeles Times*, which gave much space to opponents for them to rant and never had a good word to say about the machines. B. D. Mayson, secretary of the Watts Chamber of Commerce, declared, "Parking meters violate the rights of the people to use the streets free — streets which the people have paid for in the first place." Lionel Holland, speaking for the Atwater District Business Club, said, "We have studied the parking meter proposal and are convinced that meters will cause added congestion. With meters installed, motorists will drive around block after block, seeking a vacant place where meters will afford them unused time provided by a previous parker's nickel." A report presented by the Los Angeles Traffic Advisory Board (composed of businessmen) declared meters were meant for use in cities that were in their period of traffic adolescence, in cities that have not yet outgrown their street width." But, continued the report, Los Angeles was a traffic adult that "has outgrown its streets in an alarming fashion as have the other major cities of the United States. It is significant that New York State expressly excluded New York City from its Parking Meter Enabling Act." Philadelphia, Detroit, and San Francisco were all cited again as having disapproved meter use, while Chicago had not only no meters but no parking in its CBD. "We have definitely left the parking meter phase of city traffic growth far behind," said the advisory board. "The parking meter in Los Angeles would be an anachronism."[39]

On August 29, 1940, by a vote of eight to four, the Los Angeles City Council killed the proposal to install parking meters on a trial basis, pending the time the meter firms could show that businessmen wanted them. In moving that the matter be filed, Councilman John W. Baumgartner said that no businessman had asked for them and until they desired a tryout he was against the devices. Since the original resolution, proposing parking meters was placed before the city council by former Councilman Robert MacAlister in February 1937, said a journalist, "The idea had been kicked from pillar to post, gathering vigorous opposition along the way." Most stridently opposed of all had been the Automobile Club of Southern California, which had pointed out it would be just as fair to install turnstiles for sidewalk pedestrians as to make motorists pay for the "privilege" of parking.[40]

Just one week later, the City Council of Inglewood, California (a municipality that adjoined Los Angeles) turned thumbs down on the idea of meters for its CBD — even for a 90-day trial offered at no cost to the city. That was in spite of the fact that a chamber of commerce committee, headed by Dr. Howard Drum, had made a survey of the city's traffic and parking problems and had recommended the installation of parking meters.[41]

Vandals, at work in a Detroit suburb in early 1941, had destroyed or stolen 55 of Hamtramck's 500 parking meters since they had been installed in 1940, according to city officials. That destruction had not occurred all at once but over a period of time.[42]

Once again the issue surfaced in Los Angeles. On May 5, 1942, Councilman J. Win Austin, a member of the traffic and lighting committee introduced a resolution designed to resurrect the question of whether or not meters should be installed. It was observed that Austin was a relatively new member of the city council. Councilman Roy Hampton admonished Austin by telling him, "You don't know what you're doing. I was here when this business was before the Council more than a year ago. What a headache! You have yet to experience the wrath of the whole city of Los Angeles. You will rue the day you ever talked about parking meters." Added Councilman Robert Burns, dean of the city lawmakers, "You [Austin] are bidding for plenty of trouble." Councilman Baumgartner observed, "It's just a mell of a hess." But Austin persisted. He said he had completed a 12-page report showing that parking meters in other cities were a success, that they actually benefited merchants and were self-sustaining. However, at the end of the day the Los Angeles City Council voted seven to five to forget about the whole business, again.[43]

Even though nothing happened with Austin's Los Angeles proposal, a few groups came forward to express opposition anyway. Reaffirming its previous stand on meters, the board of directors of the junior chamber of commerce went on record as being opposed to any move that "would hinder the ultimate solution of the parking problem and traffic congestion in the city of Los Angeles." Don Petty, president of the group, said, "The curbstone slot machine is just another revenue producer in which an already tax-burdened public must pay the bill. The parking meters could be utilized to greater advantage in the current salvage campaign which is attempting to meet the shortage of iron and steel in plants producing vital implements of war." Petty argued the necessity of moving traffic in congested areas meant eventual prohibition for street parking and meters only encouraged curb parking, to the detriment of the public and merchants.[44]

What prompted the above outburst, and others, was the action of Los Angeles City Council in 1942 calling for bids for 2,000 parking meters and instructing the street traffic engineer to specify definite locations for initial and subsequent installations. The Automobile Club of Southern California, in letters of protest over the action that were sent to members of council, contended that meters had been overwhelmingly turned down in 1940 and "are just as obnoxious to Los Angeles motorists in 1942 as they were two years ago." The club raised the same objections it had brought up earlier, in the same language. S. L. Mitchell, general manager of the club, pointed out all the groups that had been in opposition in 1940 and declared, "At no time has any civic organization advocated parking meters in Los Angeles."[45]

Any projected use of the machines in Los Angeles met with determined opposition, and later in September 1942, Meade McClanahan, a steel company executive, filed an injunction suit in superior court. McClanahan, suing in the role of a taxpayer, brought the action against the city, the city council, the chief of police, and other city officials. It was contended in the suit that the use of city funds for installation and operation of the meters would be illegal.[46]

All the controversy prompted an October 12, 1942 editorial on the subject in the *Los Angeles Times,* wherein the editor railed against the devices for the same reasons he had in 1940. An extra reason against the machines that he presented in 1942 was that, with war restrictions and with men overseas, street parking and congestion were lessening, and thus also any supposed need for meters. "Some members of the City Council seem to be trifling again with the idea of installing parking meters, which is an especially ridiculous notion at this time," he fumed. "The reasons which, in peacetime, caused the parking meter scheme to be greeted here with overwhelming public disapproval are reinforced in war, with the fact of scarcities of critical materials and of labor which ought to cause the scheme to be dropped without a trace."[47]

On November 10, 1942, the Los Angeles City Council voted to adopt a resolution by Councilman Ira McDonald, putting off until after the end of the war the proposed installation of parking meters on a trial basis in various districts. Chief arguments against meters at the time were that the threatened gas rationing and the government requisitioning of extra tires was going to make plenty of parking spaces available everywhere. A couple of unnamed councilmen hinted that the Automobile Club of Southern California had a lot to do with the "death" of the proposal and claimed they were annoyed about it. A motion made by one of them to continue the proceedings on the issue a week later was voted down and McDonald's substitute proposal to postpone meters for the duration of the war was adopted by a 12 to two vote.[48]

As of December 20, 1944, the 800 meters on the streets of the CBD in Huntington Park, California, had completed their year of probationary service. According to Mayor Wendell Schooring, surveys by City Engineer Hamilton E. Robinson showing parking turnover had increased 4.5 times, which was credited with relieving traffic congestion in the downtown section it had also virtually eliminated the practice of cruising for parking space. During that first year, the meters had grossed $79,796.91. Fines for violating the city's parking meter ordinance had steadily decreased from a high of $1,000 per month to less than $500 monthly.[49]

As World War II came to an end, *Business Week* presented a lengthy article in April 1945 about parking meters. It was thought the machines had a very rosy future. When the War Production Board stopped their manufacture on August 3, 1942, about 195,000 machines had been installed in 432 American cities and towns. Annual installations had doubled every three years since the first device was introduced in 1935, reaching 47,000 in 1941. On the basis of the wartime lag, the magazine conservatively estimated that an immediate market of some 400 cities for 200,000 meters existed. However, it also estimated there were in the U.S. a maximum of 800,000 to one million parking spaces in urban areas sufficiently congested to justify meter installation. Prewar prices were $45 to $74 for the meter heads alone. The extent of replacement business was uncertain, since many of the first meters installed were still in operation. A sizeable proportion of the potential market was New York City, still excluded from New York State legislation that permitted the devices elsewhere in the state. A study of New York City's traffic and parking problems made by the Regional Plan Association strongly recommended an amendment to legalize meters to help, among other things, in expediting cross-town traffic movement. A survey of New York City motorists revealed a willingness to pay ten cents for an hour of parking, although five cents an hour prevailed in all the metered cities. New York estimated that a parking space on Fifth Avenue was worth $142 a month on the basis of land value. Revenues to cities from meters varied, but a nationwide average income was $5 per month per meter, even during the era of war restrictions. That gross was exclusive of fines (generally $1) for over-parking. Roanoke, Virginia, topped the income list with a monthly average of $13.20 per meter. Cleveland, which broke the ice among large cities by installing meters in 1940, received an average of $5.65 a month from each machine.[50]

Wrote *Business Week:* "Gradually the general principle has been established that curb parking is not an inalienable right, and that revenue obtained from a charge for such a privilege is not a tax and may legally be used in traffic regulation." The percentage of total police department expenditures paid by parking meter revenue varied from 2 percent provided by 60 meters in Mobile, Alabama, to 200 percent from 113 in Lexington, Virginia. A typical large city installation (such as Rochester's 1,855 meters) collected $90,017 in 1944, or 8 percent of all police expenditures. Cost of parts and replacements for the machines averaged less than 1.25 percent of receipts for all cities in a typical month's check. As far as the business publication was concerned, extensive studies had shown that meters facilitated the movement of traffic, mainly by reducing the amount of cruising in search of a parking space and by eliminating double parking. Merchants in the congested areas had frequently been opponents (pre-installation) of meters only to ask for an extension of the system after a brief experience with the machines. Noted was that the efficiency of meters as a traffic regulator depended upon strict enforcement: "The public shows the same disregard for meters as for limited-parking signs unless the meters are policed, which they can be at a fourth the manpower required by the chalk-and-stopwatch method."[51]

According to the article, competition between the makers of manual and automatic machines was likely to shift in favor of the latter. M. H. Rhodes, Inc., of Hartford, whose Mark-Time manual meter had been among the leaders, had announced that it would build an automatic model. Automatics were more complex and required periodic winding, but a collector called regularly at the machine anyway. Police, reportedly, had some difficulties with the crank-operated manuals; parkers had learned to cheat by inserting a coin but "forgetting" to turn the handle. The enforcement officer found a coin in the slot, but could not tell whether it had been placed there two minutes or two hours earlier. Nationwide, the ratio was then about six manuals to seven automatics. In just the first four months of 1945, 19 cities had placed contracts for meters. Biggest of those was Seattle, which was seeking 1,081 additional meters. Manufacturers were then still waiting for the war production board approval to fill such orders. The Dual Parking Meter Company had 64,866 units installed at the end of 1941 and led the field. In second place, with 26,015 meters installed, was the Duncan Meter Company of Chicago. Standing fourth in the field was the Karpark Corporation of New York with 19,284 machines in operation, as of the end of 1941. Various patent litigation suits by manufacturers revealed that the earliest patent in this area was applied for in 1926 and granted in 1930 to Charles C. Doyle of Cleveland, describing a parking timer to be used to restrict unnecessary parking and to obtain revenue. In Dallas, the installation of meters was said to have led to a 300 percent increase in the turnover in downtown parking and to have increased the traffic flow by 30 percent.[52]

Chapter 9

The General Problem and Solutions, 1945–1950

Traffic and parking problems in American cities increased dramatically and drastically from 1945 onward as the war and gas rationing ended. In Los Angeles in 1945 there was a proposal under consideration to construct an underground parking lot beneath Pershing Square in the heart of downtown, to provide space for 2,800 autos. It was a project similar to one in San Francisco where a parking area that accommodated 1,700 vehicles was built under the city's Union Square. Since the end of gas rationing there had been a rise of 10 percent in the number of cars filling Los Angeles parking lots. "Downtown auto travel," said Ralph T. Dorsey, traffic engineer for the city, "has increased noticeably" since the end of rationing. On a typical day in 1944 (with rationing) streetcars brought 5,700 more passengers to the downtown area of Los Angeles than they did on the same day in 1945 (no rationing). And that translated into 3,900 more cars and that, said Dorsey, means "that 10 acres of area would be needed in this section [downtown] to park these cars — and this just isn't available."[1]

Some 15 Murray, Utah, businessmen met on a night in May 1945 to discuss the parking problem. After two hours of deliberation, those present could decide only to hold another meeting the following week. Mayor Hansen addressed the group and said he did not favor the parking time limit idea "as a solution because the arrests do not make friends for the city." He cited instances where he had attended conventions when strangers from other cities and states had expressed to him a dislike for Murray because they had been arrested there.[2]

When *Business Week* published an April 1946 assessment of the postwar parking and traffic problems it observed that, having built all kinds of facilities for speeding motorists to their destinations, virtually every city and large town in America was refocusing its planning sights on providing parking space for motorists once they got there. Widened and one-way streets, express boulevards, rotary traffic circles, parking meters, time restrictions, and even complete parking bans were the common antidotes to traffic congestion. But the congestion increased as streets were narrowed by curb parkers. And if ordinances against curb parking were enforced by police tagging drivers, said the article, "The result is an increase in the streams of cruisers — motorists looking for places to park, estimated to form 30% of the traffic on business streets during shopping hours." Some 20 years earlier, the Harvard Bureau of Traffic Research predicted that situation. Its 1926 survey of 17 cities disclosed that 1.5 million autos were daily engaged in a competition for 232,000 places to park. Said the bureau: "The streets can never be made to handle the traffic without adequate off-street storage."[3]

The reasons cited by *Business Week* for the failure of municipalities to provide such storage were: (1) high land cost; (2) opposition of merchants; and (3) laws prohibiting cities from going into the garage business. Among the proposals then under consideration by some cities were underground parking facilities, open-air multiple-deck garages and opening building roofs to parking. As well, there were plans for extending parking meter areas, compelling new buildings to provide parking spaces, and building, operating, or leasing city-owned properties for car storage. A survey of municipal traffic departments throughout America indicated awareness that properly located parking facilities were necessary not only to aid businessmen and shoppers, but to save municipalities from "excessive decentralization. More than 200 towns and cities now own and operate congested-area parking lots."[4]

Among the various specific plans discussed by *Business Week* was that of Portland, Oregon, with the city planning to extend meter coverage. Since 1938, more than 2,000 meters had increased the city's traffic turnover by 50 percent. A comprehensive city plan developed for Chicago declared that emphasis in traffic matters had to be transferred from the building of highways to the provision of parking space. H. E. Kincaid, the former director of the Chicago Plan Commission, believed that terminal parking was an integral part of any superhighway system. There were only about 15,000 off-street parking spaces in Chicago's central area—an estimated 50,000 new off-street spaces were expected to be needed in the ensuing decade. One large Washington, D.C., store had opened a tier-parking structure for its patrons, with cars reaching the upper decks by a series of ramps. Philadelphia prohibited almost all parking in the central area on

January 2, 1946. So severe was the parking problem there that Philadelphia's city council appropriated $20,000 for an emergency study. They were thinking about two or three underground areas to hold some 4,000 vehicles. While *Business Week* mentioned that experts believed traffic congestion in many cities could be reduced by encouraging the public to make greater use of mass transit, no examples of any projects were cited. Of 80,000 to 90,000 parking tickets issued every year in Hartford, Connecticut, only 30 percent to 40 percent were paid for by the offenders — the rest being lost somewhere "along the line," according to R. W. Thompson, superintendent of streets. He said that situation discouraged garage building on expensive land by private capital. The city had then banned all parking in the downtown area between 4:00 P.M. and 6:00 P.M. and was planning a $4 million parking plaza for 3,500 cars.[5]

While passenger automobile traffic was up 52 percent in 1946 over 1945, reported *Newsweek*, parking space had decreased "alarmingly" as postwar building covered parking lots and garages were converted to more profitable uses. Also, curb parking was further curtailed. Traffic entering Chicago's downtown Loop area was 42 percent greater in 1946 than in 1945, while parking lots had decreased from 86 to 82 and garage space had diminished by nearly 25 percent. Cars entered New York City in September 1946 at a rate 57 percent higher than in January 1946, and 13 percent greater than in September 1941. Off-street parking had decreased by nearly one-third. Dallas had a daily influx of 83,000 vehicles to its downtown area, with parking facilities for only 40,000. In Kansas City, the area around Petticoat Lane was congested with 170,865 cars daily in a scramble for 15,725 parking spaces. To ease their traffic jams, Philadelphia and Cincinnati had banned all curb parking downtown during daylight hours. In Providence, Rhode Island, auto traffic was up 50 percent in 1946 over 1945, while Hartford's traffic increase for the same period was 60 percent.[6]

According to the *Newsweek* story, property values in the downtown areas of some cities were declining as auto shoppers turned away from crowded streets in favor of conveniently located suburban stores. Baltimore estimated property values in its central area had dropped some 34 percent since 1931. As most cities obtained about 25 percent of their income from property taxes on their central areas, the loss was highly significant. "This year the cities, watching suburban supermarkets springing up and big department stores opening branches on their outskirts, have been driven from talking to action," said a reporter. Downtown merchants, who in the past opposed parking restrictions with the idea they would reduce patronage, had then discovered from surveys that very little of the curb parking space was used by shoppers. More than 280 cities were operating parking lots, but it was admitted that attempts to institute bus shuttle service from parking lots on the fringes (park and ride) had met with "mixed success." Parking meters were then in use in 473 cities, reducing parking time but providing only "limited relief." Perhaps the most significant comment in the *Newsweek* piece was its conclusion: "At the bottom of the traffic stew was the fact that the average shopper refuses to walk more than 800 feet to his destination."[7]

One of the more pessimistic review articles came from Sam Shulsky, writing in February 1948 in *American Mercury*. He remarked that not a single city of any size in America claimed to have solved the auto-parking problem. Despite any and all efforts, American mid-town streets were more cluttered then than ever before. And, he declared, it would get worse as more and more people were buying cars. A survey of U.S. cities by the Institute of Traffic Engineers led them to conclude that all of them were worried about the traffic problem. In Milwaukee, automobile traffic was then 92 percent above wartime levels, while New York, Chicago, and other communities reported that traffic was up 50 percent or more. Even a small place such as Plainfield, New Jersey (35,000 population), found congestion and lack of parking space so serious that vehicle movement in the center of town was "all but impossible." Cars then, said Shulsky, required nearly 200 square feet of parking space per vehicle and the American motorist had shown he would not buy "Europe's midget cars" even during a period of emergency and "parking surveys have established that a motorist doesn't want to walk more than 1,000 feet after parking his car." Even though every community was then making some active effort, substantial or otherwise, to solve the problem — municipal lots and underground facilities were the usual proposed remedies — Shulsky concluded the situation "gets worse daily." Thanks to years of highway planning, Manhattan Island was one of the easiest centers to get to, but it was a different story when it came to storing those autos. Humorist Will Rogers had once famously advised, "If you ever find a place to park your car in New York, don't move it. Leave that car there for parking purposes and buy another one for driving around." New York City was then talking about spending between $25 million and $37 million to construct 42 garages and lots (some above ground, some below) to hold a total of 15,000 cars. Assuming two cars would use a single space each day, that measure would accommodate 30,000 cars, or just 2 percent of the automobiles that traversed the city's streets daily. In downtown New York stood the Equitable Building in the financial district. That 40-story building (just one of many of a similar size in the financial area) held 12,000 workers and was visited daily by another 65,000 people. If they all came by car (the national average was then 1.7 occupants per private auto) all of the city's proposed new parking facilities could not take care of the traffic at that building alone.[8]

It was not just New York City that had a problem. As Shulsky noted, every city was hard pressed to provide space for its motorists. "That these motorists should even expect to find space available for their convenience derives from the curious line of reasoning which holds that parking facilities can be operated at a partial, or, if necessary, total financial loss," he said, arguing that business should be held accountable. All too often businesses had built their huge office structures right up to the property line and even complained if it was suggested to them that traffic might be expedited if they provided loading docks within their buildings and away from the public road. All of those costs of cities were put on the taxpayer and, Shulsky said, "It is high time the taxpayer pointed out that he has no intention of subsidizing auto parking in mid-town Los Angeles, Boston, Utica or New Orleans. He could further argue, supported by economic law, that there would be no shortage of parking space if the market for it were allowed to find its own level. Asking the automobile owner to pay such rates for space would very quickly eliminate about 95 per cent of the demand."[9]

With respect to a Philadelphia survey that showed that 88 percent of shoppers in downtown stores arrived by public transit (8 percent came by private car; 4 percent walked), Shulsky argued, "If 88 of every 100 persons can get to the stores by public conveyance, why should I be asked to put up money to provide for the convenience of the few who insist on the luxury of private transportation?" He then added, "The American motorist has no Constitutional guarantee of the right to park on New York's Fifth Avenue, Boston's Scollay Square or Sauk Center's Main Street, and only the refusal of politicians to give him the bad news has kept the misconception alive." Any motorist who wanted to live in a community large enough to support big-city pleasure, he reasoned, had to give up to a large extent the convenience of driving to them in his own car, a "privilege he could enjoy to the full when he attended the Saturday night band concert back home in Wigwam." He wondered why a city administration should be expected to spend money catering to the 1.7 occupants of the private automobile when public transportation facilities were themselves in need of improvement throughout the country. "By what point of privilege does the motor car owner, who scorns public transportation, raise the demand that city funds be spent for his comfort?"[10]

So long as Americans sponsored the concentration of merchandising, amusements, and so on, Shulsky felt the parking problem was "insoluble." There was no prospect of finding CBD land of such low economic value that it was fit for nothing but vehicle storage, therefore, the "only logical solution to inadequate parking space and resultant traffic jams is a reduction in the number of private cars in congested areas." He wanted to see mass, not exclusive, transportation encouraged. The 50 motorists who then required 29 private cars to get downtown should be transferred to a single public conveyance, at a tremendous saving in street space. Shulsky concluded the ineffectual, half-hearted approach that had distinguished the first quarter of a century of wrestling with the traffic problem was outmoded and a new approach was needed. Among the items that were passé were such things as one-way streets, 15-minute parking here, 60 minutes there, and so forth. To end New York City's traffic mess, for example, he thought it might well require a law forbidding all private cars from being driven — let alone parked — on Manhattan Island south of 96th Street.[11]

At the other end of the spectrum from Shulsky, with an excessively optimistic article in praise of the auto and what it had wrought, was J. Robert Harris, writing in *The Rotarian* in early 1950. He enthused, "We are, for example, taking our new stores out to vacant places and facing them around to the parking lot." Harris saw the example of Los Angeles as the answer to the question of how to live most successfully with this "convenient machine" and which "has taken the form of a gradual decentralization of business from the old downtown business districts to the open areas in the environs of our city." It was a process, he continued, "which began" in the '30s, retarded by the war, but now in full momentum again, this exodus to the suburbs will cost hundreds of millions of dollars for new merchandising facilities and more millions in public expenditures for wide traffic arteries, new streets, and other facilities which the conversion will necessitate. Out of it, we expect, will come more business and better living." Harris argued that 95 percent of all customers then entered America's new stores and banks through the back doors that opened directly "upon acres of paved and landscaped customer parking areas. All our new department stores, drug stores, supermarkets, even the 5-and-10-cent stores, offer off-street parking — with their principal window displays fronting parking areas." Time was, he argued, when the value of a store location was appraised by counting pedestrian traffic passing the site, but that was disappearing in Los Angeles because, of more importance than a "busy spot on the main drag is plenty of off-street parking. Sears & Roebuck's new stores throughout Southern California are sprawling one- and two-story structures with acres of customer parking space and are well outside of existing business centers. The vanishing pedestrian did not figure in their location."[12]

Parking meters continued to be viewed as a major part of the solution, if not the solution itself. In the middle of 1946, Los Angeles City Council voted ten to three to have an ordinance drawn for the installation of the devices. That did not mean they would be installed; it simply brought the question before the council for action. Once again the *Los Angeles Times* editor was vehemently opposed. He urged those opposed to get into the fight again, since "the proponents of the plan to rent out the city streets for private use are very active and apparently well financed." He fumed that all though the proponents were overwhelmingly defeated in 1940 and again in 1942, they had never given up: "A consistent, persistent and persuasive lobby on behalf of parking meter manufacturers has infested the City Hall ever since the first hamlet decided to work the racket on its motoring citizens and visitors; and the City Council shows signs of being likely to yield to pressure unless counter pressure is applied." As far as the editor was concerned, the lure of the machines was the additional revenue and easier-to-enforce traffic regulations. He argued that meters would solve no parking problem since there would be just as much curb parking with them as without, and that a better strategy was to ban street parking in the congested areas during business hours. "Once the parking meters get their foot in the door, however, they will become increasingly hard to oust, since they will be a vested interest. The best time to deal with a vested interest is before it becomes vested. Once you let the machines in, Los Angeles will never be rid of them — or curb parking either," moaned the editor. He hammered again at the point that a city had no moral right to rent out public thoroughfares, paid for by taxes and owned by the general public, for private use. "Streets are to give access to abutting property; they should not be used for storage. The fact that revenue can be had — legally or illegally — is beside the point; there are many ways revenue can be had that no city should stoop to. The parking meter scheme should be thrown into the ash can."[13]

According to a May 17, 1947, report in *Business Week,* about 300,000 parking meters had been sold to American cities and towns since V-J Day, of which some 200,000 had been put into operation. That was more than all the meters produced and sold before the war. Approximately 1,000 American communities of all sizes were estimated to then be using more than 500,000 penny and nickel meters, both manually and automatically operated. In 1946, about 50 percent more meters were produced than in all the prewar years put together. Annual capacity of the industry was put at 200,000 meters, with a saturation point estimated at around 800,000, although the possibility of using parking meters at off-street locations, such as lots, had the potential to dramatically raise that number. In Miami and a few other cities, meters had been installed on city-owned parking lots to replace attendants; fees varied from five cents for 60 minutes to five cents for 90 minutes, or 25 cents a day. There were still around ten manufacturers with combination penny and nickel machines being most often produced, compared to the prewar single coin unit. Meters were still sold to cities generally on a no-cost, six- to 12-month trial basis, and paid for out of the revenue on a 50/50 basis, or on a 75/25 basis, favoring the maker. Sales were made by state agents on commission, who employed sub-agents. Some 150,000 meters in 323 cities in 1944 were estimated to have taken in $9,383,907 — or $62.30 per meter. Gross meter returns for the year in Buffalo, for instance, were $251,354; in Minneapolis, $146,609; and $86,754 in Oklahoma City.[14]

During 1947, U.S. cities put into operation some 255,000 parking meters with over 1,600 municipalities then having metered parking. In 26 cities alone, in 1947, meter revenues totaled $4.5 million, according to the Municipal Finance Officers' Association. San Diego had the highest 1947 collections, $329,951; followed by Denver at $327,897; Portland, Oregon at $254,504; and Seattle at $233,518. Other cities collecting more than $100,000 from meters in 1947 included Long Beach, Sacramento, San Jose, Stockton, Oakland, Akron, Cincinnati, Cleveland, Columbus, Dallas, Fort Worth, Houston, St. Paul, Newark, Minneapolis, Tampa, Wichita, Lansing, Memphis, Ogden, Salt Lake City, and Rochester. Boston and Chicago were among the largest cities that had authorized parking meters for the first time, in 1948, said the American Municipal Association.[15]

In an election on March 23, 1949, municipal voters in Bakersfield, California, tossed parking meters off the city streets for the second time in ten years. The ordinance authorizing the city's meters was repealed in the election by a vote of 3,187 to 2,832. On the following morning the machines were out of action and City Manager Carl Thornton said the company that had installed the devices would remove them from the downtown streets immediately.[16]

In May 1949, the New York Traffic Commission turned in a report in which it called for a six months' trial of meters in the city. Mayor O'Dwyer said he was "skeptical" but willing to take a chance on a trial. Meters were expected to be in operation in New York City in 1950. At the beginning of 1949, according to the Municipal Year Book, parking meters were in use in more than 1,100 cities and towns with a population of 5,000 or more, better than half of all such communities in America. And those localities included eight of the 14 U.S. cities with populations greater than 500,000 — Boston, Buffalo, Cleveland, Detroit, Philadelphia, San Francisco, Los Angeles, and Washington, D.C. Eight manufacturers were in the field with both manual and automatic models still in use.[17]

Journalist Alice Koch reported in September 1950 that nearly 2,000 towns and cities in the U.S. and Canada used parking meters, with about 650,000 of the devices in operation; seven makers remained in the field. In 1948, the machines brought in $358,000 to Oakland, California. Depositing additional coins to get more parking time was legal in about half of the cities using the machines, but traffic experts said the practice destroyed the keep-them-moving purpose of the devices. Some communities cracked down on motorists who kept feeding the machines. Syracuse, New York, for example, fined a motorist only $1 for overstaying his meter time, but the charge was $10 if the driver was caught putting an additional coin in the meter. More than half of the cities then used automatic models. City officials estimated that an average of $74 was put into each meter annually. In a reasonably busy district, where a nickel an hour was charged, the city treasury could count on $100 a year from each machine — which cost from $50 to $85 each. Several farmers in North Dakota were so angered at the installation of meters in their town's business district that they set up a rival un-metered shopping center a few miles down the highway. Their opposition finally grew into a statewide political issue with the final result being the outlawing of meters in North Dakota. Merchants in Atlantic City, New Jersey, took action to head off a similar shoppers' revolt. They made sure none of their customers was forced to cut his buying time short because time ran out on his meter by sending their clerks into the street with a handful of coins. When shoppers returned to their vehicles they found little cards on the windshield explaining what the department store had done for them. Local police, though, discouraged the practice by explaining that the purpose of the meters was to increase parking turnover.[18]

Ellis Denny of the Oak Park, Illinois, Chamber of Commerce, bizarrely proposed to the village board of that community that parking meters be installed in Oak Park in order to make enough money to buy land for parking lots in order to eliminate parking meters.[19]

Chapter 10

Conclusion

How America dealt with the problem of automobile storage, from the arrival of the machine until the end of World War II, set the stage for how America went on to deal with car parking in the economically booming post-war period and on into a new century. Today's society lives with the now all-too-obvious problems of a society overly dependent on the automobile with a system so structured that it is difficult to alter. America dealt with the automobile parking problem in the period 1910 to 1945 by effectively not dealing with it at all. Rather, it catered to the new machine. The idea in force in American law at the start of the 20th century, that thoroughfares were for the movement of traffic — with certain specific exceptions such as the loading and unloading of goods and passengers — gave way fairly quickly to the idea that took root in the popular mind that parking of vehicles on the street was a right and not a privilege.

Prior to the arrival of the automobile at the start of the 20th century, the parking of vehicles such as wagons, carts, the horse and buggy, and so on, had never been a problem. One reason was that the United States was mostly a rural and sparsely populated nation. The arrival of the automobile coincided with a dramatic increase in America's population and its shift from a rural to an urban nation. Of course, the car also played a role in that shift. From 1900 to 1920 the U. S. population increased by 30 million; there were one-third more people in America in 1920 than there were in 1900. A population split 60/40 in favor of rural over urban in 1900 had become 51/49 urban over rural in 1920. While there were 1,711,000 carriages and wagons made in 1904, cars and trucks were manufactured at a rate of three million annually in the early 1920s.

During most of the first two decades of the 1900s there was very little regulation of cars or drivers, but an increasing set of problems involving the storage of automobiles, traffic flow, and so on, caused regulations to be imposed, beginning during the last few years of that period. Large numbers of automobiles gathered at certain large public affairs, such as July 4th civic picnics, were first noticed and commented on in the media from around 1909 until near the end of World War I. It was during the time of World War I that the first rules with respect to the parking of automobiles were passed by cities. As early as 1916 it was reported that the city in America perhaps most closely associated with, and dominated by, the car — Los Angeles — had major traffic problems in its downtown business district. Gridlock had, even then, arrived. Around the end of World War I, a few cities had prohibited street parking in their downtown business districts (during the daytime) — two of which were Cincinnati and Philadelphia. Cincinnati had gone so far as to provide two large free parking lots at opposite ends of the business districts to compensate for the loss of street space. The city of Cincinnati even provided a shuttle service to the downtown area from the lots for a fare of five cents. Philadelphia's ban was in force from 8:00 A.M. to 6:30 P.M., but after intense lobbying against the measure by various groups such as area merchants, the measure was rescinded. Years later it was reinstated. It was a story repeated in other cities. Los Angeles City Council wrestled with the issue for years imposing bans, removing bans, and altering bans and definitions of just where the business district was located.

Street parking on the downtown business streets needed to be regulated, argued city officials, because such space was always full, at least during the daytime hours on Mondays through Saturdays. One reason for that was that store owners and employees arrived first, of course, each working day and often took street spaces in front of their premises for the entire day. Thus, they denied customers access to those stores — although the owners yelled the loudest when bans were proposed claiming it would interfere with their customers' access to their establishments. Another part of the parking chaos that had a spill-over effect was cruising, in which a car went around and around in order to try and find not just an empty space, but one close to the desired store. That cruising increased the overall traffic congestion. On some narrow streets there were only two lanes in each direction and one had streetcar tracks on it. When one lane allowed parking it meant the moving vehicles had to share the streetcar lane (which, ideally, should have been dedicated to the streetcars). Those mass-transit vehicles arriving at an intersection were slowed to discharge and take on passengers and probably missed a traffic signal cycle, delaying even longer all the cars in that lane. When the traffic was stopped for a signal cycle, several cars might have prevented the streetcar from reaching the safety island for passengers and perhaps the streetcar missed a second signal cycle. It was not unusual for streetcars to be blamed for the resultant traffic mess and for the solution advocated to be the removal of the streetcar tracks.

Another example of the ambivalence on the issue of parking time limits on downtown streets could be seen in the actions of the city of Long Beach, California, which, in the summer of 1923, repealed a one-hour parking limit ordinance that had been in effect for only a few months. Less than six months later, at the end of November 1923, the Long Beach City Council passed an ordinance reinstituting that one-hour limit. Generally, merchants continued to lobby loud and long against any limits on business district street parking — both in specific instances as when such measures were proposed for their cities, and in a more global, philosophical sense. The result was that full bans on downtown street parking were rare; usually what was achieved was limited to bans during the morning and evening rush hours. That was the trade-off. Chicago spent ten years, off and on, in trying to prohibit parking in the downtown area, starting in 1920 and finally implemented such a measure in 1928. Yet surveys on shoppers conducted in the 1920s indicated that only a tiny fraction of shoppers used curb space to park. Mass transit brought in 80 percent of the shoppers and most of the 20 percent who arrived by car parked off-street. Merchant protests, in fear of lost customers, were based on very little in the way of fact; they produced much noise over very little substance. What street parking did do was to produce traffic chaos and gridlock in downtown areas and discouraged shoppers from coming at all, hastening a decentralization process. As early as 1919 and 1920, some observers already argued that the process of relocating businesses outside of the downtown areas was underway. However, they argued that decentralization would flow from a banning of street parking — the reverse of reality.

By 1929, most cities had prohibited parking on their main business streets, at least during the two rush-hour periods. Other laws were passed to deal with the violators of parking time limits to aid both traffic flow and bylaw enforcement. Laws were passed to establish the legality of a traffic officer in giving a ticket to a vacant car — that is, with the operator never having been seen by the officer. Since one car parked overtime on a street in the rush hour blocked the street as effectively as if the street were full of parked vehicles, laws were passed enabling cities to tow away a violator's vehicle and hold it until the extra towing and storage fees were paid. Limits and/or bans on downtown street parking, based on studies, were described as being successful in the sense that, after the ban was imposed, the traffic moved more quickly through the area, as did the mass-transit vehicles. An increase in store patronage was also observed — more people came downtown with parking regulations in effect. Bans and time limits on street parking had their greatest effect in removing the all-day parker from the area. And that meant people did not have to cruise as much as before since parking spots opened up constantly throughout the day. Prior to regulations, so many spots were taken by all-day parkers that cruising was often close to futile. The idea that all street parking of cars, at least in the downtown sections, be abolished completely was raised only occasionally by experts and observers in the traffic field. Such suggestions were hardly ever given serious consideration.

Double parking was vigorously targeted in some areas as it was often a problem and, of course, added hugely to traffic chaos. Angle parking was gradually dropped in most places, in favor of parallel parking. Some cities used a center section of a street for parking, leaving the curb lanes for moving vehicles, with the idea being that it was easier for passing vehicles to see a store's display of goods, which was often blocked by curb parkers. But anything other than parallel-to-the-curb parking tended to increase accident risk due to trying to move a vehicle into moving traffic from an awkward parking position. Thus, parallel parking became almost universal. By 1929, a few cooperative parking ventures involving stores and parking garages were in existence. In Los Angeles, a company that owned 16 garages in the downtown area sold scrip to merchants. That scrip was then given to the merchant's customers in an amount commensurate with their purchases. In turn, those customers used the scrip to pay for all or part of their parking fees at the garages. At the same time a similar plan was in operation in Newark, New Jersey, involving 21 local merchants and 11 garages.

Traffic consultants, other experts, newspaper editors, and so on, had begun to agitate for a solution to the problem of auto parking, and traffic in general, in large numbers starting around 1920. Often, they offered their own solutions. Mostly, they saw the parking of vehicles as the most pressing of the various automobile traffic problems. Studies of the time indicated that the average automobile was driven for about two hours a day, which meant the problem of storing the machine had to be dealt with for the other 22 hours. Those observers also mostly held the idea that moving vehicles always had, or should have, preference over standing autos, yet few advocated the obvious solution of banning street parking completely. Some blamed jaywalking pedestrians as the cause of all the trouble since they gave no consideration to the smooth flow of vehicular traffic. Some wanted more streets; some wanted streets widened, and some wanted expressways. An increase in parking lots and garages was urged as well, although there was no consensus on how that could be achieved. Some believed private enterprise should be left to provide such facilities, but many felt that municipal governments should provide them, at a cost to the motorist or even for free. Failure to solve the parking problem, thought most, would intensify the decentralization efforts underway to a small degree even then. A loss of business establishments to suburban areas and towns would erode a city's tax base and bode ill for the future. Nobody among all the experts looked to an increase in mass transit as the answer. In fact, the gridlock on downtown city streets, due in no small part to street parking, was and would be used as a reason to tear up the tracks (in later years) and degrade many an efficient system. It was understood by all observers that street parking was inadequate to hold all the autos that arrived in the downtown areas, and supplementary facilities had to be available.

A few observers saw a day when there would be no street parking but that day was always safely off in the future. If all accepted the idea that moving traffic had precedence over standing vehicles, almost none challenged the more popular (and more cogent) idea that parking was a right and not a privilege. With no one having any ideas that were likely to work and with nobody willing to entertain the measures that would work, thoughts often turned to fanciful and bizarre ideas to solve the problem. Fueled by a naïve belief in science and technology's ability to solve any problem, and to do so immediately, the skyscraper garage was envisioned. This was an edifice some 20, 30, or 40 stories high and completely mechanically operated to boot. A motorist drove his car to an entrance door at street level, got a check from an attendant and happily departed. After that, machinery moved the car forward into an elevator, up to the appropriate floor, and then mechanically moved it around that floor to the specific stall selected. The vehicle was retrieved the same way. Some office buildings were envisioned to have parking on every floor, all 40 of them, with parking stalls in the center area of each floor and with offices running around the outside edge of each floor. Thus, from the street, the building looked like an ordinary office structure. There was even a portable modular parking garage with pieces stacked together like building blocks to increase the capacity. It could hold from a few cars up to many, and could be set up beside a store or in a field, or in somebody's driveway. The garage of science fiction had arrived, at least on paper. While a few of these things came into being, none succeeded.

Roofs of existing buildings and new ones were sometimes looked to as a possibility to ease the problem. And, of course, basement parking areas became a part of most new commercial buildings of any size. However, they could deal with only a small part of the problem as the basement spots, for example, were never enough for the number of employees and customers who worked in and visited the new buildings. Vacant city land was often pressed into service as a parking lot, but when the land was bought for an office building, for example, the parking problem was increased dramatically. Spaces were lost from the lot and employees and customers in the new building needed more spaces. During the 1920s, several street railways in various cities tried park-and-ride systems but none were very successful. However, a survey of such systems done in the 1920s concluded that none of the systems had been given a fair trial. For example, the Pittsburgh Street Railway Company gave its plan less than a three-week trial before declaring it unsuccessful and scrapping it. While all the experts agreed that downtown street parking could not hold all who wanted to come downtown, most agreed the solution to the parking problem was to retain street parking (at least during some part of the day) and have more parking lots and garages, and more underground parking as part of new buildings.

The Depression of the 1930s and then World War II tended to take some of the pressure off the parking problem, and the automobile problem in general. However, it meant only that the problem did not grow as fast as it did in the 1920s, but it still grew. If all agreed that parking was the biggest problem in connection with the automobile at the start of the 1920s, then all agreed that by the early 1940s it had not been solved.

The one huge technological leap in street parking came in the summer of 1935 when the parking meter was introduced and went into service in Oklahoma City. It probably was instrumental in ensuring that street parking would survive. Meters brought a certain amount of order to the parking chaos since it became much easier, cheaper, more efficient, and more reliable with respect to the enforcement of the time-limited parking then in effect in most cities. Prior to the advent of meters, the old-fashioned method of putting chalk marks on tires was used almost everywhere. It was time-consuming for police officers and not very efficient as autos were not marked as soon as they parked, and so on. Also, some motorists cheated the system by going out to their vehicles and erasing the chalk marks. Meters stopped all that but they did not eliminate cruising. Since there was a timelier turnover of spaces, meters likely reduced cruising however slightly. Since motorists then cruised not just for a spot close to their destination but also for the spot with the most unexpired time, meters increased cruising.

Opposition to meters was vocal but limited mostly to automobile clubs. The wide array of groups that opposed the regulation of street parking did not turn out in full to lobby against meters. For example, whereas most merchants opposed regulations on street parking, more of them favored meters, or were neutral. Opponents argued that meters imposed an unjust tax on motorists who had already paid for the streets. City officials were enthusiastic about meters because they represented a source of steady, reliable income for them in the Depression years of the 1930s, when most cities had to scramble to find money for their budgets. Initially, meters also brought a uniform length to parking spaces and eliminated the previous chaos of drivers parking too close to other autos in order to squeeze in, with the resultant frequent but minor fender-bender accidents. Parking meter usage spread rapidly. Less than 3.5 years after the first ones had been put in use, 85 American cities of all sizes had installed 24,610 of the devices.

With the end of World War II and gas rationing, the parking and traffic problems in American cities increased dramatically. Passenger auto traffic was up 52 percent in 1946 over 1945. Solutions said to be then in the planning stages included the usual ones trotted out in the past — widened streets, one-way streets, express boulevards, rotary traffic circles, more parking meters, and time restrictions. A 1946 estimate held that cruising accounted for 30 percent of the traffic on business streets during shopping hours. A reduction in the number of private cars in the congested areas was the one solution that might have worked — coupled with a simultaneous encouragement of mass transit, park-and-rides, and so on — was never a seriously considered option. If anything, it had less impact than the idea had in the 1920s and 1930s when its impact was negligible.

Parking meters were embraced more than ever as a solution. In the two years after V-J Day, some 300,000 of the machines were sold to American cities and towns with 200,000 of them having been put into operation. About 1,000 U.S. communities were then using them. With a belief then well entrenched that the average shopper refused to walk more than 1,000 feet to his destination, the solution of choice came quickly to be decentralization as shopping malls with their huge, free parking lots sprang up everywhere. The gutting of the downtown business sections of many American cities and the gutting and destruction of many viable, efficient mass-transit systems was then under way. Today, we live with the myriad problems created by a sprawling decentralized society with a slavish devotion to the automobile.

Not only was the option of a reduction in the number of cars not considered in post–World War II America, but the celebration of car culture was even more intense and pervasive in America. A 1950 article optimistically rejoiced in the idea that the only solution to the parking problem was the decentralization of business. The article went on to offer the thought that Los Angeles was the answer to the question of how to live most successfully with the "convenient machine." The groundwork for ideas such as that was laid in the period 1910 to 1945, when society failed to regulate the automobile in any meaningful way and gave up the idea that moving vehicles had preference over stationary ones, replaced with the idea that parking was a right.

Notes

Chapter 1

1. Harold S. Buttenheim. "The problem of the standing vehicle." *The Annals of the American Academy of Political and Social Science* 133 (September 1927): 145.
2. "Wanted — more hitching-posts for cars." *Literary Digest* 80 (February 2, 1924): 57–58.
3. "Venice throng largest ever." *Los Angeles Times*, July 6, 1909, sec. 2, p. 10.
4. Bert C. Smith. "Drag-net out for motor thieves is state-wide." *Los Angeles Times*, June 11, 1914, sec. 7, pp. 1–2.
5. "Bell puts name to traffic code." *Indianapolis Star*, July 16, 1914, p. 14.
6. "July 25th automobile day at the First Church." *Cranbury Press* [New Jersey], July 16, 1915, p. 1.
7. Harold S. Buttenheim, op. cit.
8. "Automobiles may be asked to back cars into curb." *Logansport Daily Tribune* [Indiana], December 3, 1916, p. 1.
9. Harvey E. Westgate. "Swarms of jitneys, 40,000 autos and narrow streets cause of congestion." *Los Angeles Times*, December 3, 1916, sec. 6, p. 1.
10. *Ibid.*
11. "No parking." *The Marion Star* [Ohio], April 19, 1919, p. 6.
12. "Back plans to stop parking." *Los Angeles Times*, November 30, 1919, sec. 2, p. 10.
13. "Will prohibit auto parking." *Los Angeles Times*, December 9, 1919, sec. 2, p. 1.
14. "To end parking in broad area." *Los Angeles Times*, December 19, 1919, sec. 2, p. 2.
15. "Ban on autos hard hit." *Los Angeles Times*, December 23, 1919, sec. 2, p. 1.
16. *Ibid.*, pp. 1, 5.
17. "Auto dealers smite ban." *Los Angeles Times*, December 24, 1919, sec. 2, pp. 1, 5.
18. "The raw no-parking ordinance." *Los Angeles Times*, December 24, 1919, sec. 2, p. 4.
19. *Ibid.*
20. "Others oppose parking plans." *Los Angeles Times*, December 25, 1919, sec. 2, p. 7.
21. "Compromise on parking looms." *Los Angeles Times*, December 26, 1919, sec. 2, p. 6.
22. Howard Moffatt. "Doctor scores auto zone law." *Los Angeles Times*, January 2, 1920, sec. 2, p. 10.
23. George H. Dunlop. "Blames corner tie-ups." *Los Angeles Times*, January 18, 1920, sec. 5, p. 5.
24. "Auto club hits no-parking ban." *Los Angeles Times*, January 23, 1920, sec. 2, p. 1.
25. "The perils of a parkless town." *Los Angeles Times*, February 29, 1920, sec. 2, p. 1.
26. *Ibid.*, pp. 1, 10.
27. "Two hundred in auto net." *Los Angeles Times*, April 13, 1920, sec. 2, p. 1.
28. "Parkers face court today." *Los Angeles Times*, April 14, 1920, sec. 2, p. 1.

29. "Auto ban blow to hospitality." *Los Angeles Times*, April 17, 1920, sec. 2, p. 5.
30. "Parade to point protest." *Los Angeles Times*, April 22, 1920, sec. 2, p. 1.
31. "No-parking law protest." *Los Angeles Times*, April 25, 1920, p. 19.
32. "Relief pledged from auto ban." *Los Angeles Times*, April 24, 1920, sec. 2, p. 1.
33. "Motor cars are essential." *Los Angeles Times*, April 25, 1920, sec. 6, pp. 1, 6.
34. G. Gordon Whitnall. "No parking of autos." *American City* 22 (May 1920): 484.
35. *Ibid.*
36. "Solid vote to lift auto ban." *Los Angeles Times*, April 27, 1920, sec. 2, pp. 1, 5.
37. "City's parking ban is lifted." *Los Angeles Times*, April 30, 1920, sec. 2, p. 10.
38. *Ibid.*
39. "Parking rules eased." *Los Angeles Times*, May 21, 1921, sec. 2, p. 11.
40. "Drivers resignedly accept parking law." *Los Angeles Times*, August 7, 1921, sec. 7, p. 10.
41. "Repeals parking law." *Los Angeles Times*, June 6, 1923, p. 10.
42. "Mistake nullifies auto parking law." *Los Angeles Times*, November 30, 1923, sec. 2, p. 2.
43. "Will rush ordinance on parking." *Los Angeles Times*, November 22, 1923, sec. 2, p. 1.
44. "New parking law in force." *Los Angeles Times*, November 27, 1923, sec. 2, p. 1.
45. "Retailers shown way out of troubles." *Ogden Standard Examiner* [Utah], July 20, 1923.
46. "Ogden limits auto parking." *Ogden Standard Examiner* [Utah], March 12, 1924.
47. "Roberts lectures on parking rules." *Ogden Standard Examiner* [Utah], May 16, 1924.
48. "Broadway closed to cruising cabs." *New York Times*, June 6, 1924, p. 23.
49. "Council ready on auto puzzle." *Los Angeles Times*, September 2, 1924, p. A20.
50. "Plan proposes auto seizures." *Los Angeles Times*, November 10, 1924, p. A5.
51. "Ban on parking proposed." *Los Angeles Times*, July 24, 1925, p. A1.
52. "Ordinance No. 61." *Garfield County News* [Utah], August 14, 1925.
53. George Britt. "Only the popular traffic laws get public support." *Ogden Standard Examiner* [Utah], April 11, 1926.
54. "One hour for auto parking meets favor." *Ogden Standard Examiner* [Utah], December 16, 1926.
55. "No parking of automobiles." *Ogden Standard Examiner* [Utah], January 26, 1927.
56. "Ordinance banning parking in Philadelphia strikes opposition." *Los Angeles Times*, March 20, 1927, pp. G1-G2.
57. "Remedies in traffic ills cited." *Los Angeles Times*, April 15, 1927, p. 3.
58. "Price City council passes ordinance regulating limit of parking on city streets." *News Advocate* [Utah], June 2, 1928.
59. "New parking sought in midtown." *New York Times*, May 1, 1927, p. E1.
60. "Expert advises against auto-parking ban." *Los Angeles Times*, July 22, 1928, pp. G1, G3.
61. Robert H. Nau. "No parking—a year and more of it." *American City* 40 (March 1929): 85.
62. *Ibid.*, pp. 85–86.
63. *Ibid.*, pp. 86–87.
64. *Ibid.*, p. 88.
65. "Putting parking on a somewhat higher level." *Literary Digest* 101 (May 18, 1929): 76.
66. Charles D. Gaither. "Three months' experience with no parking on two streets." *American City* 41 (July 1929): 143–144.
67. "They shall not park!" *American City* 42 (May 1930): 120.
68. Walter R. Lindersmith. "Less parking—more purchasing in Los Angeles." *American City* 43 (December 1943): 120.
69. *Ibid.*, pp. 120–121.
70. Fletcher Pratt. "No parking." *American Mercury* 39 (October 1936): 155–156.
71. *Ibid.*, pp. 157–158.
72. *Ibid.*, pp. 159–160.
73. *Ibid.*, p. 160.

Chapter 2

1. "Philadelphia's new auto parking rules." *New York Times*, July 30, 1916, sec. 2, p. 2.
2. "Police court business." *Eureka Reporter* [Utah], July 2, 1920.
3. "Warns auto row of raids today on bad parking." *Los Angeles Times*, July 10, 1920, sec. 2, p. 2.
4. "Don't park in traffic lanes." *Los Angeles Times*, September 4, 1921, sec. 6, p. 1.
5. "Parking plan tried." *Los Angeles Times*, April 9, 1923, p. 7.
6. "Proved manhood by attack on octogenarian." *Davis County Clipper* [Utah], August 17, 1923.
7. "Locks to foil wily motorists." *Los Angeles Times*, January 20, 1924, p. 2.
8. "Street parking being removed." *Ogden Standard Examiner* [Utah], April 13, 1924.
9. "Ask for teeth in parking law." *Los Angeles Times*, July 12, 1924, pp. A1, A3.
10. "Banishing the all-day parker." *Literary Digest* 82 (September 20, 1924): 76, 79.
11. "McAdoo calls jam in court inhuman." *New York Times*, October 11, 1924, p. 26.
12. "Business men ask park rule changes." *New York Times*, November 20, 1924, p. 39.
13. "Auto parking rule changed to 1 hour." *New York Times*, December 9, 1924, p. 17.
14. "Eliminate all parking waste." *Los Angeles Times*, April 26, 1925, p. H6.
15. "Loading zones hog space." *Los Angeles Times*, August 7, 1925, p. A8.
16. "Four motorists' cases disposed of." *Ogden Standard Examiner* [Utah], September 21, 1927.
17. "Auto parking ban to start April 8." *New York Times*, April 2, 1929, p. 11.
18. "Backs restrictions on auto parking." *New York Times*, April 10, 1929, p. 24.
19. "Vox populi rules city." *Los Angeles Times*, May 4, 1929, p. A8.
20. "New parking plan announced." *Los Angeles Times*, July 7, 1929, p. D3.
21. "Rigid parking order issued." *Ogden Standard Examiner* [Utah], May 6, 1929.
22. "Array of auto cases handled." *Ogden Standard Examiner* [Utah], June 14, 1929.
23. "Time limits on parking in New York State cities." *American City* 41 (October 1929): 118.
24. Lewis Amis. "Educating Newark shoppers to parking garages." *American City* 42 (January 1930): 155–156.
25. "Parking restrictions and reactions in several large cities." *American City* 42 (March 1930): 122.
26. *Ibid.*
27. *Ibid.*, pp. 122–123.
28. C. W. Trammell. "Impounding of illegally parked automobiles reduces traffic problem." *American City* 43 (September 1930): 151.
29. "123,000 cars found parked all night." *New York Times*, November 20, 1931, p. 25.
30. "59 jailed for illegal parking." *New York Times*, November 26, 1932, p. 4.
31. "Ordinance on parking revamped." *Los Angeles Times*, May 23, 1934, p. A1.
32. "That troublesome matter — parking." *American City* 50 (May 1935): 101.
33. *Ibid.*
34. "Habitual parker is target of drive." *New York Times*, November 16, 1935, p. 17.

Chapter 3

1. "Automobile parking." *Box Elder News* [Utah], July 20, 1920.
2. "The problem of the city auto." *Literary Digest* 66 (September 4, 1920): 30–31.
3. "New wide streets to solve traffic problem." *Los Angeles Times*, August 31, 1922, sec. 2, p. 1.
4. *Ibid.*, pp. 1, 3.
5. Hugh E. Young. "Day and night storage and parking of motor vehicles." *American City* 29 (July, 1923): 44.
6. *Ibid.*, pp. 44–46.
7. John Ihlder. "The parking problem." *Los Angeles Times*, June 24, 1923, sec. 6, pp. 1, 3.
8. *Ibid.*, p. 3.

9. *Ibid.*, p. 14.
10. "Overhead street cars as parking solutions." *Ogden Standard Examiner* [Utah], July 22, 1923.
11. "Parking held not a right but a privilege." *Ogden Standard Examiner* [Utah], July 15, 1923.
12. E. E. East. "Parking needs in every city." *Ogden Standard Examiner* [Utah], December 2, 1923.
13. "Parking space at premium in capital." *Garfield County News* [Utah], February 29, 1924.
14. "Vast traffic problem seen." *Ogden Standard Examiner* [Utah], January 13, 1924.
15. "Volcano expert sees menace in streets jammed with autos." *Ogden Standard Examiner* [Utah], January 24, 1924.
16. Jefferson G. Bell. "Police trying to solve parking car problem." *New York Times*, January 6, 1924, p. A6.
17. *Ibid.*
18. *Ibid.*
19. "Solved! ... Collapsible auto." *Los Angeles Times*, January 21, 1924, p. A1.
20. "Wanted — more hitching-posts for cars." *Literary Digest* 80 (February 2, 1924): 58–59.
21. *Ibid.*, pp. 59–60.
22. Miller McClintock. "Parking — when, where and why?" *American City* 30 (April 1924): 360.
23. *Ibid.*, pp. 360–361.
24. *Ibid.*, p. 361.
25. "The universal quest." *Los Angeles Times*, June 15, 1924, p. 22.
26. "Open campaign to stop all parking in streets." *Ogden Standard Examiner* [Utah], February 22, 1925.
27. "Auto parking need related." *Los Angeles Times*, October 18, 1925, p. B5.
28. *Ibid.*, pp. B5, B8.
29. "Parking space growth factor." *Los Angeles Times*, March 7, 1926, p. G20.
30. H. W. Slauson. "And we call ourselves efficient." *Scientific American* 134 (June 1926): 368–369.
31. "Traffic congestion, parking facilities, and retail business." *American City* 34 (June 1926): 664–666.
32. "Traffic congestion, parking facilities, and retail business — II." *American City* 35 (July 1926): 62–63.
33. *Ibid.*, pp. 64–65.
34. "New type of suburban shopping area proposed." *American City* 35 (August 1926): 214.
35. *Ibid.*, p. 216.
36. "Auto-parking survey made." *Los Angeles Times*, August 1, 1926, pp. B1–B2.
37. "Lots of parking space if you look closely." *Los Angeles Times*, August 8, 1926, p. G1.
38. "To park or not to park." *American City* 35 (October 1926): 461–462.
39. *Ibid.*, pp. 462–463.
40. "Autoists ignore 30-minute parking law." *New York Times*, October 1, 1926, p. 4.
41. "Says parking doomed to go." *Ogden Standard Examiner* [Utah], May 2, 1926.
42. "Solving the traffic problem." *Box Elder News* [Utah], September 21, 1926.
43. Miller McClintock. "Must provide car storage places to solve parking and business problems." *Ogden Standard Examiner* [Utah], October 3, 1926.
44. "Main Street parking is hazardous and uninviting." *Garfield County News* [Utah], December 10, 1926.
45. "Auto storage big need now." *Ogden Standard Examiner* [Utah], December 19, 1926.
46. "Parking hogs assailed." *Los Angeles Times*, July 31, 1927, p. B12.
47. "Overtime parking." *Los Angeles Times*, August 4, 1927, p. A4.
48. Austin F. Macdonald. "Parking facilities outside the traffic zone." *The Annals of the American Academy of Political and Social Science* 133 (September 1927): 78–79.
49. *Ibid.*, p. 79.

50. *Ibid.*, p. 80.
51. *Ibid.*, pp. 80–81.
52. Harold S. Buttenheim. "The problem of the standing vehicle." *The Annals of the American Academy of Political and Social Science* 133 (September 1927): 153.
53. *Ibid.*, p. 155.
54. "No street parking." *Ogden Standard Examiner* [Utah], November 6, 1927.
55. "Double-deck boulevards get place in new traffic plans of big cities." *Ogden Standard Examiner* [Utah], July 31, 1927.
56. "How many shoppers park autos in street?" *American City* 38 (February 1928): 163
57. "Auto parking balks experts." *Los Angeles Times*, May 12, 1928, p. A6.
58. John A. Miller Jr. "The chariots that rage in the streets." *American City* 39 (July 1928): 111.
59. *Ibid.*, pp. 112–113.
60. *Ibid.*, pp. 113–114.
61. "Parking held vital to Fifth Av. Trade." *New York Times*, December 16, 1928, p. N1.
62. *Ibid.*, pp. N1–N2.
63. "A change needed." *Columbia Missourian* [Missouri], November 25, 1929, p. 4.
64. R. T. Dorsey. "The curb-parked car and its purchasing power." *American City* 47 (August 1932): 74.
65. *Ibid.*
66. John A. Miller. "They're all afraid to mention it." *Review of Reviews* 94 (August 1936): 54–55.
67. *Ibid.*, pp. 55–56.
68. *Ibid.*, p. 56.
69. *Ibid.*
70. William Chevalier. "What price parking?" *American City* 51 (November 1936): 75.
71. E. L. Yordan. "City parker studied." *New York Times*, November 29, 1936, sec. 13, p. 1.
72. T. T. McCrosky. "Only 216 automobiles cause Yonkers' jam." *American City* 53 (January 1938): 97.
73. "Cities try out traffic cures." *New York Times*, January 2, 1938, sec. 11, p. 1.
74. *Ibid.*, pp. 1, 5.
75. Arthur Pound. "No parking." *Atlantic Monthly* 161 (March 1938): 387–388.
76. *Ibid.*, p. 388.
77. "Where to leave the car." *The New Republic* 95 (June 1, 1938): 87.
78. "Devouring the parking problem." *American City* 54 (December 1939): 65.
79. "Traffic survey shows need for regulation." *Murray Eagle* [Utah], December 14, 1940.

Chapter 4

1. "Storage charges as the mainstay of a garage." *Literary Digest* 46 (April 12, 1913): 853–854.
2. *Ibid.*, pp. 854–855.
3. "The skyscraper garage." *Scientific American* 121 (September 13, 1919): 247, 259.
4. Robert G. Skerrett. "Every automobile its own elevator." *Scientific American* 124 (January 22, 1921): 65+.
5. "No more parking in busy cities?" *Ogden Standard Examiner* [Utah], February 14, 1925.
6. "New parking sought in midtown." *New York Times*, May 1, 1927, p. E1.
7. "City meeting garage needs." *Los Angeles Times*, July 10, 1927, p. E8.
8. Hawley S. Simpson. "Downtown storage garages." *The Annals of the American Academy of Political and Social Science* 133 (September 1927): 87–88.
9. *Ibid.*, pp. 88–89.
10. "Roof parking forecast." *Los Angeles Times*, April 29, 1928, p. G1.
11. Lee J. Eastman. "The parking garage merits encouragement as an important factor in traffic relief." *American City* 40 (January 1929): 156–157.

12. George Horace Lorimer. "Where to park." *Saturday Evening Post* 201 (February 16, 1929): 24.
13. *Ibid.*
14. "Putting parking on a somewhat higher level." *Literary Digest* 101 (May 18, 1929): 72.
15. *Ibid.*
16. *Ibid.*, pp. 74, 76.
17. "High garages required." *Los Angeles Times*, June 23 1929, p. E8.
18. "Car space is urged in office buildings." *New York Times*, October 6, 1929, p. W18.
19. "Automobile parking machine developed." *American City* 41 (November 1929): 100.
20. *Ibid.*
21. "A Ferris wheel car parking machine." *Scientific American* 142 (January 1930): 64.
22. "Parking autos in a pile." *Literary Digest* 109 (May 16, 1931): 19.
23. "One lock with 24 different keys." *Literary Digest* 112 (March 26, 1932): 37.
24. "Push a button; park your car." *Los Angeles Times*, May 1, 1932, p. E2.
25. "Plans steel tower over mile high." *Vernal Express* [Utah], October 13, 1932.
26. E. L. Yordan. "City parker studied." *New York Times*, November 29, 1936, sec. 5, p. 5.
27. C. T. MacGavin. "Parking stems trade ebb." *New York Times*, October 27, 1940, sec. 10, p. 3.
28. "Parking solution." *Business Week*, February 8, 1941, p. 22.

Chapter 5

1. "Public parking place is unpopular." *The Daily Courier* [Connellsville, Pennsylvania], May 16, 1916, p. 1.
2. "Parking facilities for industrial employees." *American City* 31 (September 1924): 239.
3. "Chicago to open large parking area." *Ogden Standard Examiner* [Utah], May 1, 1927.
4. "Capital beauty plans prove aid to parking." *Murray Eagle* [Utah], June 23, 1927.
5. "Auto parking quiz planned." *Los Angeles Times*, November 28, 1929, p. A22.
6. "Auto park law change requested." *Los Angeles Times*, December 5, 1929, p. A3.
7. "Parking lot owner held not liable." *Los Angeles Times*, February 10, 1933, p. A5.
8. "That parking problem." *American City* 51 (June 1936): 7.
9. "Parking lot law sought." *Los Angeles Times*, July 27, 1936, p. A2.
10. "Parking lot law scored." *Los Angeles Times*, August 6, 1936, p. A5.
11. "Parking lots curb planned." *Los Angeles Times*, November 18, 1936, p. A2.
12. "Los Angeles parking lots now exceed 1250 in number." *Los Angeles Times*, December 12, 1937, p. E1.
13. E. L. Yordan. "The lowly parking lot thrives." *New York Times*, March 14, 1937, sec. 12, p. 1.
14. *Ibid.*
15. *Ibid.*
16. "Parking lots: a new city activity." *American City* 53 (December 1938): 59.
17. "Working at the parking problem." *American City* 54 (February 1939): 62–63.
18. "A.B.C. of the parking problem." *American City* 54 (July 1939): 89.
19. "Merchants to build free parking lots." *Murray Eagle* [Utah], April 3, 1941, pp. 1, 8.
20. "Free parking lots open for public use." *Murray Eagle* [Utah], July 24, 1941.

Chapter 6

1. "Parking floors for autos now suggested." *Los Angeles Times*, August 2, 1914, sec. 7, p. 10.
2. "Seaboard Bank provides auto parking services." *Los Angeles Times*, January 5, 1926, p. 4.
3. "Janss offers novel service." *Los Angeles Times*, May 30, 1926, p. E9.

4. "Autos parked in skyscraper on twenty-two floors." *Popular Mechanics* 76 (September 1926): 438–439.
5. "Roof parking forecast." *Los Angeles Times*, April 29, 1928, pp. G1-G2.
6. Leon R. Brown. "Suburban parking-stations." *American City* 40 (February 1929): 81.
7. *Ibid.*, pp. 81–82.
8. "Car space is urged in office buildings." *New York Times*, October 6, 1929, p. W18.
9. H. M. Gould. "Staggered parking in Detroit." *American City* 42 (January 1930): 155.
10. Al Parmenter. "Auto parking to be barred in downtown area." *Los Angeles Times*, November 30, 1930, pp. F1-F2.
11. "Underground garage to end parking problem." *Popular Mechanics* 55 (February 1931): 180.
12. "Roof parking to relieve street overcrowding." *American City* 52 (January 1937): 44.
13. "Park and shop." *American City* 52 (October 1937): 71–72.
14. "Auto parking area on roof." *Los Angeles Times*, October 19, 1939, p. B1.
15. "Park-N-Shop plan." *Business Week*, December 16, 1939, pp. 46–47.
16. "Park-N-Shop in '41." *Business Week*, June 21, 1941, pp. 41–43.
17. "Study made of parking." *Los Angeles Times*, June 16, 1940, p. E1.
18. C. T. MacGavin. "Parking stems trade ebb." *New York Times*, October 27, 1940, sec. 10, p. 3.

Chapter 7

1. "Parking meters in Oklahoma City." *American City* 50 (August 1935): 61.
2. *Ibid.*
3. "Park-O-Meters." *Business Week*, October 5, 1935, p. 31.
4. O. M. Mosier. "Our experience with parking meters." *American City* 51 (January 1936): 77.
5. *Ibid.*
6. *Ibid.*
7. C. G. Beckenbach. "Dallas installs 1,000 parking meters." *American City* 51 (January 1936): 95.
8. *Ibid.*, pp. 95, 97.
9. "Freedom of the streets." *Los Angeles Times*, May 12, 1936, p. A4.
10. "America's new gadget." *The New Republic* 87 (May 20, 1936): 34.
11. "Parking meters gain." *Business Week*, June 27, 1936, p. 16.
12. "Canadian cities ban parking meter plan." *Murray Eagle* [Utah], September 24, 1936.
13. "Park-O-Meters may decrease S. L. business." *Murray Eagle* [Utah], August 13, 1936.
14. A. F. Thomasson. "Parking meters in St. Petersburg, Fla." *American City* 51 (July 1936): 7.
15. "A promising solution of the parking problem." *American City* 51 (August 1936): 59–60.
16. *Ibid.*, p. 60.
17. "Nickel-in-meter regulates parking." *Literary Digest* 122 (August 22, 1936): 35.
18. *Ibid.*
19. *Ibid.*
20. *Ibid.*, p. 36.
21. "Parking meter previewed." *Los Angeles Times*, September 26, 1936, p. 8.
22. "Auto clubbers battle tax." *Los Angeles Times*, November 22, 1936, p. 2.
23. "Long Beach cold first day to parking meters." *Los Angeles Times*, November 29, 1936, p. 12.
24. "A.A.A. assails parking meters." *Davis County Clipper* [Utah], January 22, 1937.
25. "Parking meters to stay." *Times Independent* [Utah], January 7, 1937.
26. "Auto parking meters urged." *Los Angeles Times*, February 15, 1937, p. A2.
27. "Clash at Albany on parking meters." *New York Times*, February 25, 1937, p. 2.
28. "Parking meters here urged by merchants." *New York Times*, March 3, 1937, p. 14.
29. "Parking meters now in service." *Los Angeles Times*, March 13, 1937, p. 6.

30. "An all-weather parking meter." *American City* 52 (July 1937): 117.
31. "Parking meters are two years old." *American City* 52 (July 1937): 7.
32. *Ibid.*
33. "Speaking of parking meters." *Business Week*, August 7, 1937, p. 27.
34. Leon R. Brown. "Effective control of parking meters." *American City* 52 (August 1937): 53–54.
35. *Ibid.*
36. "Meter matters." *Time* 30 (September 6, 1937): 44.

Chapter 8

1. C. G. Beckenbach. "Eighteen months of intelligent parking-meter operation." *American City* 52 (September 1937): 60.
2. *Ibid.*, pp. 60–61.
3. "Parking meters." *Scientific American* 157 (November 1937): 288, 290.
4. Lewis R. Greene. "Westerly comments on parking meters." *American City* 52 (November 1937): 107.
5. A. E. Dowell. "Metered parking safe and efficient." *American City* 53 (January 1938): 73.
6. *Ibid.*
7. Paul S. Robinette. "Eliminating business-district congestion in Toledo." *American City* 53 (March 1938): 79.
8. *Ibid.*
9. *Ibid.*, p. 81.
10. *Ibid.*, p. 83.
11. *Ibid.*
12. "Parking meters an unqualified success in 18 cities." *American City* 53 (May 1938): 7.
13. Benjamin F. Turner. "Passaic likes parking meters." *American City* 53 (May 1938): 52.
14. *Ibid.*, pp. 52–53.
15. *Ibid.*, pp. 53–54.
16. L. W. Tazewell. "Results of Norfolk's parking meters." *American City* 53 (July 1938): 47.
17. *Ibid.*, pp. 47–48.
18. "Metropolitan parking meters." *San Juan Record* [Utah], November 24, 1938.
19. "85 cities operate parking meters." *American City* 53 (November 1938): 7.
20. "Parking meters." *Fortune* 18 (November 1938): 12.
21. *Ibid.*
22. "Parking meters: best solution yet found." *American City* 53 (December 1938): 73.
23. Merrill Folsom. "External use of meters." *New York Times*, December 11, 1938, sec. 11, p. 16.
24. "The editor's column." *Murray Eagle* [Utah], March 30, 1939.
25. "Free parking in Murray." *Murray Eagle* [Utah], April 13, 1939.
26. "The editor's point of view." *Murray Eagle* [Utah], May 9, 1940.
27. "Working at the parking problem." *American City* 54 (February 1939): 62.
28. "Board files plan for parking meters." *Los Angeles Times*, October 4, 1939, p, A1.
29. Donald M. McNeil. "Motorists overwhelmingly favor Pittsburgh's parking meters." *American City* 54 (December 1939): 63.
30. "Motorist smashes parking meters." *Los Angeles Times*, March 14, 1940, p. 22.
31. "Parking meters defense made." *Los Angeles Times*, April 9, 1940, p. 11.
32. "Parking meters." *Los Angeles Times*, April 17, 1940, p. A4.
33. "Police Commission weights parking meter protests." *Los Angeles Times*, April 24, 1940, p. A1.
34. "Added congestion predicted if city tries parking meters." *Los Angeles Times*, May 5, 1940, p. F6.
35. "Council's parking meter project scored by auto club." *Los Angeles Times*, May 15, 1940, p. B2.

36. "Foes of meters urged to protest." *Los Angeles Times*, May 26, 1940, p. F4.
37. "Parking meter foes increase." *Los Angeles Times*, June 9, 1940, p. A3.
38. "Civic-minded citizens rise against parking meter plan." *Los Angeles Times*, August 23, 1940, p. A2.
39. "Parking meters declared violation of people's rights." *Los Angeles Times*, August 27, 1940, p. A10.
40. "Council kills meter plan." *Los Angeles Times*, August 30, 1940, p. A1.
41. "Inglewood rejects parking meters." *Los Angeles Times*, September 5, 1940, p. A10.
42. "Parking meters sabotaged." *Wall Street Journal*, April 24, 1941, p. 3.
43. "Council suffers recurrence of parking meteritis disease." *Los Angeles Times*, March 6, 1942, p. A1.
44. "Parking meter plan condemned." *Los Angeles Times*, September 3, 1942, p. 11.
45. "Meter plan on parking hit." *Los Angeles Times*, September 4, 1942, p. A2.
46. "Injunction sought against proposed parking meter plan." *Los Angeles Times*, September 18, 1942, p. A1.
47. "We want no parking meters in Los Angeles." *Los Angeles Times*, October 12, 1942, p. A4.
48. "Parking toll fight shelved." *Los Angeles Times*, November 11, 1942, p. A2,
49. "Parking meters gross $79,796." *Los Angeles Times*, December 20, 1944, p. A2.
50. "Curbstone future." *Business Week*, April 21, 1945, pp. 41–42, 44.
51. *Ibid.*, p. 44.
52. *Ibid.*, pp. 46–47.

Chapter 9

1. "Steadily growing traffic tangle's seriousness disclosed by survey." *Los Angeles Times*, August 29, 1945, p. A1.
2. "Merchants ask mass meeting on parking difficulty." *Murray Eagle* [Utah], May 24, 1945.
3. "Off-street parking drive." *Business Week*, April 6, 1946, p. 21.
4. *Ibid.*
5. *Ibid.*, pp. 21–22.
6. "Cities: no parking." *Newsweek* 28 (October 28, 1946): 28.
7. *Ibid.*, p. 29.
8. Sam Shulsky. "America's traffic headaches." *American Mercury* 66 (February 1948): 151–153.
9. *Ibid.*, p. 154
10. *Ibid.*, pp. 155–156.
11. *Ibid.*, pp. 156–157.
12. J. Robert Harris. "Los Angeles: the city that automobiles rebuilt." *The Rotarian* 76 (February 1950): 18–19.
13. "Let's not rent out the streets." *Los Angeles Times*, August 16, 1946, p. A4.
14. "Meter makers look for boom." *Business Week*, May 17, 1947, pp. 28–29.
15. "Parking meters put millions in cities' coffers." *Los Angeles Times*, May 30, 1948, p. 9.
16. "Parking meters voted out for second time." *Los Angeles Times*, March 24, 1949, p. 24.
17. J. Anthony Lewis. "Taxation on time." *New York Times* Magazine, November 6, 1949, p. 48.
18. Alice Koch. "Curbstone gold mine." *The Rotarian* 77 (September 1959): 15–16.
19. "Sounds complicated." *Morgan County News* [Utah], February 14, 1947.

Bibliography

"A.A.A. assails parking meters." *Davis County Clipper* [Utah], January 22, 1937.
"A.B.C. of the parking problem." *American City* 54 (July 1939): 89.
"Added congestion predicted if city tries parking meters." *Los Angeles Times*, May 5, 1940, p. F6.
"America's new gadget." *The New Republic* 87 (May 20, 1936): 34.
Amis, Lewis. "Educating Newark shoppers to parking garages." *American City* 42 (January, 1930): 155–156.
"An all-weather parking meter." *American City* 52 (July 1937): 117.
"Array of auto cases handled." *Ogden Standard Examiner* [Utah], June 14, 1929.
"Ask for teeth in parking law." *Los Angeles Times*, July 12, 1924, pp. A1, A3.
"Auto ban blow to hospitality." *Los Angeles Times*, April 17, 1920, sec. 2, p. 5.
"Auto club hits no-parking ban." *Los Angeles Times*, January 23, 1920, sec. 2, p. 1.
"Auto clubbers battle tax." *Los Angeles Times*, November 22, 1936, p. 2.
"Auto dealers smite ban." *Los Angeles Times*, December 24, 1919, sec. 2, pp. 1, 5.
"Auto park law change requested." *Los Angeles Times*, December 5, 1929, p. A3.
"Auto parking area on roof." *Los Angeles Times*, October 19, 1939, p. B1.
"Auto parking balks experts." *Los Angeles Times*, May 12, 1928, p. A6.
"Auto parking ban to start April 8." *New York Times*, April 2, 1929, p. 11.
"Auto parking meters urged." *Los Angeles Times*, February 15, 1937, p. A2.
"Auto parking need related." *Los Angeles Times*, October 18, 1925, pp. B5, B8.
"Auto parking quiz planned." *Los Angeles Times*, November 28, 1929, p. A22.
"Auto parking rule changed to 1 hour." *New York Times*, December 9, 1924, p. 17.
"Auto-parking survey made." *Los Angeles Times*, August 1, 1926, pp. B1-B2.
"Auto storage big need now." *Ogden Standard Examiner* [Utah], December 19, 1926.
"Autoists ignore 30-minute parking law." *New York Times*, October 1, 1926, p. 4.
"Automobile parking." *Box Elder News* [Utah], July 20, 1920.
"Automobile parking machine developed." *American City* 41 (November 1929): 100.
"Automobiles may be asked to back cars into curb." *Logansport Daily Tribune* [Indiana], December 3, 1916, p. 1.
"Autos parked in skyscraper on twenty-two floors." *Popular Mechanics* 76 (September 1926): 438–439.
"Ban of autos hard hit." *Los Angeles Times*, December 23, 1919, sec. 2, pp. 1, 5.
"Ban on parking proposed." *Los Angeles Times*, July 24, 1925, pp. A1-A2.
"Banishing the all-day parker." *Literary Digest* 82 (September 20, 1924): 76, 78, 79.

Beckenbach, C. G. "Dallas installs 1,000 parking meters." *American City* 51 (January 1936): 95, 97.
Beckenbach, C. G. "Eighteen months of intelligent parking-meter operation." *American City* 52 (September 1937): 60–61.
Bell, Jefferson G. "Police trying to solve parking car problem." *New York Times*, January 6, 1924, p. A6.
"Bell puts name to traffic code." *Indianapolis Star*, July 16, 1914, p. 14.
"Board files plan for parking meters." *Los Angeles Times*, October 4, 1939, p. A1.
Britt, George. "Only the popular traffic laws get public support." *Ogden Standard Examiner* [Utah], April 11, 1926.
"Broadway closed to cruising cabs." *New York Times*, June 6, 1924, p. 23.
Brown, Leon R. "Effective control of parking meters." *American City* 52 (August 1937): 53–54.
Brown, Leon R. "Suburban parking stations." *American City* 40 (February 1929): 81–82.
"Buck plans to stop parking." *Los Angeles Times*, November 30, 1919, sec. 2, p. 10.
"Business men ask park rule changes." *New York Times*, November 20, 1924, p. 39.
Buttenheim, Harold S. "The problem of the standing vehicle." *The Annals of the American Academy of Political and Social Science* 133 (September 1927): 144–155.
"Canadian cities ban parking meter plan." *Murray Eagle* [Utah], September 24, 1936.
"Capital beauty plans prove aid to parking." *Murray Eagle* [Utah], June 23, 1927.
"Car space is urged in office buildings." *New York Times*, October 6, 1929, p. W18.
"A change needed." *Columbia Missourian* [Missouri], November 25, 1929, p. 4.
Chevalier, Willard. "What price parking?" *American City* 51 (November 1936): 75.
"Chicago to open large parking area." *Ogden Standard Examiner* [Utah], May 1, 1927.
"Cities: no parking." *Newsweek* 28 (October 28, 1946): 28–29.
"Cities try out traffic cures." *New York Times*, January 2, 1938, sec. 11, pp. 1, 5.
"City meeting garage needs." *Los Angeles Times*, July 10, 1927, p. E8.
"City's parking ban is lifted." *Los Angeles Times*, April 30, 1920, sec. 2, p. 10.
"Civic-minded citizens rise against parking meter plans." *Los Angeles Times*, August 23, 1940, p. A2.
"Clash at Albany on parking meters." *New York Times*, February 25, 1937, p. 2.
"Compromise on parking looms." *Los Angeles Times*, December 26, 1919, sec. 2, p. 6.
"Council kills meter plan." *Los Angeles Times*, August 30, 1940, p. A1.
"Council ready on auto puzzle." *Los Angeles Times*, September 2, 1924, p. A20.
"Council suffers recurrence of parking meteritis disease." *Los Angeles Times*, May 6, 1942, p. A1.
"Council's parking meter project scored by auto club." *Los Angeles Times*, May 15, 1940, p. B2.
"Curbstone future." *Business Week*, April 21, 1945, pp. 41–42+.
"Devouring the parking problem." *American City* 54 (December 1939): 65.
"Don't park in traffic lanes." *Los Angeles Times*, September 4, 1921, sec. 6, p. 1.
Dorsey, R. T. "The curb-parked car and its purchasing power." *American City* 47 (August 1932): 74.
"Double-deck boulevards get place in new traffic plans of big cities." *Ogden Standard Examiner* [Utah], July 31, 1927.
Dowell, A. E. "Metered parking safe and efficient." *American City* 53 (January 1938): 73.
"Drivers resignedly accept parking law." *Los Angeles Times*, August 7, 1921, sec. 7, p. 10.
Dunlop, George H. "Blames corner tie-up." *Los Angeles Times*, January 18, 1920, sec. 5, p. 5.

East, E. E. "Parking needs in every city." *Ogden Standard Examiner* [Utah], December 2, 1923.

Eastman, Lee J. "The parking garage merits encouragement as an important factor in traffic relief." *American City* 40 (January 1929): 156–157.

"The editor's column." *Murray Eagle* [Utah], March 30, 1939.

"The editor's point of view." *Murray Eagle* [Utah], May 9, 1940.

"85 cities operate parking meters." *American City* 53 (November 1938): 7.

"Eliminate all parking waste." *Los Angeles Times*, April 26, 1925, p. H6.

"Expert advises against auto-parking ban." *Los Angeles Times*, July 22, 1928, pp. G1, G3.

"A Ferris wheel car parking machine." *Scientific American* 142 (January 1930): 64.

"59 jailed for illegal parking." *New York Times*, November 26, 1932, p. 4.

"Foes of meters urged to protest." *Los Angeles Times*, May 26, 1940, p. F4.

Folsom, Merrill. "External use of meters." *New York Times*, December 11, 1938, sec. 11, p. 16.

"Four motorists' cases disposed of." *Ogden Standard Examiner* [Utah], September 21, 1927.

"Free parking in Murray." *Murray Eagle* [Utah], April 13, 1939.

"Free parking lots open for public use." *Murray Eagle* [Utah], July 24, 1941.

"Freedom of the streets." *Los Angeles Times*, May 12, 1936, p. A4.

Gaither, Charles D. "Three months' experience with no parking on two streets." *American City* 41 (July, 1929): 143–144.

Gould, H. M. "Staggered parking in Detroit." *American City* 42 (January 1930): 155.

Greene, Lewis R. "Westerly comments on parking meters." *American City* 52 (November 1937): 107.

"Habitual parker is target of drive." *New York Times*, November 16, 1935, p. 17.

Harris, J. Robert. "Los Angeles: the city that automobiles rebuilt." *The Rotarian* 76 (February 1950): 18–20.

"High garages required." *Los Angeles Times*, June 23, 1929, p. E8.

"Inglewood rejects parking meters." *Los Angeles Times*, September 5, 1940, p. A10.

Ihlder, John. "The parking problem." *Los Angeles Times*, June 24, 1923, sec. 6, pp. 1, 3, 14.

"Injunction sought against proposed parking meter plan." *Los Angeles Times*, September 18, 1942, p. A1.

"Janss offers novel service." *Los Angeles Times*, May 30, 1926, p. E9.

"July 25th automobile day at the First Church." *Cranbury Press* [New Jersey], July 16, 1915, p. 1.

Koch, Alice. "Curbstone gold mine." *The Rotarian* 77 (September 1950): 15–16.

"Let's not rent out the streets." *Los Angeles Times*, August 16, 1946, p. A4.

Lewis, J. Anthony. "Taxation on time." *New York Times Magazine*, November 6, 1949, p. 48.

Lindersmith, Walter R. "Less parking—more purchasing in Los Angeles." *American City* 43 (December 1930): 120–121.

"Loading zones hog space." *Los Angeles Times*, August 7, 1925, p. A8.

"Locks to foil wily motorists." *Los Angeles Times*, January 20, 1924, p. 2.

"Long Beach cold first day to parking meters." *Los Angeles Times*, November 29, 1936, p. 12.

Lorimer, George Horace. "Where to park." *Saturday Evening Post* 201 (February 16, 1929): 24.

"Los Angeles parking lots now exceed 1250 in number." *Los Angeles Times*, December 12, 1937, p. E1.

"Lots of parking space if you look closely." *Los Angeles Times*, August 8, 1926, p. G1.

Macdonald, Austin F. "Parking facilities outside the traffic zone." *The Annals of the American Academy of Political and Social Science* 133 (September 1927): 78–81.

MacGavin, C. T. "Parking stems trade ebb." *New York Times*, October 29, 1940, sec. 10, p. 3.

"Main Street parking is hazardous and uninviting." *Garfield County News* [Utah], December 10, 1926.

"McAdoo calls jam in court inhuman." *New York Times*, October 11, 1924, p. 26.

McClintock, Miller. "Must provide car storage places to solve parking and business problems." *Ogden Standard Examiner* [Utah], October 3, 1926.

McClintock, Miller. "Parking — when, where and why?" *American City* 30 (April 1924): 360–361.

McCrosky, T. T. "Only 216 automobiles cause Yonkers' jam." *American City* 53 (January 1938): 97.

McNeil, Donald M. "Motorists overwhelmingly favor Pittsburgh's parking meters." *American City* 54 (December 1939): 63.

"Merchants ask mass meeting on parking difficulty." *Murray Eagle* [Utah], May 24, 1945.

"Merchants to build free parking lots." *Murray Eagle* [Utah], April 3, 1941, pp. 1, 8.

"Meter makers look for boom." *Business Week*, May 17, 1947, pp. 28–29.

"Meter matters." *Time* 30 (September 6, 1937): 44.

"Meter plan on parking hit." *Los Angeles Times*, September 4, 1942, p. A2.

"Metropolitan parking meters." *San Juan Record* [Utah], November 24, 1938.

Miller, John A. "They're all afraid to mention it." *Review of Reviews* 94 (August 1936): 54–56.

Miller, John A. Jr. "The chariots that rage in the streets." *American City* 39 (July 1928): 111–114.

"Mistake nullifies auto parking law." *Los Angeles Times*, November 30, 1923, sec. 2, p. 2.

Moffatt, Dr. Howard. "Doctor scores auto zone law." *Los Angeles Times*, January 2, 1920, sec. 2, p. 10.

Mosier, O. M. "Our experience with parking meters." *American City* 51 (January 1936): 77.

"Motor cars are essential." *Los Angeles Times*, April 25, 1920, sec. 6, pp. 1, 6.

"Motorist smashes parking meters." *Los Angeles Times*, March 14, 1940, p. 22.

Nau, Robert H. "No parking — a year and more of it." *American City* 40 (March 1929): 85–88.

"New parking law in force." *Los Angeles Times*, November 27, 1923, sec. 2, p. 1.

"New parking plan announced." *Los Angeles Times*, July 7, 1929, p. D3.

"New parking sought in midtown." *New York Times*, May 1, 1927, p. E1.

"New type of suburban shopping area proposed." *American City* 35 (August 1926): 214–216.

"New wide streets to solve traffic problem." *Los Angeles Times*, August 31, 1922, sec. 2, pp. 1, 3.

"Nickel-in-meter regulates parking." *Literary Digest* 122 (August 22, 1936): 35–36.

"No more parking in busy cities?" *Ogden Standard Examiner* [Utah], February 14, 1925.

"No parking." *The Marion Star* [Ohio], April 19, 1919, p. 6.

"No-parking law protest." *Los Angeles Times*, April 25, 1920, p. 19.

"No parking of automobiles." *Ogden Standard Examiner* [Utah], January 26, 1927.

"No street parking." *Ogden Standard Examiner* [Utah], November 6, 1927.

"Off-street parking drive." *Business Week*, April 6, 1946, pp. 21–22.

"Ogden limits auto parking." *Ogden Standard Examiner* [Utah], March 12, 1924.
"One hour for auto parking meets favor." *Ogden Standard Examiner* [Utah], December 16, 1926.
"123,000 cars found parked all night." *New York Times*, November 20, 1931, p. 25.
"One lock with 24 different keys." *Literary Digest* 112 (March 26, 1932): 37.
"Open campaign to stop all parking in streets." *Ogden Standard Examiner* [Utah], February 22, 1925.
"Ordinance banning parking in Philadelphia strikes opposition." *Los Angeles Times*, March 20, 1927, pp. G1–G2.
"Ordinance No. 61." *Garfield County News* [Utah], August 14, 1925.
"Ordinance on parking revamped." *Los Angeles Times*, May 23, 1934, p. A1.
"Others oppose parking plans." *Los Angeles Times*, December 25, 1919, sec. 2, p. 7.
"Overhead street cars as parking solutions." *Ogden Standard Examiner* [Utah], July 22, 1923.
"Overtime parking." *Los Angeles Times*, August 4, 1927, p. A4.
"Parade to point protest." *Los Angeles Times*, April 22, 1920, sec. 2, p. 1.
"Park and shop." *American City* 52 (October 1937): 71–72.
"Park-N-Shop in '41." *Business Week*, June 21, 1941, pp. 41, 43.
"Park-N-Shop plan." *Business Week*, December 16, 1939, pp. 46–47.
"Park-O-Meters." *Business Week*, October 5, 1935, p. 31.
"Park-O-Meters may decrease S. L. business." *Murray Eagle* [Utah], August 13, 1936.
"Parkers face court today." *Los Angeles Times*, April 14, 1920, sec. 2, p. 1.
"Parking autos in a pile." *Literary Digest* 109 (May 16, 1931): 19.
"Parking facilities for industrial employees." *American City* 31 (September 1924): 239.
"Parking floors for autos now suggested." *Los Angeles Times*, August 2, 1914, sec. 7, p. 10.
"Parking held not a right but a privilege." *Ogden Standard Examiner* [Utah], July 15, 1923.
"Parking held vital to Fifth Av. Trade." *New York Times*, December 16, 1928, pp. N1–N2.
"Parking hogs assailed." *Los Angeles Times*, July 31, 1927, p. B12.
"Parking lot law scored." *Los Angeles Times*, August 6, 1936, p. A5.
"Parking lot law sought." *Los Angeles Times*, July 27, 1936, p. A2.
"Parking lot owner held not liable." *Los Angeles Times*, February 10, 1933, p. A5.
"Parking lots: a new city activity." *American City* 53 (December 1938): 59.
"Parking lots curb planned." *Los Angeles Times*, November 18, 1936, p. A2.
"Parking meter declared violation of people's rights." *Los Angeles Times*, August 27, 1940, p. A10.
"Parking meter foes increase." *Los Angeles Times*, June 9, 1940, p. A3.
"Parking meter plan condemned." *Los Angeles Times*, September 3, 1942, p. 11.
"Parking meter previewed." *Los Angeles Times*, September 26, 1936, p. 8.
"Parking meters." *Scientific American* 157 (November 1937): 288, 290.
"Parking meters." *Fortune* 18 (November 1938): 12.
"Parking meters." *Los Angeles Times*, April 17, 1940, p. A4.
"Parking meters an unqualified success in 18 cities." *American City* 53 (May 1938): 7.
"Parking meters are two years old." *American City* 52 (July 1937): 7.
"Parking meters: best solution yet found." *American City* 53 (December 1938): 73.
"Parking meters defense made." *Los Angeles Times*, April 9, 1940, p. 11.
"Parking meters gain." *Business Week*, June 27, 1936, p. 16.
"Parking meters gross $79,796." *Los Angeles Times*, December 20, 1944, p. A2.
"Parking meters here urged by merchants." *New York Times*, March 3, 1937, p. 14.

"Parking meters in Oklahoma City." *American City* 50 (August 1935): 61.
"Parking meters now in service." *Los Angeles Times*, March 13, 1937, p. 6.
"Parking meters put millions in cities' coffers." *Los Angeles Times*, May 30, 1948, p. 9.
"Parking meters sabotaged." *Wall Street Journal*, April 24, 1941, p. 3.
"Parking meters to stay." *Times Independent* [Utah], January 7, 1937.
"Parking meters voted out for second time." *Los Angeles Times*, March 24, 1949, p. 24.
"Parking plan tried." *Los Angeles Times*, April 9, 1923, p. 7.
"Parking restrictions and reactions in several large cities." *American City* 42 (March 1930): 122–123.
"Parking rules eased." *Los Angeles Times*, May 21, 1921, sec. 2, p. 11.
"Parking solutions." *Business Week*, February 8, 1941, p. 22.
"Parking space at premium in capital." *Garfield County News* [Utah], February 29, 1924.
"Parking space growth factor." *Los Angeles Times*, March 7, 1926, p. G20.
"Parking toll fight shelved." *Los Angeles Times*, November 11, 1942, p. A2.
Parmenter, Al. "Auto parking to be barred in downtown areas." *Los Angeles Times*, November 30, 1930, pp. F1-F2.
"The perils of a parkless town." *Los Angeles Times*, February 29, 1920, sec. 2, pp. 1, 10.
"Philadelphia's new auto parking rules." *New York Times*, July 30, 1916, sec. 2, p. 2.
"Plan proposes auto seizures." *Los Angeles Times*, November 10, 1924, p. A5.
"Plans steel tower over mile high." *Vernal Express* [Utah], October 13, 1932.
"Police Commission weighs parking meter protests." *Los Angeles Times*, April 24, 1940, p. A1.
"Police court business." *Eureka Reporter* [Utah], July 2, 1920.
Pound, Arthur. "No parking." *Atlantic Monthly* 161 (March 1938): 387–393.
Pratt, Fletcher. "No parking." *American Mercury* 39 (October 1936): 155–160.
"Price City Council passes ordinance regulating limit of parking on city streets. *News Advocate* [Utah], June 2, 1928.
"The problem of the city auto." *Literary Digest* 66 (September 4, 1920): 30–31.
"A promising solution to the parking problem." *American City* 51 (August 1936): 59–60.
"Proved manhood by attack on octogenarian." *Davis County Clipper* [Utah], August 17, 1923.
"Public parking place is unpopular." *The Daily Courier* [Connellsville, Pennsylvania], May 16, 1916, p. 1.
"Push a button; park your car." *Los Angeles Times*, May 1, 1932, p. E2.
"Putting parking on a somewhat higher plane." *Literary Digest* 101 (May 18, 1929): 72, 74, 76.
"The raw no-parking ordinance." *Los Angeles Times*, December 24, 1919, sec. 2, p. 4.
"Relief pledged from auto ban." *Los Angeles Times*, April 24, 1920, sec. 2, p. 1.
"Remedies in traffic ills cited." *Los Angeles Times*, April 15, 1927, p. 3.
"Repeals parking law." *Los Angeles Times*, June 6, 1923, p. 10.
"Retailers shown way out of troubles." *Ogden Standard Examiner* [Utah], July 20, 1923.
"Rigid parking order issued." *Ogden Standard Examiner* [Utah], May 6, 1929.
"Roberts lectures on parking rules." *Ogden Standard Examiner* [Utah], May 16, 1924.
Robinette, Paul S. "Eliminating business-district congestion in Toledo." *American City* 53 (March 1938): 79+.
"Roof parking forecast." *Los Angeles Times*, April 29, 1928, pp. G1-G2.
"Roof parking to relieve street overcrowding." *American City* 52 (January 1937): 44.
"Says parking doomed to go." *Ogden Standard Examiner* [Utah], May 2, 1926.
"Seaboard bank provides auto parking services." *Los Angeles Times*, January 5, 1926, p. 4.

Shulsky, Sam. "America's traffic headaches." *American Mercury* 66 (February 1948): 151–157.
Simpson, Hawley S. "Downtown storage garages." *The Annals of the American Academy of Political and Social Science* 133 (September 1927): 82–89.
Skerett, Robert G. "Every automobile its own elevator." *Scientific American* 124 (January 22, 1921): 65, 75, 79.
"The skyscraper garage." *Scientific American* 121 (September 13, 1919): 247, 259.
Slauson, H. W. "And we call ourselves efficient." *Scientific American* 134 (June 1926): 368–369.
Smith, Bert C. "Drag-net out for motor thieves is state-wide." *Los Angeles Times*, January 11, 1914, sec. 7, pp. 1–2.
"Solid vote to lift auto ban." *Los Angeles Times*, April 27, 1920, sec. 2, pp. 1, 5.
"Solved! ... Collapsible auto." *Los Angeles Times*, January 21, 1924, p. A1.
"Solving the traffic problem." *Box Elder News* [Utah], September 21, 1926.
"Sounds complicated." *Morgan County News* [Utah], February 14, 1947.
"Speaking of parking meters." *Business Week*, August 7, 1937, p. 27.
"Steadily growing traffic tangle's seriousness disclosed by survey." *Los Angeles Times*, August 29, 1945, p. A1.
"Storage charges as the mainstay of a garage." *Literary Digest* 46 (April 12, 1913): 853–855
"Street parking being removed." *Ogden Standard Examiner* [Utah], April 13, 1924.
"Study made of parking." *Los Angeles Times*, June 16, 1940, p. E1.
Tazewell, L. W. "Results of Norfolk's parking meters." *American City* 53 (July 1938): 47–48.
"That traffic problem." *American City* 51 (June 1936): 7.
"That troublesome matter — parking." *American City* 50 (May 1935): 101.
"They shall not park!" *American City* 42 (May 1930): 120.
Thomasson, A. F. "Parking meters in St. Petersburg, Fla." *American City* 51 (July 1936): 7.
"To end parking in broad area." *Los Angeles Times*, December 19, 1919, sec. 2, p. 2.
"To park or not to park." *American City* 35 (October, 1926): 461–464.
"To park or not to park." *Ogden Standard Examiner* [Utah], October 10, 1926.
"Traffic congestion, parking facilities, and retail business." *American City* 34 (June 1926): 664–666.
"Traffic congestion, parking facilities, and retail business — II." *American City* 35 (July 1926): 62–65.
"Traffic survey shows need for regulation." *Murray Eagle* [Utah], December 14, 1940.
Trammell, C. W. "Impounding of illegally parked automobiles reduces traffic problem." *American City* 43 (September 1930): 151.
Turner, Benjamin F. "Passaic likes parking meters." *American City* 53 (May 1938): 52–54.
"Two hundred in auto net." *Los Angeles Times*, April 13, 1920, sec. 2, pp. 1, 12.
"Underground garage to end parking problem." *Popular Mechanics* 55 (February 1931): 180.
"The universal quest." *Los Angeles Times*, June 15, 1924, p. 22.
"Vast traffic problem seen." *Ogden Standard Examiner* [Utah], January 13, 1924.
"Venice throng largest ever." *Los Angeles Times*, July 6, 1909, sec. 2, p. 10.
"Volcano expert sees menace in streets jammed with autos." *Ogden Standard Examiner* [Utah], January 24, 1924.
"Vox populi rules city." *Los Angeles Times*, May 4, 1929, p. A8.
"Wanted — more hitching posts for cars." *Literary Digest* 80 (February 2, 1924): 57–60.

"Warns auto row of raids today on bad parking." *Los Angeles Times*, July 10, 1920, sec. 2, p. 2.
"We want no parking meters in Los Angeles." *Los Angeles Times*, October 12, 1942, p. A4.
Westgate, Harvey E. "Swarms of jitneys, 40,000 autos and narrow streets cause congestion." *Los Angeles Times*, December 3, 1916, sec. 6, p. 1.
"Where to leave the car." *The New Republic* 95 (June 1, 1938): 87.
Whitnall, G. Gordon. "No parking of autos." *American City* 22 (May 1920): 484.
"Will prohibit auto parking." *Los Angeles Times*, December 9, 1919, sec. 2, p. 1.
"Will rush ordinance on parking." *Los Angeles Times*, November 22, 1923, sec. 2, p. 1.
"Working at the parking problem." *American City* 54 (February 1939): 62–63.
Yordan, E. L. "City parking studied." *New York Times*, November 29, 1936, sec. 13, pp. 1, 5.
Yordan, E. L. "The lowly parking lot thrives." *New York Times*, March 14, 1937, sec. 12, p. 1.
Young, Hugh E. "Day and night storage and parking of motor vehicles." *American City* 29 (July 1923): 44–46.

Index

absolute ban, advocated 29–30
advertising 118–119
aerial photos 46
Alabama 129
Albertson, J. 12
Alhambra, California 38
all-day parkers 35, 40, 80, 142
alleys 26, 46
all-night parking 50
American Automobile Association 122, 125, 127, 128
American City 83–84, 101
Amis, Lewis 40–41
angle parking 23, 33
angle vs. parallel 38
apartment buildings 83
arrests, for parking offenses 15
Asbury Park, New Jersey 65
Atlanta 42
Atlantic Monthly 81–82
attendants, lots 102
attitudes, to meters 131, 134, 139, 146
Austin, J. Win 152
auto thefts, from lots 101–102
automatic systems 92–93
Automobile Club of Philadelphia 33
Automobile Club of Southern California 9, 13, 149
automobiles: linked to disasters 52–53; as necessity 49; and number of spaces 157; numbers of 97; rights of 11; and society 11–12, 17, 31–32, 45–46, 64–65, 74, 78–79; in the United States (1924) 52
available space 91

Babson, Roger W. 21
Bagby, E.H. 15–16
Bakersfield, California 129–130, 163
Baltimore 28–29, 42
Banham, W. 43
banks, branch locations 73

banning, acceptance of 20
bans 8; downtown Chicago 24, 26–28; removed 18
Barrellas, Harry 26
basements 8
Baumgartner, John W. 151
Beckenbach, C.G. 120, 134
Bell, Jefferson 53–54
benefits, of meters 120–121
Bentel, George 10
Boston 41
Boston Elevated Railway 70
Breuning, Joseph 98
Britt, George 23–24
Brown, Leon R. 110, 132
Buffalo, New York 42
building core facilities 109
buildings with parking 88–89
Burby, John J. 101
Burnett, T. R. 131
Burns, Robert 152
buses 59, 110–111, 138; free 115
business districts 8
business lobbying, Los Angeles 9–18
Business Men's Cooperative Association 15
Business Week 118
businesses: paying for parking 39; provision of 25, 67, 109
Butler, J.L. 37, 58
Buttenheim, Harold 71

cage parking 97–98
California 128–129
Canada 123
carriages and wagons 6
C.C. Bet Tractor Co. 99
center-of-street 34
chain-driven facility 94–95
chalk marks 120
Chevalier, Willard 78–79
Chicago 26–28, 70, 80–81, 99–100

190

Index

Chicago Association of Commerce 27
Cincinnati 8, 42
circling the block 48
city tax base 82
Cleveland 41
Cohen v. Mayor 5
coin-in-slot feature 95
collection of coins 124
Collins, Morgan A. 66
Columbia, Missouri 75
commercial vehicles 14
congestion 13, 17, 31–32, 46, 157; cost 46–47, 61, 76–77, 88; Los Angeles 191; losses from 73; solutions 83–84
Connellsville, Pennsylvania 99
coop efforts 114–115
Cooperative Customer Parking Plan 40–41
courts: cases 36; decisions 37; proceedings 21, 43; and regulations 35
Crossley, John R. 146
cruising 91, 118, 154, 157
curbs: ownership 50; painting 36–37; parking 8, 33; space 30–31, 63; usage 43, 72; vs. lot vs. garage 64

Dallas 43, 134
Davis, William T. 53
decentralization 52, 56, 59, 71, 82, 97, 158–159, 162
Denny, Ellis 164
department stores 60
Depression (economic) 82, 102; and meters 119
Detroit 81, 103, 111–112
Doherty, Frank P. 150
doormen of stores, enforcing 19
Dorsey, Ralph T. 156
Dorsey, R.J. 75
double parking 27, 33–34, 54, 57, 132, 142
Dowell, A. E. 136
Doyle, Charles C. 155
drive-in facilities 109
Dual Parking Meter Company 177–118, 126, 144, 155
Duffy, Michael P. 130
Dunlop, George 13
durability, of meters 131

East, E.E. 25, 51
Eastman, Lee J. 90–91
economics 66; costs 79; loss 48
editorials, newspaper 11–13, 24, 45, 50–51, 64–65, 68, 75, 91, 121–122, 147–1153, 162
education campaigns 24
efficiency of meters 142–143, 145, 147; survey 139–140
Eighth Avenue Association 38
elevators 92
Eliot, Samuel 97
Ellison, Franklin Hugh 97

El Monte, California 34
employers, providing 99
enforcement of regulations 28, 56, 60, 117, 120, 138, 141
English law 5
Equitable Building (NYC) 159–160
Erickson, Orlando 106–107
Europe 8
evaluation of meters 131–132
Evanston, Illinois 116
expressways 24
extent of problem 80–81

facilities, outside downtown 69–70
fanciful ideas 53–54
Faries, David 13
Faulkner, M.G. 12
Fifth Avenue (NYC) 74
Fifth Avenue Association 36
fines 32, 33, 37
fire department 92
Fisher Brothers Building (Detroit) 90
fistfights 34
floors, sloping 98
Ford, Michael 43
Fort Worth, Texas 70, 136
Fred Meyer, Inc. 113
Fredericks, John D. 6

Gaither, Charles 29
garages: benefits 92–94; economics of 1913 85–86; large commercial 14, 20, 59; Los Angeles, 1927 88; mechanized 92–93; necessity of 89–90; Philadelphia 98; private 54; public 47; public vs. private 89; and transit 89
Garner, R.E. 101
Garson film studio 16
gasoline rationing 156
gasoline sales 86
Goodrich, Ernest P. 45–46
Gottlieb, William 128
Gould, H.M. 111–112
Grant Park, Chicago 81
Greene, Lewis R. 135–136
Greer, P.R. 10
Griffin, Jack 10
growth of congestion 60
Gunnison, Utah 67

Haldeman, R.C. 74
Hamlin, Ralph 10
Hampton, Roy 152
Harrington, J.E. 25, 88
Harris, J. Robert 161–162
Harriss, John A. 23–24, 55–56
Harvard University 26
Hayes, William 34
Heath, Cleveland 35
Hendricks, John A. 39–40

Highway Research Board 43–44
highways, use of 5
Hill, Frank 34
hitching posts 5
Hobbs, Clark S. 77
Holey, Horace 37
Holland, Lionel 151
honor system 40, 65
d'Humy, Fernand E. 87
Huntington Park, California 153–154
Hurst, J.T. 88

Ihlder, John 48–49
Indianapolis 6, 42
Inglewood, California 151
Ithaca, New York 40

Jackson, Walter 65
Jagger, Thomas A. 52–53
James, H.D. 95
jaywalking 47
Jensen, Alonzo 39–40
Jeweler's Building (Chicago) 109
Jordan, Edward S. 52, 59–60
Jordy, J.N. 127
Joscelyn, W.J. 85–86

Kansas City, Missouri 42
Kilday, Owen W. 131
Kincaid, H.E. 157

La Guardia, Fiorello 103
Lawrence, Ruth 34
laws, businesses, parking 71
lawsuits: and lots 100; meters 119, 124, 129, 133, 135, 153
Leahy, D.J. 127
legislative battles 129
length of parking time 23, 36
licensing 8
limitation vs. prohibition 44
limited entry, to downtowns 74
Lindersmith, Walter 30
Literary Digest 28–29, 92
loading merchandise 11
loading zones 37
Logan, Utah 35
Logansport, Indiana 7
Long Beach, California 20, 127
Lorimer, George Horace 91
Los Angeles 7–8, 9–20, 35, 43, 63, 100–102, 112, 147–150, 162
Los Angeles Chamber of Commerce 15–16
Los Angeles City Council 9–11, 13, 16–18, 21, 54–55, 152–153
Los Angeles Fire Commission 99–100
Los Angeles Police Department traffic squad 7
Los Angeles Times 11–13, 14, 68, 121, 147–148
lots: capacity, Detroit 81; economics 106;
elaborate 103–104; fees 104; images of 103; largest 99; municipal 8, 55, 101–102, 104–105; and municipalities 159; numbers of 103; NYS 104; private 105–106

MacDonald, Austin 69
MacGavin, C.T. 97, 116
machine controlled units 94–96
machines, parking 83
Magee, Carlton Cole 125–126
Manhattan 25
Mansfield, Frederick 136–137
manual vs. automatic meters 134, 135–136
Mark-Time meter 130, 144
Marsh, Edward 66
Marshall Field Company 113
mass transit 69–70, 73
Massachusetts Supreme Court 135
Mayson, B.D. 151
McAdoo, William 36
McClanahan, Meade 153
McClintock, Miller 26, 56, 66–67, 111
McCrosky, T.T. 80
McDowell, James 15
Meads, Roy R. 10
mechanized facilities 98, 109, 112–113
merchants: free storage 89–90; and garages 58, 115; Manhattan 74; parking services 62; surveyed 60–61
Merchants Association of New York 128
meters: economics 123–124, 131, 133, 136, 144–145, 146–147, 154–155, 163, 164; first 117–118; invention of 125–126; numbers of 122, 132, 144, 145, 154, 162, 163–164; philosophy of 82–83; public reaction 126, 128; receipts 119–120, 133, 142, 144
M.H. Rhodes Inc. 144
Miami 80, 163
Miller, John 76
Miller, John A. 72–73
Miller Meter 144
Milwaukee 103
Mitchell, S.L. 108
modular facility 94–95
Moffat, Howard 12
Montreal 123
Morrison, George C. 139
Moseley, Hal 121
Mosier, O.M. 118
Motor Car Dealers' Association (Los Angeles) 10
Motor Mart (Boston) 90
movement vs. storage 26, 31–32, 43–44, 48, 50–51, 56–57, 73–74, 82
multiple dwellings 116
multi-purpose buildings 90–91
municipal ownership, of lots 111
municipal vs. private lots 104–105
municipalities, failure of 157–158
Murray City, Utah 84, 106

National Association of Building Owners and Managers 93
National Automobile Chamber of Commerce 25
Nau, Robert 26–28
necessity of autos 17
necessity of regulations 45
The New Republic 82–83, 122
New York City 22, 38, 43, 80, 103, 127; theater district 32–33
New York City Merchants Association 36
New York State 145–146
Newark, New Jersey 40–41
Norfolk, Virginia 142–143
North Dakota 164

Oakland Downtown Merchants Parking Association 84
objections, to meters 122–123
off-street facilities 49, 67–68, 106
off-street parking 28; public vs. private 78; vs. on-street, survey 76
office buildings 108
Ogden, Utah 21, 24, 39–40
Oklahoma Agricultural and Mechanical College 126
Oklahoma City 117–118
Olsen, E.S. 37
one-side parking 25, 79–80, 112
one-way streets 11, 46
Ontario Motor League 123
opposition to meters 121, 145, 150
opposition to regulations 56
ordinances 116; legal principle 118
over-parking 79–81
overstaying 135

Pacific Mutual Building (Los Angeles) 55
Panguitch, Utah 22
park-and-ride systems 69–70, 110
park and shop markets 113–114
Park-N-Shop 114–116
parking spaces, required 116
parking survey 84
parking systems, by business 14
parks 53
Parmenter, Al 112
Passaic, New Jersey 140–141
patent litigation 155
Peabody, H.B. 25
Pedrick, William J. 74
pessimistic forecast 159–160
petitions 26, 38
Petty, Don 152
Philadelphia 8, 24, 41, 98, 157–158
Philadelphia Rapid Transit Company 69–70
philosophical considerations 46–50
physicians 12–13, 21; exemptions 9
Pittsburgh 42, 147
Pittsburgh Chamber of Commerce 42

Pittsburgh Railway Company 70
police 18, 22, 34–35, 39–40, 45, 67–68, 138
population, USA, 1900–1920 5
Portland, Oregon 157
Pound, Arthur 81–82
Pratt, Fletcher 31–32
Price, Utah 25–26
Pridham, R.W. 22
prohibitions, Los Angeles 9–19
property values, downtown 158
protests 39; against parking laws 16
public relations efforts 21, 41, 118–119, 130–131
public transit 10, 27, 160
Pure Oil Building (Chicago) 93

ramp garages 88
ramps 87, 92
Rampton, R.M. 37
Red Ball Meter 144
Redd, John H. 26
referendums 14
repairs, rate of 134, 141
repeals, of bans 20
residences, private 50
retail trade 21, 116
revenues, city 119
Rex v. Cross 5
Roach, Hal 57–58
Roberts, D.R. 21
Robinette, Paul 137
Roche, J.L. 39
Rochester 110–111
Rockett, F.K. 12
Rogers, Will 57–58, 159
rooftop facilities 54, 110, 113, 114

St. Louis 114–115
St. Petersburg, Florida 123–124
Salt Lake City 123, 128, 143–144
San Francisco 42, 81
Saturday Evening Post 91
Schneider, John J. 141
Schurman, Jacob 44
Scientific American 95
scrip 39
Sears (Los Angeles) 114
seized vehicles 38
Shannahan, J.N. 58
shoppers 27, 29, 61, 72, 73–74, 77
Shulsky, Sam 159–160
shuttle services 8
Simpson, Hawley S. 89–90
Skerett, Robert G. 87–88
skyscrapers 8, 86, 91, 93
Slauson, H.W. 60
Smith, B.B. 131
Smith, Bert C. 6
Snyder, Meredith 19
stabling of horses 85–86

Steinberg, Irwin 100
Stoeckel, R.B. 72
storage 51
streetcars 7, 13, 17–18, 58, 65, 66, 110, 156
streets: cleaning 26, 38; elevated 72; markings 7; parking survey 76; railway systems 58, 69–70; vs. off-street 66–67; widening 46; width of 13, 50, 60
strip malls 113–114
subsidized facilities 114–115
suburban shopping centers 62
Subway Terminal Building (Los Angeles) 111
surveys 27, 48–49, 63

taxation 111; double 121; effects 148
taxis 7, 9, 66
Tazewell, L.W. 143–144
thefts, auto 6
Thomas, J. Fred 131
Thomasson, A.F. 123–124
Thompson, L.G. 15
Thompson, R.W. 158
tickets 35; fixing 138
time limits 6; NYS 40; survey 61–62
Toledo, Ohio 122, 137–139
Toledo Automobile Club 139
Toronto 123
tourists, arrests of 20
towing, of parking violators 29, 38, 43
trade from auto shoppers 59
Traffic Committee of the Broadway Association 25
traffic: lights 18, 45; movement 5; patterns 158; speed 27–29
Transit Journal 131–132
Turner, Benjamin 140–141
Tuttle, Harold 12

Ullman, William 35–36
underground facilities 112–113, 156

underground garages 89
United States Chamber of Commerce 72
United Railways and Electric Company (Baltimore) 70
urban planners 45–46
Utah 145

valet parking 14, 109
vandalism 147, 152; and lots 100
Venice, California 6
vertical parking 96
violations of regulations, survey 68
Von Hoffman, Bernard 116

Wacker Drive, Chicago 72
Walker, John O. 29–30
Washington, D.C. 41–42, 52, 81, 100, 114
Watt, John 118, 124
Weaver, Robert S. 12
West Palm Beach, Florida 71
Westgate, Henry 7–8
Westinghouse Electric company 94–95
Whalen, Grover 32–33
Wherry, Styles W. 123
White, Harry 66
Whitehead, H.H. 130–131
Whitnall, G. Gordon 17
women: drivers 38–39, 120; and meters 119
Woodhill, Gilbert 12
World War II 156–164
World's Fair (1933) 97
Wright, Harry F. 9
Wright, Henry C. 7

Yonkers, New York 80
Yordan, E.L. 79–80, 97, 102–103
Young, Clara Kimball 16
Young, Hugh E. 47–48, 55

zoning 9–17, 94

www.ingramcontent.com/pod-product-compliance
Ingram Content Group UK Ltd.
Pitfield, Milton Keynes, MK11 3LW, UK
UKHW042011140426
5217IPUK00015B/1098